When The Senate Halls Were Hallowed

When The Senate Halls Were Hallowed

Dorothye G. Scott

Carillon Press
Los Angeles

Carillon Press is an imprint of Belle Publishing.

Belle Publishing
3875 Wilshire Boulevard, Suite 802
Los Angeles, CA 90010
213-385-7771

Printed in the United States of America

Library of Congress Cataloging-in-Publication Data
Scott, Dorothye G., 1921–
  When the Senate Halls were Hallowed / Dorothye G. Scott -- 1st ed.
  p.   cm.
  includes index
  LCCN: 99-69676
  ISBN 0-9649635-6-6
  1. Scott, Dorothye G., 1921– 2. Congressional secretaries--Biography 3. United States Congress. Senate--Biography 4. United States Congress Senate--History--20th century 5. United States Congress--Officials and employees--Biography 6. Presidents--United States--Biography I. Title

JK 1257.S36 2000   328.092
                                                QBI99-500582

Interior & Cover Design by Sparrow Advertising & Design
Editorial Assistance by Margaret Burk
Cover photo: Tom Brewster, Palm Springs, California

Printed and bound in the United States of America
International Standard Book Number: 0-9649635-6-6

10 9 8 7 6 5 4 3 2 1

The entire Congress of the United States has been the object of great criticism in recent years. Efforts of many legislators have been overlooked because of the disappointing actions of a few.

As one who served in the United States Senate for over thirty-one years, I wish to tell of an earlier time "when the Senate halls were hallowed."

My personalized inside story, shares the unique and exciting experiences with the reader of my day-to-day life in the United States Senate, the "Greatest Deliberative Body in the World."

TABLE OF CONTENTS

CHAPTER NINE

CHAPTER TEN

CHAPTER ELEVEN

CHAPTER TWELVE

CHAPTER THIRTEEN

CHAPTER FOURTEEN

ACKNOWLEDGEMENTS

In loving memory of my beautiful mother, **Mildred Scott Fausset,** who lit up every room she entered.

In dearest memory of my kind, sentimental and sensitive father, **Thomas F. Scott,** who was always an inspiration to me.

In sincere appreciation to my dear cousin, **Deborah Arnold,** for her interest and important contribution in the processing of my manuscript, and her mother **Marilyn Arnold,** for her support.

My gratitude to **Donald A. Ritchie,** the Senate Associate Historian, who prepared the oral history of my Senate career and commented that, "It reads like a novel;" also for his continued cooperation in researching Senate material for this book.

In fond memory of my attendance at a great many literary luncheons of Round Table West in La Quinta, California, which inspired me to write **my** story.

To **Margaret Burk,** my treasured friend, the Chairman of Round Table West, who encouraged and persevered with me to write this book, with her understanding, enthusiasm and expertise.

Thanks to **Tray Burk,** Belle Publishing, for producing a book of my life.

And with love for all those dear friends who strode the Senate's hallowed halls with me.

INTRODUCTION

**An Ode to Dorothye Scott
on her Departure from the U. S. Senate**

I first saw Dorothye Scott about 20 years ago. She was in the Senate restaurant indulging in two of her favorite pursuits— eating and talking. I was amazed at how anyone so skinny could eat so much and how anybody would have so much to say so early in the morning.

Later, I came to know that Dorothye Scott had a secret passion even more formidable than food and conversation. That passion was the Senate of the United States. None has served it better or more faithfully. Few people have served this institution for a longer period of time. When it comes to the Senate, Dorothye Scott is a totally dedicated person. She puts the Senate ahead of me and I know she likes me. She has been here through almost a complete change in the membership of the Senate. As a matter of fact, on the Senate seniority list, she is number four! Only three Senators still here came to the Senate before Dorothye Scott. I can only say that her seniors on that list look like her seniors and, so, too, do her juniors.

As for Secretaries of the Senate, Dorothye has seen them come and go—three or four at least. All the while, Dorothye has endured.

It is almost impossible to envision a Senate without Dorothye Scott. Her influence on this institution has been very great, so great that it is likely to reflect something of her many contributions for decades to come. Dorothye and I have worked together for eleven years. She has gone on eating and talking through all those years. But she has also done something more. She has not only made it possible for me to function as Secretary of the Senate, she has become an inseparable part of my personal life. She is a friend to me and to people very dear to me and I shall miss her at least as much as the Senate will miss her.

Yet, I know that the only constant in life is change and there is no life without it. So, I welcome this departure even as I regret it. I welcome it because I know it will open new horizons. And Dorothye Scott rates this opportunity to confront new challenges. She is an immensely talented, energetic and tenacious human being. I have never known a person who works harder to contribute and in so doing finds her own fulfillment.

Dorothye leaves the Senate with the love and admiration and gratitude of everyone who has known her. My personal gratitude is great and so is my affection.

With love,
Francis R. Valeo
Secretary of the Senate

PREFACE

The United States Capitol—a symbol of freedom; its majestic white dome, recognized throughout the world, is the most important monument in a city of many beautiful edifices. It is a palace with a purpose, impressive with its white marble pillars, beautifully hand-painted corridor walls, the frieze of the entire history of the United States pictured inside the magnificent dome of the rotunda, as it reaches skyward; finally, the bronze Statue of Freedom at the very top presides over the city of Washington.

The inspiration which this building stirs in the minds and hearts of all who gaze upon it stems from the life and energy within. It is the towering summit of the Congress whose members labor both in the adjoining Senate and House of Representatives office buildings enacting the laws that govern our country. Thus, visiting our national legislature in these buildings, referred to as Capitol Hill, is an American custom as well as a privilege shared by visitors from every country in the world.

The Capitol building, this great edifice, is something very personal to me. It was a warm home where I spent over thirty-one years of my life. Amidst the dignity and elegance of its hallowed halls I found an air of dedication where my duties in assisting in the fashioning of our laws gave me great satisfaction. The long hours when the Senate was in session, although filled with work, were stimulating and inspiring, knowing that my efforts formed a part of the pattern of our democracy.

In addition to my respect for the members and officers of the Senate, I found a real family of dear friends and associates in the various offices where we kept the wheels of the Senate turning.

As one who served in the Senate for so many years, I wish to tell of an earlier time, when the halls were hallowed. Those of us sharing our day-to-day activities became a family in our Washington Senate home. As my loving "sister," Rose Mary Woods (Executive Assistant to President Nixon) said, "We all grew up together." It was this family who gave us the warmth and love to find our places under the dome.

Numerous colleagues and statesmen of the time, as well as members of the press who were my friends, have written books about the Congress, about life on Capitol Hill, about the Presidents, and about Washington, the city.

Mine is a more personal inside story, sharing the interesting and exciting experiences of my extraordinary everyday life in the United States Senate, the living, throbbing, pulsating greatest deliberative body in the world.

Dorothye Grant Scott

CHAPTER ONE

Inauguration Day in Palm Springs—January 20, 1997

The day dawned bright and frigid in our Nation's Capitol. Washington was filled to overflowing with happy Democrats, including officials of the present administration, and not so happy Republicans, although their party had won control of both Houses of Congress in the election. Visitors from all over America had come to see the historic second term swearing in of William Jefferson Clinton. Clinton is the only Democratic President to be voted a second term since Franklin D. Roosevelt, whose record of four terms would never be repeated, as by law the terms are now limited to two. Everyone gathered at the Capitol, bundled up like Eskimos . . . in many cases with scarves tied right up to their cold noses.

Far from the glitter and excitement of inaugural festivities in Washington, I sat in the warm, sun-drenched den of my home adjoining the golf course of the Palm Springs Country Club reliving my thirty-one years in the United States Senate. My political education provided a tapestry of wonderful experiences.

The background for the television's presentation of the ceremonies in my den was most appropriate. One wall of the room is covered with a colored photograph of the United States Capitol at dusk in the center. This photograph is surrounded on each side, as well as above and below, with autographed photographs of many members of the Senate and other associates with whom I worked during my Senate career. Prominent is a photograph of the Senate proceeding in a body from the Senate chamber to a joint session of Congress in the House of Representatives chamber. Three Presidents are in this photograph: at that time Vice President Nixon, Senator John F. Kennedy, and Senator Lyndon Johnson.

Several of my pencil portraits of Senators Johnson, Kennedy and Mansfield, among others, decorate my den wall. Mementoes of Senate and Capitol memorabilia complete my "Capitol Corner."

The balmy Palm Springs weather lived up to its reputation with spring-like temperatures on Inauguration Day, quite a contrast to the deep freeze in Washington! I was filled with nostalgia as I watched the ceremonies. Memories came tumbling out of all the inaugurations I had attended while working at the Senate, including those of six Presidents, from Harry Truman's to Jimmy Carter's.

I glanced out of my den window to see golfers clad in shorts, whose main hope on this day was to hit a hole in one. What a contrast this world offered to the vital and historic proceedings in Washington on this most American of days.

It was exalting to see our young President looking vital and energetic and enthusiastic. Despite the chill he removed his overcoat, and as he repeated the words of the oath of office, I felt they came from his heart.

Afterward he encompassed both his wife, Hillary, in her colorful deep peach outfit, and daughter, Chelsea, in her blue coat, in a huge bear hug. All three looked delighted. It was very moving to share the happy emotions of this American family on this very special day. A wave of optimism washed over me when he seemed to also embrace the crowd with a warm ecstatic smile. Remembering that he had served as a messenger in the Senate Foreign Relations Committee during my Senate career, I was thrilled to realize how far he had come.

Later in the ceremonies, as he was seated on the platform a little distance from his family, the President stretched his arm over several chairs to touch his wife's hand. There was tender warmth in this gesture.

Following the conclusion of the program, the President was led to the President's Room in the Capitol. This room is the most richly decorated and ornate in the building. It was originally designed to be an office for the President. He occasionally came to this room to sign last minute bills and appointments before the expiration of his term in office. After 1933, the room was no longer needed for that purpose, but it is sometimes used for symbolic reasons. On

August 6, 1965, President Lyndon Johnson signed the Voting Rights Act of 1965 in this room—100 years to the day after Abraham Lincoln had in the same room signed a bill freeing slaves who had been pressed into service under the Confederacy. The first Civil Rights legislation was enacted when President Johnson was Majority Leader of the Senate.

As Fred J. Maroon states in his book, *The United States Capitol,* "What the President's Room lacks in purpose, it makes up in splendor." The frescoes on the ceiling and the oil paintings on the walls show Constantino Brumidi's art beautifully. He wove together portraits and allegory to illustrate the role of the chief executive. Because the room was carpeted for many years, the Minton tiles on the floor have retained their original vibrancy. The chandelier that dominates the room is one of the few original, and certainly one of the largest, chandeliers in the Capitol. It was spared after a serious gas explosion in the Capitol in 1898. It was electrified and enlarged. In 1915 six additional extensions were added to the eighteen original ones. This room, with its beautiful fireplace, its paintings and decorations, all blended in gold, is virtually unchanged since the late nineteenth century. It is considered the finest room in the Capitol.

I loved showing visitors this historic room. There are floor-to-ceiling gold framed mirrors at each side of the room. I would light a match over the large round table in the center of the room, and its flame would be reflected in both mirrors, giving the effect of a long lighted highway going for miles in each mirror.

Inauguration Day this year was the first time in recent years that a President had entered this room. There, President Clinton signed a proclamation of friendship and hope, providing a unique conclusion to the ceremonies.

Watching the Presidential party and guests at the customary luncheon in the Capitol rotunda, too, brought back many memories. Following the luncheon the President and his family led a motorcade to the White House. When he and his family alighted from his car to walk the last short distance to the White House I was caught up in the warmth and spontaneous response of the crowd of spectators lined up to see the procession. As she was walking down Pennsylvania Avenue, the first lady spotted Bertie Bowman sitting in one of the grandstands. He was the African-American messenger under whom President Clinton served for two years in the Senate Foreign Relations Committee. Hillary Clinton had left the procession to go over and shake hands with him. Our first family seemed to be genuinely enthusiastic and buoyed up. Those watching in other countries surely observed these emotions.

After the President's party entered the reviewing stand at the White House and the parade had begun, my musings returned me to the exhilarating thirty-one years of my life spent in the United States Senate. It all came back to me so clearly! Each day when I arrived at my office under the majestic Capitol dome was one day of fulfillment, memories of which I would like to share with you now.

CHAPTER TWO

Under the Capitol Dome: My First Years in the Senate

The cab wound its way slowly up Pennsylvania Avenue to the Capitol building on this quiet afternoon in the fall of 1945. I was the excited passenger anticipating an interview for a position in Washington, the most historic city in the world. The sun was sparkling on the trees dressed in autumn foliage. The hectic pace of wartime Washington was but a memory. An air of calm and serenity hung over the city as though it had given its all to the war effort and now could be restored to dignified tranquillity in the satisfaction of a job well done.

Peace was breaking out. I was twenty-four years old, and I previously had spent five years frozen in my job at the War Department. In the military service you can't get out unless they *let* you out. I was living with my father in the lovely suburb of Silver Spring, Maryland. His thirty-year career as a salesman and sales agent for the National Cash Register Company, paralleled my five-year career at the War Department. We both worked in New York City as well as Washington, D.C. Since my office, the Caribbean Division of the Corps of Engineers, had moved, bag and baggage, to New York and me with it, I was able to join Dad who had also been transferred to the Big Apple.

After one year, we both returned to Washington; I to my job in the office of the Chief of Engineers and he to the Washington office of NCR. Subsequently, I was offered an appointment as personal secretary to General Farrell, special assistant to General Leslie R. Groves, head of the very *secret* Manhattan Project, the department which handled the atomic bomb. I later learned that even General Groves' wife hadn't known about the bomb until the day it was launched!

I accepted instead a position in private industry and struggled for a long period before being released from the War Department.

The freeze policy designed to retain War Department personnel only provided for release due to illness or a spouse's transfer to another location. Finally, after three months of negotiations all the way up to the War Manpower Commission, I obtained a release based on "utilization of capabilities" on advice of attorneys associated with my new position. With the war winding down, it seemed that entering private industry would be timely, but when the Senate called, I responded, proud to serve my country in any capacity.

We felt that way then. Ours had been a popular war with a distinct purpose of which we approved and we had cheerfully embraced working incredible hours, black-outs, brown-outs, rationing, no gas, and no nylons either! We gals had experimented with painting our legs stocking-color while silk went to the war effort for parachutes.

It was now November of that year, 1945, and in the nine months since it began, the war had climaxed. In April, 1946, President Franklin D. Roosevelt died only eighty-three days into his fourth term and his Vice President, Harry S. Truman, succeeded him. In the same month, it was announced that Adolf Hitler had committed suicide in Berlin. By May, we celebrated V-E Day (Victory over Europe) with Germany's unconditional surrender. In July, the first atomic bomb was detonated in New Mexico, and in early August President Truman authorized the bombing of Hiroshima and Nagasaki. Japan, too, surrendered unconditionally and, on August 15th, we celebrated V-J Day.

We had won! A nice clear-cut victory. Our war had indeed been the war to end all wars, to make the world safe for democracy. We believed the devastating bomb was a weapon for peace. The United Nations had been launched in San Francisco. For months we had been singing a song about the day when "the lights go on again all over the world, and our boys come home again all over the world." That day had come. We were jubilant!

I wish you, too, could remember the end of World War II. It was a unique moment in American history. We would care for our wounded, mourn our dead, but we were sure their sacrifices had not been in vain. Most of us actually believed during those brief months of euphoria that we could build a brave new world without further struggle. The earthly paradise!

* * * * *

In the cab, I surveyed a mood of quietude. Every so often in my life I have had this feeling—a moment when everything seemed to be in sharp focus. I felt very alive and vibrant, sensitive to expectation, feeling the drama of driving to the United States Capitol and knowing there was someone inside waiting to meet me.

Until this moment, the Capitol had been only an impersonal, though majestic, symbol. The cab turned right off of Pennsylvania Avenue, up historic Jenkins Hill to the Capitol Plaza, and suddenly the beautiful white dome and stately columns loomed before me. As I thought of the appointment ahead, it became an effort to subdue my excitement. My friend, Betty Euler, had arranged this interview. She was assistant to Leslie Biffle, who had been elected Secretary of the Senate after having served as Secretary for the Majority of the Senate. He was predecessor to Mr. Felton Johnston, the man awaiting my arrival.

There were uniformed Capitol policemen on duty, guarding all the official parked cars in the spaces across the plaza from the Capitol building. I turned around in my seat to take it all in. Across the beautiful grounds of planted, walled walkways stood the Supreme Court in all its awesome splendor.

The cab pulled to a stop in the driveway that curved under the Senate steps. More excited than ever, I jumped out, ran up the inside steps, and pushed through the revolving door. I approached the Capitol guard's desk and told him of my appointment. He made a phone call and within minutes a young man in black knickers, white shirt and a black tie appeared. He was one of the elite group of twenty-one Senate pages, patronage appointees allotted by the Patronage Committees to individual Senators, who attended the Congressional Page School at the Library of Congress from 6:15 to 9:15 every morning prior to the convening of the

Senate. In addition to manning the telephones in the Democratic and Republican cloakrooms behind the chamber, when the Senate is in session, the pages are seated at the foot of the rostrum facing the members, there to be beckoned by a snap of the fingers to serve each sitting Senator. They are on duty each day and night the Senate is in session until the recess or adjournment bell rings.

My personal page boy guide courteously led me into the elevator and told the operator to stop at the third floor—the gallery level. By the time the elevator door opened again, I had learned that he was from South Carolina. His ingratiating manner and pleasant southern accent left no surprise on that score. Next stop, the office of the Honorable Felton M. Johnston, Secretary for the Majority of the Senate.

> *There are four officers of the United States Senate elected by the Senate: the Secretary of the Senate; the Sergeant-at-Arms; the Secretary for the Majority (the majority party in the Senate); and the Secretary for the Minority (the minority party).*

Mr. Johnston had been elected over six other candidates. He was a graduate of "Ole Miss" University, had served in the office of Senator Pat Harrison of Mississippi, and had been Chief Clerk of the powerful Senate Finance Committee. Included in his career was a tour of duty as assistant to Under-Secretary of State Dean Acheson, serving as the State Department's liaison to the Senate. The elections of the officers of the Senate are held at the beginning of every Congress, every two years.

The corridor to Mr. Johnston's office was high-ceilinged, with a rich, dark dignified feeling. The walls were in a muted "cream of tomato soup" red. Rather plain light fixtures led me to the very tall mahogany double doors.

Taking a deep breath, I made my big entrance, hoping my correct black gabardine suit, crisp white blouse, black hat and white gloves would make a good first impression.

In the very large, high-ceilinged room, with a beautiful marble fireplace at one end, sat this quiet, dignified-looking man. Mr. Johnston was of medium build, with dark brown hair and blue gray eyes. I immediately noticed the deep shadows under his eyes, and for one mad moment it seemed a thoughtful raccoon was sitting at the large formal desk. His face held a petulant expression, making me wonder what was troubling him. (This, I later discovered, was his normal expression and not a reaction to me!) He had a subdued sense of humor and even when he laughed his face seemed set in serious lines. On rare occasions I was to find his eyes would hold a knowing twinkle as he relaxed.

"How do you do, Miss Scott? Come, have a seat. Betty has told me about you." I sat down next to his large desk, smiled at him and waited. Quiet poise seemed to be called for and I thought, I can do that. I think he noted my calm air and unaffected manner. I didn't try to make any strong impression, which he seemed to like. "As you may know, Leslie Biffle has been elected Secretary of the Senate, and I have been elected to replace him as Secretary for the Majority, so I am looking for a secretary." So, I thought to myself, a job as the Secretary's secretary wouldn't be all that bad—hadn't I graduated from The Washington School for Secretaries?

"Yes," I replied, "Betty told me this was her former job." I was observing him and decided he was the type who would appreciate an unassuming approach. I felt it would be best to let him take the initiative in this interview.

"You've been working in government?"

"Yes, sir. I've been personal secretary in the War Department for nearly five years, first with the Caribbean division of the Engineer Corps. I moved with that office from Washington to New York, then back to Washington with the office of the Chief of Engineers." At this point, I brought out my personal efficiency report, which had been graded "excellent," and passed it to Mr. Johnston.

"You know," he said, glancing at it, "I don't put much stock in these reports." He smiled as he spoke, but I thought to myself, if it had been anything but "excellent," I'll bet he would have paid attention to it. I mentioned my education, telling him of my having been an honor graduate of the Washington School for Secretaries and presented samples of the kinds of work I performed.

He suddenly interrupted the interview to invite me to see the view from the window behind his desk. I had to take a big step up to the recessed window ledge. It was awe-inspiring to look down at the Washington Monument and the Lincoln Memorial, a familiar Washington scene. After returning to the chair next to his desk, I thought he seemed to be judging me by my manner rather than my experience record.

When I had settled back into my chair, he seemed a little friendlier and confided that in his last position as special assistant to the Under-Secretary of State, his secretary had been a woman older than him, who wanted to come with him into his new job at the Senate. "But I can't tell her what to do," he complained. "She'd be telling me what to do. I've also interviewed some others for this opening." I felt I was getting to know him better now and I relaxed.

There was a short silence and then he picked up the phone and asked the operator to get Mr. Biffle for him. "Les?" he said, "do you have a minute?" Silence, and then, "Fine, I want to send Miss Scott down and have you meet her. She'll be right down. Okay." Hanging up, he swung around in his chair and said, "I would like you to meet Mr. Biffle, Secretary of the Senate. You know where his office is–one floor below and around to the left." He paused. "Betty will meet you and show you in. Then I'd appreciate it if you would come back up here."

I rose. "All right, yes, I can find it. Thank you, Mr. Johnston, I'll see you later." As I walked to the door, I could feel his eyes following me. Guess I'll have to pass the Biffle Test next, I muttered to myself.

I took the elevator down to the second floor, referred to as the "floor" level, as the Senate floor in the Senate chamber is located on this level. Once in the elevator, I was evaluating the reason Mr. Johnston wanted me to be approved by Biffle, who had been his predecessor. I felt this was a key to Mr. Johnston's possible lack of confidence in his own decision. I knew of his vast experience in the Senate and the State Department, and that he must have had knowledge of the operations of the Senate as well as insight into getting along with its members.

His election attested to that. He seemed, however, to be bowing to Biffle for confirmation of his decision. I was to discover during the twenty years I worked for him that his attitude was one of service to the institution he loved, and not self-aggrandizement. Although his duties were performed with humility, he was not unappreciated. Majority Leader Lyndon Johnson expressed his appreciation in a letter to Mr. Johnston some years later. "We lean upon you heavily for the strength and steadfastness which you have amassed in a lifetime devoted to the Senate and to your country, and characterized by wisdom and honor."

Then on the floor level, I was welcomed by Betty, whom I now deemed my fairy godmother. I looked forward to my next interview. As I walked down an English-tiled corridor toward the Senate chamber, I noticed a large, plain chandelier hanging down immediately in front of tall, forbidding-looking doors. It had a single white bulb burning. This, I learned later, signified that the Senate was in session. In this connection, a light burns in the lantern below the Statue of Freedom above the dome when either House of Congress is in session. This was a tradition begun when the first gaslight was lit in the newly completed dome.

On either side of the entrance to the Senate floor, straight ahead, sat a dignified gentleman, one of the many "doormen" whose job it was to guard the all-important portals to the Senate chamber so that only members and officials of the Senate were permitted entry. I walked to the left, as Mr. Johnston directed, and discovered excitedly that I was walking around the outside of the Senate chamber. I ended up between another well-guarded entrance to the Senate floor on the right and a portal marked "Office of the Secretary" on the left. The huge, polished mahogany doors were open and I passed through a white archway, very high and very beautiful. I walked slowly by several roll top desks, lined up with edges touching as they were, which seemed a continuous counter of some kind. Before me at the end of this very long reception room was a magnificent marble fireplace over which hung a very ornate gold mirror. The carpet and draperies were burgundy, and it looked like a beautifully furnished drawing room right out of the theater, befitting my feeling of entering upon one of the scenes of the world stage.

Mr. Biffle's office boasted a gorgeous crystal chandelier that was reflected in another elaborate gold framed mirror over a most imposing black marble fireplace. Ceiling high mahogany cabinets with glass doors draped in beige silk looked as if they contained state secrets. He was not at his desk but in the adjoining conference room, and I entered yet another graceful room in this unbelievable suite. Over the large mahogany conference table was yet another very ornate crystal chandelier, reflected in the mirror over another marble fireplace. It was as though I was being conducted through a royal palace.

Mr. Biffle's slight build, soft voice, and unassuming manner masked a very savvy, Washington-wise politician. I learned later of his reputation for speaking in hushed tones, mouth concealed behind a hand, to Senators on the Senate floor accomplishing parliamentary miracles. His considerable talent in the successful performance of his duties was well known among the Senators and the Washington establishment.

Upon meeting me, Mr. Biffle was polite, interested in my background, and the perfect host for what seemed like more of a social occasion than an interview.

It was really charming. He had as his guest in the conference room Senator Carl Hatch of New Mexico, a nice looking, relaxed and jovial man. He asked both Betty and me to come in, and we were all served coffee and pastries by one of his staff of waiters. I remarked that it reminded me of a currently popular Washington radio program with Eddie Galaher, called "Coffee with Congress."

When I returned to Mr. Johnston's office he was speaking to Mr. Biffle on the phone. Evidently he approved of me. Mr. Johnston seemed pleased with the conversation as I was told to report the following Monday. Retracing my steps to the Senate entrance of the Capitol I could hardly believe my good fortune. From now on I would be a real "congressional secretary!"

Leaving the Capitol I was walking on air, and that evening at our home in suburban Washington I could hardly wait to give my father the big news.

* * * * *

My father and I had become very close—really good pals. He was delighted to hear my news and his words, accompanied by a big hug were, "You have arrived!" He was a tall, thin man with serious Irish blue eyes, whose sensitive nature found expression in playing the piano (by ear) for hours on end. At parties in our recreation room, our friends would not allow him to get up from the piano bench but kept requesting more and more songs, which we all joined in singing. Frequently, too, on summer evenings when my Dad would play the other piano in the living room, an unseen audience of small neighbors would gather on the opposite corner outside of our home to listen. It was really a "concert," heard through the open windows and doors, for the children. The frustrated actor in my father came out, too, in his colorful recitations, such as "The Face on the Barroom Floor," "Casey at the Bat," etc.

After my mother and father divorced and she remarried, within a few months she passed on very suddenly. She was only forty-two. "Mamadear" lit up every room when she entered, and everyone loved her. My mother and father had a pact before I was born, that if I were a boy she could name me and, if a girl, my father would have his choice. Although she had several boys' names picked out, he won and chose Dorothy. My mother whimsically insisted that an "e" be added. It was to be spelled "Dorothye" so that it would be fancier—with the emphasis on the "e!"

While I inherited my mother's brown eyes and slight figure, (both size eight), my hair was dark, though she was a decided blond. (She had "decided.") Her hair was worn soft around her face, while mine was styled in an upswept, curly-topped do. Most of all, I always hoped I had inherited her happy disposition and love of life.

When my mother died, my grandmother "Nana," offered to live with my stepfather and me. She was too young to be called "Grandma," very clothes conscious with hennaed hair and she even naughtily smoked a little, using a long cigarette holder *a la FDR*. However, my father took me instead to Washington to live with him. Nana's contribution was the baby grand piano in our living room!

Daddy's white Cape Cod colonial home with grass terraces sat on a picturesque corner in residential Silver Spring, Maryland, just nine miles from downtown Washington. When I came to live with him, he planted a small "Dorothye's bush" at the corner of the side porch, making me feel a part of his home. Miss Hay, our Pennsylvania Dutch housekeeper, a quiet little woman, lived with us and took care of us. Our big friendly and lovable police dog, "Silver Scott from Silver Spring," got his name from silver hair mixed with his tan and black fur. He completed our family.

A few months prior to her death when I was thirteen-years-old, my mother, stepfather and I made a brief automobile trip to Washington. The first evening we drove to the Capitol. It was a still, moonlit night and we drove past the beautiful Capitol building with the white dome gleaming in the moonlight. We were entranced even though we got lost and drove round and round the Capitol grounds before finding our way back to the Carlton Hotel. This was my first sight of this historic landmark making a lifelong impression.

These memories kept me from sleeping. Mr. Johnston called me at home and said not to wait until Monday to report, but to come in the next day, which was Armistice Day. The Senate wouldn't be in session so he thought it would be a good idea for us to get together on a holiday when things were quiet.

I was so keyed up thinking about the next day when I would make my official entrance as a Senate employee that sleep was impossible.

In the midst of this pleasant reverie abruptly returned the memory of another visit when I was fifteen. At the invitation of my friend, Betty Euler, I went to hear a speech by Huey Long, the maverick Senator from Louisiana. I remembered the thrill of entering the Senate gallery and being escorted to a front row seat by one of the doormen.

> *The Senate gallery is a balcony on the third floor level of the Capitol building overlooking the Senate floor below. The Senate press and radio galleries above the presiding officer's desk and speaker's rostrum accommodate representatives of the media. The other three galleries are diplomatic, staff, and visitors' galleries, each requiring tickets of admission.*

Huey Long was the current Senate sensation, a forty-two year old Democrat who had worked miracles in the South to help elect Franklin D. Roosevelt to his first term. There was an excited air of anticipation as we all looked down into the dignity of the Senate chamber and awaited the arrival of this Senator. The other members on the floor seemed to share this feeling. Finally, Senator Long arrived and the presiding officer recognized "the Senator from Louisiana." He had lost faith in the New Deal as a quick way to end the depression and eliminate poverty and was attacking President Roosevelt for betrayal openly and violently on the Senate floor. He was exciting and always drew a standing room only crowd, but when Betty got me a pass it was part of my education in democracy, so I went. (Of course, the fact that Betty's mother's dog was named after him intrigued me, and made my attendance to hear him more interesting. I will never forget hearing her call, "Here, Huey" from the kitchen door of her home next to ours!)

Betty often brought her puppy, named "Huey Long," to her office which was near the Senate Press Gallery. One day her office door was open and one of the reporters spotted the puppy asleep on a couch and took a picture. It was published on the front page of the *Washington Post*, with the caption, "Huey Long discovered asleep in Secretary of the Senate's office."

The Senator sent for Betty and she went to his office wondering if she would be fired. He asked her why she had given her puppy his name. She didn't tell him the real reason. It was that her puppy always pushed aside the other puppies in the litter while feeding, and reminded her of the way Senator Long acted in pushing aside the double doors then leading to the Senate restaurant before others. She told him it was because it was her favorite puppy!

The Senator, like Betty's mother's bulldog, was short and pudgy. He had a doughy white face; his clothes were awful. My father was a sporty, though conservative dresser and I noticed such things. Huey wore a fawn-colored suit, a purple shirt with mangy red and brown tie, and brown and white shoes. In this stately body, the Senator looked like a clown. And then he began to speak and I had my first glimpse of the drama and magic that can happen on the hill.

He waved his arms, ranted, pounded on his desk, but somehow managed to hold us all spellbound. I didn't understand much of what he was saying, still he seemed to cast a spell that held his whole audience enthralled. It was magic all right, but black magic. It pushed all the dark buttons inside me—fear, prejudice, anger, violence. What was it? I didn't like it at all.

I was to experience the power of charisma many times over the next thirty-one years, an inspired quality of leadership that could unify and uplift. This was the exact opposite, a violent quality that seemed to suck you down into a spooky black whirlpool. Was this the quality, I wondered vaguely, that Daddy was talking about when he held forth on a former Austrian house painter named Schiklgruber who had become Adolf Hitler, *Der Fuhrer*, supreme leader and chancellor of Germany? *Der Fuhrer* had my father worried. He, too, was a funny looking fellow, but a master, so said my dad, of "passionate, magnetic oratory."

"He is a demagogue," said my father, "who had all of Germany and half of Europe hypnotized. Beware the demagogue!"

Was Huey Long a "demagogue?" I had heard he wanted to be President. What was the lesson in democracy that I was supposed to learn? That he could speak, but that "we the people" could make sure he never got elected? I am positive I was not thinking in those words. At the tender age of fifteen I was thinking "yuk!" And, when I reported my dramatic adventure to my eagerly awaiting friends at school, all I said was that Huey Long was a "mushmouth." I had mixed feelings when a few months later the Senator from Louisiana was shot to death in the marble halls of his own Capitol in Baton Rouge. Ironically, the experience went full circle when I took a trip with the Congressional Secretaries Club years later and sat on the very same sofa in the Governor's office in Baton Rouge where he had died. I was naturally shocked to hear of his assassination, but I had been so disillusioned by his manner and his speech that I felt our country was lucky to be rid of such a hypocrite. I had expected, while sitting in the Senate gallery, to hear patriotic and inspirational words, not the ones I witnessed.

I did not return to the Capitol for nine years. But this night, nine years later, I finally put Senator Long out of my mind, and returned to the exultation of the coming day. These happier thoughts finally lulled me to sleep, and the big day arrived.

I felt very official as I entered the Capitol on my first day as a Senate employee. This time I knew my way around and went directly to Mr. Biffle's office, room S-221, opposite the Senate chamber. Being there on a holiday made the experience more casual. He, Betty Euler and Senator Alben Barkley from Kentucky were in the outer office, conferring about arrangements for the funeral of Senator Thomas, one of the Democratic Senators.

I had heard of the colorful Senate Majority Leader, Senator Barkley, and it was a great surprise to meet him, especially in such informal circumstances. As the strong and powerful Democratic leader of the Senate, his reputation was well respected. I remembered that at one time he had resigned as Majority Leader in objection to a tax bill, and he was immediately re-elected. He was formally escorted back to the Senate chamber at that time and this grandstand move obviously made quite an emotional impact. He had also locked horns with President Roosevelt on occasion. Years later, of course, he was to be elected President Truman's colorful "Veep."

There he was, shaking hands with me, his friendly blue eyes twinkling. He wasn't tall, but his slight stocky build added to his dignity. To me, his graying hair and dapper manner befitted his role. To put me at ease upon being introduced, Senator Barkley said, "My wife's name is Dorothy, too."

When Senator Barkley asked if I'd had any Congressional experience I replied, "No, I worked in the War Department." I was elated when he said, "That's good, because you don't have any bad habits that you're going to have to break!"

That was my first lesson in the art of politics from one of its real masters! I knew there would be many more lessons to be learned, but I was indeed fortunate to have such a wonderful teacher from day one.

CHAPTER THREE

I Hear the Bells (They Ran My Life)

The Capitol elevator didn't move quickly enough for me on the day I started my Senate career. As I opened one of the huge mahogany doors of my new office, Mr. Johnston looked up from his desk. Room G-43 was quiet except for the cozy sound of crackling logs in the fireplace. The warm red carpet with a black scroll design softening the bright color seemed to complete the feeling of warmth. To the right of the fireplace was a tall gold stand proudly holding an American flag. Spotting it brought the drama of the moment to me, and I felt both humble and proud as I walked to my desk in this lovely room.

Mr. Johnston's perfunctory "Good morning, Miss Scott" included a half smile. He looked very serious in a good looking gray suit, and I felt he fit into this formal office with dignity befitting an officer of the United States Senate. I tried to control my delight and thought "What an exciting world I am entering!"

After taking care of routine organizational matters, my first job was taking dictation—a statement made by the Majority Leader when the Senate would convene listing those Democratic Senators who were absent and why. This would be needed to respond to the first quorum call.

When that was prepared, Mr. Johnston took it and abruptly left the office without a word. I was mystified and wondered where he was going. A few minutes later a bell rang—one long ring and shortly after that two short rings. It dawned on me that the long ring was to announce that the Senate was convening! The two bells that followed indicated a quorum call.

The beautiful sound of the Senate bells on the Senate side of the Capitol and throughout all Senate office buildings announce that the Senate is in session.

When the bell for the daily convening of the Senate rings, the Vice President or, in his absence, the President Pro Tempore, the

Secretary of the Senate, and the Senate chaplain, walk onto the Senate floor. The session is opened by prayer by the Senate chaplain. The Vice President announces that the Senate is in session.

Immediately the "absence of a quorum" is suggested, usually by the Majority Leader, and two bells are rung for a quorum call. The roll is called by the Chief Clerk of the Senate (of the staff of the office of the Secretary of the Senate) and all Senators present answer to their names.

Then the Majority and Minority Leaders each announce the reasons for the absence of the Senators on their sides of the aisle following the formal quorum call—and then the debate begins.

The nicest sounds of all are at the end of the day, either six bells, which is "recess," or four bells, which is "an adjournment." A recess stays in the same legislative day and an adjournment goes to the next legislative day which involves the work of the parliamentarian to see what is pending from the previous day.

From then on I realized that my office life would be run by the Senate bells. One long bell, very long, would indicate a roll call vote, usually proceeded by a quorum call, and late in the afternoon, or by midnight, or at 3:00 in the morning or even the next day, two short bells would blissfully announce a recess in the same legislative day. Four bells would indicate an adjournment (still welcome!) to a new legislative day. Bells would also announce executive sessions to consider Presidential nominations.

That day the Senate never recessed for lunch, and Mr. Johnston didn't return to the office until the session was over for the day. I called on one of the page boys to stay in my office at lunch time and took the opportunity to go out and sit on the Capitol steps. I found myself musing about the historic past of life on Capitol Hill.

After 100 years of sleeping, Capitol Hill was coming awake. The old rundown federal townhouses, where giants of history had lived and worked were now being restored. One could easily picture Chief Justice Oliver Wendell Holmes strolling slowly along the tree-shaded streets to the awe-inspiring Supreme Court building across from the Capitol. Horse drawn carriages could be pictured crossing the wide expanse of the plaza.

All of a sudden a deep voice behind surprised me with "Excuse me, Miss," I turned to see Senator Tom Connally of Texas looking for all the world as though he had stepped out of a movie—gray hair curling over his high collar, black string tie and frock coat. I scrambled up, jerked out of my musing to realize this was *now*, and I need no longer daydream about the Capitol Hill of the past! His shy, almost boyish smile made my day!

My first reaction was to wonder why he wasn't at work on the Senate floor. Rather than playing "hooky," I realized that Senators left the chamber from time to time while the Senate remained in session and deliberations continued. Thus, the reason for all the bells to call them back which sounded throughout all Senate offices in the Capitol building and the Senate office buildings.

Little did I realize that instead of thinking of the past Congresses and members who made them come to life, I would experience in my Senate service association with many outstanding statesmen, among them the three colorful and yet tragic Kennedy brothers. Throughout their rejoicing and triumphant times to their devastating and disastrous experiences, I would be a witness to the roles played under the Capitol dome—and beyond.

My Office

I served on the Senate staff for thirty-one plus years, from 1945 to 1977, as Administrative Assistant to three different Secretaries of the Senate.

> *The Secretary of the Senate is nominated by the majority party of the Senate and then elected by the entire Senate. The Secretary's job is to handle all the administrative matters necessary to make the Senate run smoothly.*

Mahogany doors open during each day and night session, lead to the Secretary of the Senate's suite of impressively high-ceiling rooms, across the hall from the Senate chamber in the Capitol. Our outer office was an introduction to what has been referred to as the "chandeliered atmosphere" of the Senate. Towering windows with heavy beige and gold drapes on either side of beautiful marble fireplaces, under gold-leaf mirrors and ceiling-high mahogany cabinets completed the background. The color scheme was blue-gray, gold and tan throughout. One wall contained a gallery of framed photographs of all the previous Secretaries of the Senate.

On our desks were lovely arrangements of fresh flowers that were picked up by one of our chauffeurs from the Botanical Gardens twice weekly.

To the right was seated the Chief Clerk whose service as a State Senator in the Kentucky legislature predated his term of over thirty years with the US Senate. He was a calm, no-nonsense man, well known to all the Senators whose historic duty besides serving as liaison for all the administrative offices under the Secretary was to call the roll on the Senate floor. This was done after each quorum call and before each roll-call vote. He also performed this duty at all the Democratic National Conventions.

A left turn, and then through a high archway would bring you to my office where my second assistant secretary and I sat at large mahogany desks. A ceiling high window with beige and gold draperies was on each side of our marble fireplace topped with its gold leaf framed five foot high by three and a half-foot wide mirror. The gold leaf scrollwork at the top was very ornate, extending another two and a half feet, the elegant design befitting a royal palace.

One of the specialists in the Senate cabinet shop whose job it was to restore and maintain all Senate furniture occasionally renewed the gold leaf work by hand, rubbing layers of gold leaf into the frame.

The fragrance of mixed flowers in crystal vases, gladiolus, carnations and others welcomed members of the Senate and other visitors when they first stepped through the high arched entrance to my office. It provided an enticing air of refinement and graciousness, a background to my attractive, well-groomed assistants at their desks.

On St. Patrick's Day the Irish Ambassador always sent green carnations to us and, of course, we carried out the tribute to the day in our "wearing of the green."

In addition to my desk phone was a personal line and a direct telephone line to the White House. Each time a Presidential message was brought to the Senate by one of the White House messengers he had to come into my office and report on my White House phone that "the message had been delivered to the Senate."

As hectic as the daily activities in our office were, with Senators, VIP visitors, Senate page boys and members of the press present, the atmosphere remained tasteful and dignified.

The magnificent impressive views from our Senate windows overlooking the Washington Monument and reflecting pool elicited deep emotions of patriotism, flag and America.

Highlights on the Job

My friend, Harold Beckley, Superintendent of the Senate Press Gallery, frequently said he wanted to "die with his boots on" serving under his beloved Capitol dome.

We felt that—the Capitol was filled with the spirit of all who labored there. It was alive with the warmth and good fellowship of the members of Congress and their busy staffs. Sincere feelings of camaraderie and devotion among all existed. We enjoyed going to work each day.

From the lighted halls during long night sessions that made the drama being enacted there resemble a glamorous theater, to the Congressional ball games between members of the House and Senate, it was a world of its own.

Frank Valeo and I attended Congressional ball games and when we Senate fans yelled "Charge!" it was as exciting as any big league game. The members of Congress fought for runs as they did legislation, looking for all the world like ordinary American boys.

Indeed they were, important lawmakers for our country and little boys at heart.

After sharp debates on the Senate floor, the Senators, even as they did as players in the ball games, would come away with their arms entwined, moods jovial and respectful.

One night when the Senate was still in session and the House was awaiting its passage of the adjournment resolution, so they could also adopt it, I was talking to Charlie Marston, a friend from the House Press Gallery. He turned his telephone so I could hear the House members, filling in the wait with their voices raised in song in the House chamber.

During joint sessions held in the House chamber, the Congress appeared as gracious hosts to the officials or guests addressing them. The dignity of these occasions was always striking.

I felt so at home in my warm and beautiful office under the magnificent dome, that it made me homesick to leave after my thirty-one years of service. Mr. Charles Watkins, the Senate parliamentarian, called it home for fifty years, as did Mr. Mark Trice, former Secretary for the Minority and then Secretary of the Senate. Vernon Talbertt, the chief messenger in the office of the Secretary of the Senate, also served for fifty years.

The devotion of these loyal servants so enriched the life of the Senate that we all shared in the love of our jobs, no matter how important or unimportant they were. Our exuberance in feeling an integral part in the running of our country helped us endure long sessions, day and night. The spirit of loyalty and accomplishment, with thoughtfulness and cooperation between the political parties made the United States Senate an inspiring and meaningful place to work.

* * * * *

Greeting President Eisenhower on his return to Washington, Senator Mansfield, Senator O'Mahoney and I welcomed the President back to Andrews Air Force Base. Another highlight.

* * * * *

Attending an official ceremony of LBJ's Presidential signing of legislation at the White House, an assignment to escort representatives of the Chinese liaison office in Washington on election day to three local District of Columbia precincts, explaining the voting procedures to them.

* * * * *

Attending embassy receptions at Ambassadors' homes in Washington and a reception at the Organization of American States at the Pan American Union.

* * * * *

Frank Valeo, at a convention of the Secretaries of the Senates and Clerks of the Houses of Representatives of the State Legislatures, introducing me as the "real Secretary of the United States Senate" (in Washington). That evening I attended their reception with our Senate Parliamentarian Murray Zweben. (It turned out to be doubly enjoyable for me as a distant cousin of mine, who was assistant to the presiding officer of the Illinois state Senate from Chicago, was there. It was a complete surprise, and we had an interesting visit together.)

* * * * *

We were invited to go on the "maiden voyage" of the new District of Columbia tourmobile. This was instituted to take tourists all over Washington to special places of interest such as Arlington, Smithsonian, other museums, the Capitol and the Treasury. It stopped at each place and passengers had time to visit at their leisure until the next bus would come to take them further.

CHAPTER FOUR

The Official Senate
Cast of Characters

At times the United States Senate resembles a theater on the stage of which the roles of historic characters are played. The cast during my run in its performances is as follows:

Aiken, George, Senator from Vermont

Aiken, Lola, Asst., (later wife) to Senator Aiken of Vermont

Anderson, Muriel, Staff Member

Barkley, Senator Alben of Kentucky, Senate Majority Leader, later Vice President under President Truman, the beloved *Veep*.

Bell, Jack, Press

Byrd, Senator Robert of West Virginia

Cooper, Ed, Assistant Head, Motion Picture Association

Cosgrove, Rose Ann Johnson, Staff Member

Craig, May, Press

Cutter, Johnnie, Press

Dozier, Ellsworth, Chief Messenger

Frazier, Emery, Secretary of the Senate

Griffin, Henry, Press

Hatch, Senator Carl of New Mexico

Johnson, Christine, Staff Member

Johnston, Felton M., Secretary of the Senate

Johnson, George, Chief Messenger

Johnson, Senator Ed of Colorado

Johnson, Senator Lyndon of Texas

Ketchum, James, former Curator at the White House and later Senate Curator of Arts and Antiquities

Kimmitt, Stan, Secretary for the Majority

Lane, John, Senator Brien McMahon's office

Lincoln, Evelyn, Secretary to President Kennedy

Lucas, Senator Scott of Illinois

Malkie, Del, House Press Gallery

Mansfield, Senator Mike of Montana

McCarty, Dorothy, Chief Clerk to three successive Senate Sergeant-At-Arms

McClendon, Sarah, Press

McFarland, Senator Ernest of Arizona

McGrory, Mary, Press

McNaughton, Frank, Press

Nicholson, Marjorie, Senator McClellan's Secretary

Novella, Angie, Senator Robert Kennedy's Secretary

O'Brien, Larry, President Kennedy's staff, later head of the Democratic National Committee

Peek, Scott, Senator Smathers' office

Potter, Orlando, formerly with Senator Pell of Rhode Island

Riddick, Dr. Floyd, Senate Parliamentarian

Ridgely, Bill, Senate Financial Clerk, later Chief Clerk, Secretary's office

Roberts, Juanita, Secretary to Pres. Lyndon Johnson

Rowell, Mrs. Betty Euler Darling, Assistant to Mr. Leslie Biffle, Secretary of the Senate.

Sahagian, Salpee, Senator Mansfield's Secretary

Schering, Lois, Staff Member

Shaffer, Sam, Press

St. Claire, Darrell, Assistant Secretary of the Senate

Stewart, Joe, Bobby Baker's staff, later elected Secretary of the Senate

Talbertt, Vernon, Chief Messenger for fifty years

Tames, George, Press

Thomas, Helen, Press

Tucker, Juliette, Mr. Biffle's office

Tucker, Margaret, Bobby Baker's Secretary

Tyler, Carole, Bobby Baker's Secretary

Valenti, Jack, President, Motion Picture Association

Valeo, Francis R., Secretary of the Senate
Vaughn, Bill, Senator Barkley's office
Wannall, Bill, Senate Printing Clerk, later elected Senate
    Sergeant-At-Arms
Watkins, Charles, Senate Parliamentarian fifty years
Watt, Ruth, Chief Clerk of the Senate Investigating Committee
Watt, Walter, husband of Ruth Watt, Senate Doorkeeper and
    later Superintendent of the Senate Folding Room
Woods, Rose Mary, Exec. Assistant to President Nixon
Wynn, Florence, Staff Member
Guests:
Acheson, Dean, Secretary of State
Bellamy, Ralph, Actor
Dickerson, Nancy, Television Reporter
Dubbs, Mary Ann Parsons, Secretary
Durante, Jimmie, Actor/Comedian
Eden, Sir Anthony, English Prime Minister
Ford, Gerald, Vice President and later, President
Glenn, John, Astronaut and later Senator
Godfrey, Arthur, Entertainer
Mansfield, Jayne, Actress
McCormack, John W., Speaker of the House
Rayburn, Sam, Speaker of the House
Skelton, Red, Comedian
Rockefeller, Nelson, Vice President
Rosenberry, Loraine, Secretary

Majority Leaders Of The Senate

The contrast in personalities of the many Majority Leaders who
served during my thirty-one years in the Senate was interesting.
These were Senators Barkley, Lucas, Ed Johnson, McFarland,
Lyndon Johnson, Mansfield and Byrd.

* * * * *

Skeeter Johnston was Secretary for the Majority before being elected Secretary of the Senate. Senator Barkley, before his election as Vice President, and Senator Walter George of Georgia, good friends even then, would come to our office in Room G-43, (the "gallery" level of the Capitol). They would always say, "Now, Dorothye, why aren't you married yet?" "Because neither of you is available," I would answer.

Alben Barkley, whom I met on my first day in the Senate, was outstanding. He was a jovial man whose dignity was only enhanced by his warm sense of humor. He used to come into the archway of my office and greet my two assistants and me by singing, "Beautiful Girls."

Former Senator Harry S. Truman had served as Vice President to President Franklin D. Roosevelt, assuming the Presidency upon his death. In the election of 1948, President Truman and Senator Alben Barkley were elected, whereupon Vice President Barkley was known as the beloved "Veep." After his first wife's death he courted Jane Hadley, sometimes penning love letters to her while presiding over the Senate. A member of his staff, Bill Vaughn, would take the letters from him and hurry to the Senate Post Office to mail them. Some of the reporters in the Senate Press Gallery became aware of this practice, watching from their gallery seats and at one time tried to follow Bill. He became aware he was being tailed and took an unusual route with the letter. He was also the staff member who drove the Veep's wedding present to his fiance—a new car—out to her in St. Louis. His bride gave him a handsomely fitted picnic basket.

They were deeply in love.

He was always a warm and memorable person. After the Veep was not nominated again for Vice President, he had been elected junior Senator from Kentucky. He and Senator Walter George, had their luncheons constantly in our private dining room after other official luncheons were over.

After they were married, his wife had a luncheon in our private dining room. She was full of life, attractive and graceful, with an unusual slightly husky voice.

One of my assistants, Rose Ann Cosgrove, a cute, red-haired Irish girl, was standing in front of my desk on one of Senator Barkley's visits. The Senator came in and stood by her. He touched her hand and slowly, slowly moved his fingers up higher and higher on her arm. Her eyes got bigger and bigger as he proceeded and finally Mr. Johnston, who was watching, had to burst out laughing! The Senator was known for his affinity for the ladies. One time he spotted a woman reporter who had written an article about him and this weakness. She stepped into one of the phone booths in the Senate hall, and he bounced in after her and gave her a big kiss—all in fun.

It was said that the Senator was quite a storyteller. There were occasions when tempers would get short in committee meetings and he could soothe feelings by saying, "That reminds me . . ." he would then tell a story, and all would be well. He even wrote a book with that title.

We called them the "Gold Dust Twins," a name which Senator Barkley coined; the soft spoken dignified President Pro Tempore of the Senate, Senator Walter George, and the new "junior" Senator from Kentucky, Honorable Alben Barkley.

Nearly every day the Senate was in session I greeted these two aging pals as they stopped at my desk on their way into our private dining room. They were served a quiet luncheon by the respectful waiters on our staff. Beneath the beautiful crystal chandelier and sometimes to the accompanying crackle of logs burning in the marble fireplace, the crusty humor of Senator Barkley would delight and bring forth a chuckle from Senator George. The dignified, high-ceilinged room with its beautiful mahogany banquet table with its fine appointments became, for a short time each day, a cozy corner for two of the Senate's most illustrious members.

This grew to be a happy habit for the two elder statesmen. On a few occasions they had to wait briefly until other luncheon meetings were over before they could be seated. They then good-naturedly joked about being the juniors who had to take the "second shift." They were deeply revered by their colleagues and this was observed as a warm, rather sweet tradition.

* * * * *

Senator George of Georgia was a quiet, patrician, silver-haired southern gentleman. His Georgian background was reflected in his kindly, gentle and patient manner. At one of the Democratic fund raising dinners in his honor, I well remember a gasp that went through the Mayflower Hotel ballroom in Washington when Governor "Happy" Chandler of Kentucky, in his speech, referred to Senator George by his first name—Walter! We all knew Governor Chandler by reputation but he shocked us all that night with such familiarity.

Senator George's wife didn't even call him by his first name— even by her it was always "Mr. George."

When Henry Talmadge ran for the Senate, Senator George decided not to run against him as he had beaten Senator Talmadge's father years ago when he was elected to his Senate seat. Upon his retirement, Senator George was appointed Ambassador-at-Large to Europe by President Eisenhower. Before he left on his tour of duty, he was thoughtful enough to ask me if he could bring me some perfume from Paris. He brought me Shalimar, still my favorite.

Senator Barkley seemed to be in robust good health, but when down in Kentucky, he was making a speech on what he said was the "happiest day of his life." He ended with, "I'd rather be a servant in the House of the Lord then sit in the seats of the mighty." These were his last words. He keeled over on the platform and died.

When Senator Barkley died and we returned from his funeral, Senator George came in by himself to have his usual lunch. It was sad to see him walk into our office without his old pal, his head bent in sorrow. One of my secretaries, Christine Johnson, jumped up and hugged him and then Rose Ann, my other assistant, did too. When he approached me my heart went out to him. I embraced him, too, wordless, as we all were, at his loss. I guided him inside to Skeeter's private office and though usually undemonstrative, he clasped the Senator in his arms. It was a deeply moving moment, and I'm sure we all hoped our love and caring was of help to the "Gold Dust Twin" who was left alone. Skeeter Johnston immediately called Lyndon Johnson and he rushed over and joined Senator George for luncheon. He dropped everything and did this for several days following, to help fill the void.

* * * * *

After his death, his wife Jane Barkley worked at George Washington University as a secretary to the Dean. She wrote a book entitled, *I Married The Veep*. She died at a comparatively young age a few years later.

* * * * *

Following Barkley, Senator Scott Lucas from Illinois was the next Democratic Majority Leader. He was handsome and a very hard worker. At one time he was incapacitated by an ulcer and spent time at the National Institutes of Health in Bethesda, Maryland.

At the same time, Leslie Biffle, then Secretary of the Senate, was hospitalized there for bursitis. To make it worse, Secretary for the Majority, Felton Johnston, had a nervous breakdown and joined the other two at the same hospital. During the many night sessions of the Senate at that time, Senator Earle Clements from Kentucky, the assistant Majority Leader, worked long hours in Senator Lucas' place. Bobby Baker, then assistant Secretary for the Majority (to Mr. Johnston) would telephone me at my office and dictate all the announcements for the roll call votes. At that time we had many important votes.

That year we had a very long session of the Senate, continuing through the fall elections and Senator Lucas, after his recuperation, could not leave Washington to go back to Illinois to campaign for re-election. Congressman Everett Dirksen won Senator Lucas' Senate seat. Disappointment and sadness were obvious during his election night party as the returns came in.

After Senator Lucas was defeated he developed circulation problems in his leg and had one leg amputated. My last memory of him was a sad picture. At a party at the National Press Club in Washington, he seemed so embarrassed and downhearted as he sat in a wheelchair.

Not long after that he went on a train trip with the "Ex-Senate Employees Club." Senator Lucas became ill on board and the train was stopped. He died on that trip. The next day, Margaret McMahon, his principal assistant, placed flowers on his former desk in the Senate chamber in his memory.

* * * * *

Senator Everett Dirksen, who had defeated Senator Lucas, was elected Minority Leader by the Republican side of the Senate.

* * * * *

Lyndon B. Johnson was the next elected Democratic Majority Leader of the Senate, and he towered over Senator Dirksen, on occasion leaning down and grabbing his lapels with his face up to his, *coaxing* him into cooperation on legislation.

Senator Dirksen had a golden velvet voice. He was warm-hearted and I remember one time he rose on the Senate floor to take umbrage against a member of the House who had made cruel remarks about the "women of the Senate."

Senator Dirksen made a televised tour of the Senate side of the Capitol which many of us, including Jim Ketchum, the Curator of Arts and Antiquities of the Senate, under our office, watched. We heard some discrepancies in his velvet-voiced descriptions, however, Jackie Kennedy later took a television audience on a similar tour of the White House.

* * * * *

After gregarious and colorful, that "can do" man Lyndon Johnson, was elected Vice President, Senator Mike Mansfield of Montana was elected Majority Leader. Mansfield was a tall, quiet, rather taciturn, serious man. His speeches were delivered like lectures or, as some thought, in the tones of a funeral director. He worked hard in this position and had a special interest in foreign policy. He took many trips out of the country. He was accompanied by Secretary of the Senate, Frank Valeo. They provided very comprehensive reports to the Senate. One of these trips was to China soon after President Nixon had opened our relations with that country. Included were Senate Minority Leader Hugh Scott of Pennsylvania, the Capitol physician and some staff members.

Upon his return Senator Mansfield invited my staff and me to an informal reception in his office. Slides of his trip, as well as those taken on the use of acupuncture by the Chinese were shown, including a picture of a woman giving birth while eating a banana, undergoing this treatment.

I also attended a reception where Senator Mansfield was feted, celebrating his seventeen years as Majority Leader.

After he retired, he was named Ambassador to Japan by President Carter. During a trip to Japan I called his office but he was not in Tokyo. He was traveling in the country. The daughter of a friend of mine went to Japan shortly after that while working on her thesis for college graduation on the Japanese economy. I gave her a letter of introduction to the Ambassador hoping she could meet with him. I later received a very warm letter from him saying that when she arrived in Tokyo, President Carter was also there, so he could not give her an appointment. He did, however, have his secretary help the young lady with her assignment.

At this writing, Senator Mansfield is in his nineties and he still receives visits from Japanese officials when they come to Washington.

* * * * *

After Senator Mansfield retired as Majority Leader, Senator Robert Byrd of West Virginia was elected (calling in his "chits" while serving as assistant Majority Leader, in the way of votes). Some thought Senator Ted Kennedy, who had assisted the leadership, might be elected to this post, but it was Senator Byrd who made it. His hobby was "fiddling" on the violin. One evening after the Senate session was adjourned one of my assistants and I were invited into the Democratic cloakroom (headquarters of the Democratic pages, just off the Senate floor) to hear Senator Byrd play the violin. My assistant taped it and the next day the Senator came into our office and we played it for him—hearing it all over again.

I attended a Democratic fund-raising dinner where Senator Byrd was the main speaker. His personal secretary, Elizabeth Lowe, and her husband took me to the dinner and told me he had kept changing his speech as she was typing it.

Unfortunately, we all had to agree the speech was not good. He spoke again and again of driving in West Virginia and seeing old deserted houses with paint chipping off and overgrown yards, which reminded him of the Republican party. Prior to this dinner, I had attended a luncheon in the old Senate office building where Senator Byrd spoke. This speech was very well done in contrast. When the Senator came into my office the day after the big dinner where his speech had fallen flat, he asked me how I liked it. I couldn't lie, but just said, instead, how much I had enjoyed the previous one at the luncheon. He agreed and said he should have done some fiddling instead!

The Secretary of the Senate
Who He Is and What He Does

Departmental Structure of the
Office of the Secretary of the Senate

Administrative Assistant and Assistant Secretaries
Bill Clerk
Chief Clerk
Chief Messenger and eight assistants
Enrolling Clerk

Executive Clerk's office
Journal Clerk's office
Legislative Clerk
Office of the Curator of Artifacts and Antiquities
Parliamentarian's office
Printing Clerk's office
Public Records office
Registration Clerk
Senate Disbursing office
Senate Document Room
Senate Historical office
Senate Law Library branch
Senate Library

I served in the United States Senate for thirty-two years (1945–1977) as Administrative Assistant to three different Secretaries of the United States Senate as each succeeded the other over this period when elected by the Senate, and six Presidents.

> *The Secretary of the Senate is always nominated by the majority party of the Senate and then elected by the entire Senate. Many of the administrative functions in the overall operation of the Senate are performed by individuals and offices under the jurisdiction of the Secretary of the Senate. The Senate consists of 100 members, two from each state. One-third of the Senate is up for re-election each year. Every time there is an election (every two years), there is a new "class of Senators" who are elected.*

Leadership of the Senate

After the election there are two conferences—one the Democratic Conference of all Democratic Senators; the other, the Republican Conference of all Republican Senators. These meetings include the entire membership for each party separately to organize the Senate. At the Democratic Conference the Majority Leader is elected, the majority whip is elected and the other officers of the Senate are elected. The President Pro-tem is the one who actually keeps the Senate in order by presiding over the Senate, that is his main function. He, under the Vice President, presides over the Senate when the Vice President is not there. The Secretary for the Majority is elected at the Democratic Conference. When the Democrats are in the majority, the Secretary for the Minority is elected at the Republican Conference. When the Republicans are in the majority, of course they are allowed to elect their Secretary of the Senate, the Sergeant-at-Arms and the Secretary for the Majority.

These elections are really not so much elections as they are nominations. The parties nominate these people and they are elected by the full Senate after having been nominated by each of the individual parties. The Democratic Majority Leader is also the Chairman of the Democratic Conference itself and the Chairman of the Democratic Steering Committee that appoints all Senators to membership on all the standing committees. He is also the Chairman of the Democratic Policy Committee, whose function it is to work out the policy agenda for the entire program of the Senate.

Offices Under the Secretary of the Senate

Under the office of the Secretary of the Senate are various offices starting with the Senate parliamentarian. This office, as the name implies, is to keep everything going according to *Robert's Rules of Order*, the parliamentary proceedings on the Senate floor each day. The Secretary of the Senate also has under his jurisdiction the Senate Disbursing Office which is run by the financial clerk of the Senate. It is his staff which expends all moneys of the Senate including all Senators' salaries, Senate employees' salaries, funds spent on furniture and fixtures, maintenance of the Senate chamber and Senate disbursing office. Another office under the Secretary of the Senate is the Senate Library. This office is for all reference purposes for the entire membership of the Senate. The

Senate Document Room, which has copies of all bills, amendments and everything that is presented for work on the Senate floor is also under the Secretary of the Senate. The Executive Clerk's office, which handles Presidential nominations, is also under the Secretary of the Senate. There is a calendar of business each day for legislation scheduled for debate in the Senate chamber. There is always an executive session of the Senate in addition to the legislative session. The Stationery Room is also under the Secretary of the Senate's office. It stocks all the necessary materials for each Senator's office. The Printing Clerk's office is also under the Secretary of the Senate. This office is in charge of the printing of the legislative and executive calendars and is the liaison with the government printing office to send in everything that is printed. The official reporters of the Senate are not under jurisdiction of the Secretary of the Senate but they do record every spoken word on the Senate floor that is sent through the Printing Clerk's office to the government printing office. *The Daily Digest* is a joint office of the Senate and the House. The employees of the Senate side of *The Daily Digest* are under the Secretary of the Senate. *The Daily Digest* is in the back of each issue of the Congressional record each day giving a summary of the work on each side of the Capitol, the work on the Senate floor, the work of all Senate committees and the entire programs for the Senate side. The House side has its employees also in the same *Daily Digest* office, but they are only for the House. Also under the Secretary of the Senate is the registration clerk who registers lobbyists and another office called the Public Records office which has available for members of the press pre-election and post-election reports which have to be submitted before and after each Senatorial election.

Duties of the Administrative Assistant to
the Secretary of the Senate

Preparation of notices to nominees for election to the Senate, instructions, mailing of forms to file with the Public Records office, etc. Another function of the Administrative Assistant is writing letters to the State Governors to instruct them about certification of members of the Senate when they are elected. When each Senator reports in person he has orientation meetings in the office of the Secretary of the Senate in his office suite. These are attended by the newly-elected Senators and representatives of all the different offices that are to serve them. For instance, a representative from the Senate Rules Committee has to come over and tell the newly-elected Senators what office spaces they are going to be allotted. The financial clerk who is the head of the Senate Disbursing Office under the Secretary of the Senate, tells them how much money they have to spend for staff and so forth. All these details are taken care of in the office of the Secretary of the Senate.

Office Hours of the Secretary of the Senate

The Secretary of the Senate accompanies the Vice President and the Senate chaplain to open the sessions of the Senate each day. In connection with the various conferences, meetings and luncheon meetings in our suite of offices, I supervised two assistants and nine messengers. We had one head messenger, two chauffeurs, and waiters who served us. We had the Democratic Policy Committee luncheons in our office and frequently luncheons for committee chairmen, frequently also with liaison offices helping us get the Senate program that the President requested enacted.

The Secretary of the Senate's office is always open during the hours when the Senate is in session that sometimes lasts until three to four o'clock in the morning, or all night long. The Senators frequently come in during the hours the Senate is in session to wait for roll call votes to occur on the Senate floor even in the small hours of the night. Therefore, the Secretary of the Senate's office is always open and its staff is available to serve all the members of the Senate.

Processing of Electoral College Votes

In connection with record-keeping, when we had the joint session to count the electoral votes, I was responsible for getting everything done regarding contacting Governors, preparing official letters, preparing for the joint session, which is the electoral college vote to officially certify the President's election. This is a joint session with the House in the House chamber and there are three tally clerks among the members of the House appointed by the Speaker of the House. Everything is counted to record the Presidential votes in each state by the Electoral College. In this regard, our office put out several publications, factual campaign information, manner of selecting delegates to conventions and the Electoral College. All this information I distributed after my various talks to the Congressional seminars. The tally clerk meeting, the joint session of the House and Senate, is very interesting because it is the final vote for the President. The Speaker of the House and the Vice President have to be the ones in attendance to determine that this is the *final function for the election of the President* and they are there historically.

Luncheon Conferences in our Conference Room

In addition to the Democratic Policy Committee luncheons, Committee Chairmen luncheons, Liaison White House luncheons and the Senators' personal luncheons, we had diverse groups. For instance, Mr. Valeo had what they call the I-House (International House) which was a group similar to a "junior" United Nations. The participants came down from New York and we had some members of the Senate and House address them. We had all types of official and semi-official luncheon meetings in our conference room that doubled as our private dining room.

I was with Felton M. Johnston, Secretary for the Majority, for ten years. At that time we had a two-year period when the Republicans were in the majority and we changed the signs on the door to "minority" and changed our letterhead, but we still served the Democratic side of the Senate. After Johnston's retirement, he left after having served as Secretary of the Senate himself for ten years and I worked with his two successors when they were elected by the Senate.

Messages from the President

One of our interesting functions in the office of the Secretary of the Senate was to receive messages from the President. The White House messenger always had to come into our office after delivering a message to the Senate floor. I had one telephone that was a direct line to the White House on a table next to my desk. He had to call the White House and say, "the message has been delivered."

Legislation Enacted by Both Houses of Congress

When we had bills that were signed both in the House and the Senate by the Speaker of the House and by the Vice President of the Senate after adoption by both houses of the conference reports, we had our chauffeur take these bills down to the White House to the President. That was following a function of one of the offices under the Secretary of the Senate, the "Enrolling Clerk's" office.

There is also the Clerk of Enrolled Bills. These are individuals who have to check every word, every bit of punctuation, every comma and every period to be sure everything is exactly right before the legislation goes down in final form to the White House.

Journal Clerk's Office

The Journal Clerk's office is also under the Secretary of the Senate. The journal is a summary of the action on the Senate floor each day.

Secretary of the Senate's Role in Inaugurations

We had various functions in connection with inaugurations, as the Secretary of the Senate is a member of the group that goes out on the inaugural platform. He accompanies the Supreme Court members who come in a body to get into robes in our conference room in which they appear out on the platform when the President is inaugurated. The Secretary of the Senate has a lot to do with the seating and official functions of the inaugural ceremonies. There is a Joint Inaugural Committee—members of the Senate and House—that distributes tickets to the official receptions in connection with the inauguration. We also had many official inaugural functions in our suite of offices that I arranged.

Summary

This covers the overall picture of how the Secretary of the Senate is nominated by the Democratic Conference, then elected by the Senate by resolution.

After having served eleven years, Frank Valeo retired because another man was elected to that position. When he retired, I also did.

Three Different Secretaries of The Senate

It was educational and revealing to work as Administrative Assistant for these three different Secretaries of the Senate: Felton M. Johnston, Emery L. Frazier, and Francis R. Valeo, as they were elected in succession. They were entirely different from each other; in personality, disposition, and approach to the job.

* * * * *

I worked with Mr. Johnston for ten years when he was Secretary for the Majority (serving just the Democratic side of the Senate). For this position, he was also elected by the Senate. His nickname was "Skeeter," as when he was a boy he was "no bigger than a mosquito." When elected the eighteenth Secretary of the Senate he brought to this office the same thorough, detailed, and very conscientious manner of working which was his trademark. In this new role he supervised many departments in the administration of the Senate, comprising over 150 employees. In our immediate office I supervised two secretarial assistants and nine messengers; the chief messenger, who also served as headwaiter at our luncheons, the assistant chief messenger, two waiters, two chauffeurs, and three additional messengers.

As Secretary for the Majority, Mr. Johnston, during night sessions when any roll call votes were taken, would work for hours after the Senate adjourned, as would I. We checked on each of those Senators who had been absent for each vote, trying to get their positions. This practice was important for their individual voting records. These were used in their campaigns for re-election.

Most of the time his expression was thoughtful and a bit down-hearted. It was only because his deep concentration was reflected in his face. A friend of mine, Walter Watt, used to call him "laughing boy." During the twenty years I worked closely with him I could anticipate his moods and what his directions to me would be. At first I frequently worried that I'd done something wrong, but realized that was only his manner. He would say to me, "I don't tissue around, but when I like you, I'll be devoted to you." He was cross to telephone operators and others, including our chief messenger, Ellsworth Dozier. So nervous did he make him that Dozier came to me to ask what he could do to please Mr. Johnston. I advised him when Mr. Johnston was giving orders for our luncheons in our private dining room, to make him repeat, if necessary, rather than to make mistakes and have the wrong food served. Our waiters brought the orders up from the Senate restaurant. I think this advice smoothed out their relationship.

Mr. Johnston's wife, Wanda, was a lovely young woman, used to his moods. One day I received a newspaper cartoon from her. It showed a wife opening the door for her husband when he arrived home from work. He had a big scowl on his face—with a note saying she thought I would appreciate it! I did.

The Senators appreciated Johnston's diligence, especially Lyndon B. Johnson, when he was Majority Leader of the Senate. He was devoted to Mr. Johnston, expressing in many ways his admiration. One letter from him described Mr. Johnston as the "Ninety-seventh Senator."

Johnston had served as Congressional liaison to the Senate from the State Department under Honorable Dean Acheson when he was Under-Secretary of State. Earlier his career had started immediately after his graduation from "Ole Miss" university when Senator Pat Harrison from Mississippi appointed him to the staff of the powerful Senate Finance Committee. He became Chief

Clerk of the committee. He later triumphed over six other candidates when he was elected Secretary for the Majority of the Senate.

He had some very interesting visitors—one, a friend from his State Department days when he was special assistant to Under-Secretary of State Dean Acheson—came to our office on a Saturday morning dressed in a sport shirt—no tie, and slacks. As he was still in an executive position I was surprised that he didn't appear in "diplomatic dress" which I pictured as striped trousers and frock coat! However, on another occasion Honorable Dean Acheson, then Under-Secretary of State, came for a visit and I went down to meet him at the revolving door of the Senate entrance of the Capitol and escorted him to our office. I was fascinated to discover a very dapper figure in an expensive suit, with a black cape, similar to President Franklin Roosevelt when photographed at Yalta wearing *his* black cape. The Johnstons entertained Mr. Acheson and his son, who was a carbon copy of his handsome dad at their home. I was one of their guests, and was particularly interested in hearing about Mrs. Acheson who was quite an artist whose work was displayed at various places in Georgetown. (I was a "Sunday painter," too, doing portraits).

It was during Mr. Johnston's tenure that Ralph Bellamy, Arthur Godfrey, and Jayne Mansfield visited our office.

Mr. Johnston was not at the office the day of Jayne Mansfield's visit but Bobby Baker (Secretary for the Majority) and I received her. Many of the Senators came in to meet her.

When Mrs. Johnston was undergoing a brain tumor operation, many of the Senators wrote very kind and thoughtful letters to him, some of which I dispatched to him during the many hours he waited during her operation.

Upon his retirement after thirty-five years of government service, Mr. Johnston was honored at a very elaborate reception at the Statler Hotel in Washington. The members of the Senate who served on the committee planning this affair spared no expense. The decorations included a huge buffet table with an ice sculpture of the Capitol. The food was delicious and 700 formally attired guests attended. Speeches by many of the Senators were highly complimentary and sincere. I enjoyed every minute of his sentimental evening and looking around at the devoted company assembled, felt privileged to share the honor being paid to him. Mr. Johnston's family and his proud mother, her eyes sparkling, accompanied him.

One of the highlights of the evening was the presence of President Lyndon Johnson. I was touched and deeply pleased and felt a few tears well up when Mr. Johnston gave his appreciation speech citing my service to him. He said in part that I had been a loyal, dedicated and devoted person who next to his immediate family, was the closest to him, etc.

This occasion to me was one of the most memorable of my Senate career.

After twenty years of being so close to him, getting to know him so well, I had also become close to his family. In my memories the image of his daughter Wray, at age twelve, playing duets on the piano with my father at our home in Silver Spring and of his son when a small boy trying out my typewriter at the office kept returning.

I remembered his Air Force lieutenant son, Mac, surprising his mother at the twenty-fifth anniversary dinner honoring his mother and father at the Metropolitan Club in Washington. Mr. Johnston and I had taken pains to arrange his leave from his duties in Texas to surprise her. Many of the Senators and friends had presented a silver money tree for the occasion.

Another of my treasured memories was seeing Mr. Johnston on his way to the Senate floor, grinning ear-to-ear when his daughter gave birth to her second child. He announced that he was a "second grandfather."

I remember his good friend, "Beck," Harold Beckley, Superintendent of the Senate Press Gallery. They always argued over who had the best job in Washington.

And so, as our chief messenger Dozier and I bid our boss a tearful goodbye the warm and happy, nostalgic recollections overwhelmed me. The next day Dozier said he thought he should have gotten a floor mop, to mop up our tears.

The next day, when I answered the morning's first phone call and said, "Mr. Frazier's office," it was Mr. Johnston, laughing and saying, "good morning."

Following his retirement, it was known that Senator Mike Mansfield from Montana, then Majority Leader, was going to nominate Francis Valeo for the post of Secretary of the Senate. As a temporary honor to Emery Frazier for his many years as Chief Clerk of the Senate, he was elected to serve in this post for a short time.

* * * * *

My relationship with Emery Frazier, was that of an old friend. I had always called him "Emery" and I was "Scottie" to him. After he became my superior, I addressed him as "Mr. Secretary."

Mr. Darrell St. Claire, who inherited Frazier's job of Chief Clerk of the Secretary's office, gave a party at his home honoring the two previous Secretaries of the Senate, Johnston, and Frazier, and Mr. Valeo, who would be the incoming secretary. It reminded me of a Lucy-Desi television program where three Santa Clauses had appeared.

Emery Frazier was a homespun, wholesome man who had an abiding interest in the US Coast Guard and his cottage he and his wife enjoyed on Chesapeake Bay, Maryland. He was a "hail fellow, well met" type of person who highly respected the traditions and history of the Senate. A man of quiet good nature, he also relished the weekly poker games, a tradition among the seasoned officers of the Senate. He called for the "yeas" and "nays" in each roll call vote on the Senate floor when he was Chief Clerk. His duty it was to push the buttons on the Senate rostrum, signaling by bells quorum calls, roll call votes, and recess or adjournment. These sounded in each office in the Senate side of the Capitol as well as all offices in the Senate office buildings, named the "Russell" and "Dirksen" buildings, honoring the memories of Senator Russell of Georgia and Senator Dirkson of Illinois. Some years later, a third Senate office building was constructed and named the "Hart" building, honoring Senator Hart of Michigan.

Emery Frazier also served at numerous Democratic National Conventions in this capacity, calling the roll of states for their votes in nomination of the candidates for President and Vice President. His deep voice was familiar to all. During my service at the Democratic Convention in Philadelphia, I had a late dinner with him after one of the night sessions. It was more of a "midnight snack" as we both had to remain at Convention Hall until the late night recess.

Emery's duties as Secretary of the Senate after his thirty-two years as Chief Clerk finally caused him to sit at my desk shortly before the end of his term and say, "Scottie, this job is getting to be a job!" He, of course, had been elected to this post to serve as a bridge following Mr. Johnston's retirement and the expected election of Mr. Francis R. Valeo. Many of the Senators urged him to campaign for longer service in this capacity. I offered to write letters to each of the Democratic Senators during the evenings from home for him but he refused. Emery was given a very sentimental retirement luncheon at the Capitol. He was presented with a sword by the Coast Guard. This he cherished as a fitting close to his long Senate career. I watched with mixed emotions as he gracefully accepted the sword and said his farewell to the institution he loved. The Senate was losing a devoted servant.

* * * * *

The third secretary was Francis R. Valeo. He was dark-haired, good looking and quiet, but a somewhat sophisticated Italian. His was said to be the true "Horatio Alger" success story. His father, when he immigrated to this country, had sold peanuts on the streets of New York. Mr. Valeo lived in Brooklyn in his youth and worked for Brooks Brothers in New York City. Every day he would study languages on the subway going to and from work. The result was that he was prolific in five languages.

Senator Mansfield first met Frank when he was a speechwriter at the Library of Congress and borrowed him, ultimately adding him to his own Senate staff. Mr. Valeo was a very talented writer and served Senator Mansfield well. He also accompanied the Senator to some sessions of the United Nations in New York.

After Bobby Baker, who was Secretary for the Majority of the Senate, was forced to resign, Mr. Valeo was appointed temporarily and subsequently elected to that position.

Following Mr. Frazier's retirement as Secretary of the Senate, Mr. Valeo was elected to that post.

He proved to be an affable boss, immediately calling the head of each department under his jurisdiction in for a personal "get acquainted" meeting. He also went to some of our departments personally to meet with their staffs and present himself as their new boss. He retained my staff and all our messengers.

One day I had gone on my lunch hour to Garfinckels downtown, to get a fur jacket. Who should come in the store but Red Skelton! We talked a while and I remember his suit looked like he had slept in it—it was all wrinkled—and he had a tape recorder and a camera hanging on his arms. He explained that he carried them whenever he went to a new place. Invariably when he took a cab he would talk to the driver and get funny material for his show.

He asked me where he could find Attorney General Mitchell and I directed him to the Justice Department. (I mentioned that he should really meet Mitchell's wife, Martha!)

I invited him to visit my office in the Capitol building but didn't expect to see him too soon, so when he arrived I quipped "What took you so long?" He was a warm, friendly, humorous man.

(About Martha: She, at that time, was Washington's primary "gossip." She had caused the Attorney General and the Nixon administration a great deal of embarrassment by making late night telephone calls to key administration members and others on the Washington scene. It made all the national papers.) Because of her outbursts and irresponsibility, she was sent to Palm Springs, California and literally "hidden away."

* * * * *

Frank Valeo was versatile in his duties. One snowy morning, for instance, the staff of the official reporters of the Senate had all been snowed in. They were late getting to work. The Senate convened and the necessary reporter did not arrive to report the proceedings. Valeo flew back into our office and got his tape recorder. The opening had to be repeated and he recorded the proceedings, saving the day.

Valeo accompanied Majority Leader Senator Mansfield on many foreign fact-finding trips during his tenure as Secretary of the Senate and he prepared reports for the Senator's presentation to the Senate.

Following President Nixon's initial trip to recognize and open relations with China, Valeo again accompanied Senator Mansfield on his trip. He studied Mandarin Chinese in preparation. Occasionally on entering his private office we were surprised to hear the Chinese language coming from the tape recorder on his desk. He was then able to address official dinners in China in Chinese.

Valeo's first trip to China, in what was then Peking, was traumatic. He became ill, but refused to go to a hospital there. Instead, he stayed in his chilly hotel room while the rest of his party went on to other cities. He told me he thought he was going to die in that cold room with its bare bulb hanging from the ceiling.

During his term Frank and I became close friends. His mother was a sweet little white-haired lady with big brown eyes. She came down from New York state frequently and at times officiated with Italian specialties at his dinner parties. She and I were drawn to each other. I took her on a tour of the White House one day and to breakfast afterward at the Washington Hotel Roof restaurant, overlooking the Washington skyline. While at the White House we visited the restroom used for official functions. To our surprise it was arranged for both men and women, one sex at a time!

Frank and his son, Jamie, and I went to the circus together and one time Jamie hiked with Sixta, their Spanish housekeeper, all the way from their home in Northwest Washington to the Capitol.

Carrying out his father's instructions about climbing steps whenever possible, Jamie and I climbed the Capitol steps and, to his surprise, I beat him to the top!

Frank's affectionate big brown-eyed police dog, "Vicky," frequently attended his dinner parties under the dining room table. Major Holthusen, Frank's friend, loved that dog. Frank entertained many members of the Senate and others at his condo which, with the help of his housekeeper, he termed the "best restaurant in Washington." He received birds' nests and shark fins from friends in Hong Kong for preparation of the Chinese dinners. He furnished his guests with three sets of chopsticks—beginners, intermediate and expert. At the first of these Oriental dinners at his home I didn't do so well and he asked me wiltingly, "Would you like a fork?" He enjoyed bringing recipes back from all his trips with Senator Mansfield.

We assisted the members of the Chinese Liaison Office in arranging a Congressional reception for them, and Frank jokingly said to me that if I should retire I could get a job as social secretary for them. I remember attending a dinner there with him at which baby octopus was served.

I had an interesting experience with them when they requested that Mr. Valeo take them to see some polling places on Election Day in Washington. He delegated this duty to me. I took them to three precincts where the voting was being held. They were vitally interested in the procedure and I felt proud to answer their questions and explain "democracy in action" to them. I was invited to tea back at the embassy but another engagement kept me from accepting.

During Valeo's term I attended with him and Skeeter Johnston, one of the Administrative Assistants' receptions. I felt very official, with a Secretary of the Senate on each arm! I was an active member of the Administrative Assistants' Association, serving as secretary in that organization. One of the parties I arranged was an Easter bonnet contest. This was attended by some of the Senators, two of whom, Senator Frear of Delaware and Senator Lausche of Ohio, served as judges.

Another unusual assignment I had was to take a group of Senate wives and their children on a private tour of the Washington zoo. This was in the evening and the manager served a light buffet supper to the group. It was after dark when we went through all the animal houses and I felt sorry to have the lights turned on in each building to awaken the animals. It was a fun evening and Frank's son Jamie also came with us.

Some time later their dog, "Vicky" had to be put to sleep and my heart went out to Frank and Jamie when they had to take her to the vet. They said the dog seemed to sense the place where they had been before and it was a *sad* trip. I felt like putting my arms around Jamie, the blond, usually smiling boy, as he stood by his father's desk in the inner office, his broken heart reflected in his eyes. It was a *sad* picture—they both looked so helpless. Our chief messenger, Dozier, lived close to them and sometimes took Vicky for a walk. He, too, was touched when he heard the news.

The Secretary of the Senate is re-elected every two years, at the beginning of each new Congress. In January of 1977, just prior to the Democratic Conference, Frank confided to me that two of the Democratic Senators were going to endeavor to have the Secretary for the Majority, Stan Kimmitt, elected to his job. He didn't want me to discuss it with office personnel and we began calling some of the Democratic Senators to get their reaction and support. They were deeply shocked and Frank did obtain support from several. The next day at the Conference, Stan Kimmitt was elected and Frank was defeated. This ended his Senate career.

After the Conference, when the bells rang for the Senate's convening, Frank walked to the Senate floor as usual, knowing he had been replaced. I sincerely admired him for his grace and dignity at that moment and told him so.

Upon his retirement he opened an office in Washington representing some clients whom he advised on relations with Congress. I had moved to Palm Springs, California, planning to spend winters there and to return to Washington each summer. He asked me when

I was in Washington if I would work with him. He assumed I might become bored! Impossible! I was always busy visiting old friends.

I value Frank's autographed keepsake to me describing me as "a strength of the Senate."

In Palm Springs I play tennis, swim, play bridge, attend literary luncheons, concerts, etc. I've also done many oil portraits of friends, relatives and pets.

The Senate Pages

The term "page" is of Middle English origin. According to the *Oxford English Dictionary,* the word dates from the fifteenth century when it meant a youth employed as a personal attendant to a person of rank. Hence, because of the similarity of their ages and the services they provide to members of Congress, this word is used to describe the young Congressional employees.

The first page was appointed in 1789. In 1827 the House employed three and the number has increased to twenty-one. They must be up, dressed, and in the Capitol Page School by 6:15 A.M. When their school day is over (at 10:30 A.M. unless the Senate convenes earlier) they report to the Senate cloakrooms (Democratic and Republican) to which they've been assigned. Their duties begin by placing on each Senator's desk in the Senate chamber the Calendar of Business (list of legislative agenda), Executive Calendar (list of Presidential nominations), all Senate bills, resolutions, and Senate committee reports. They place telephone calls, deliver messages and letters to Senate and House offices, and run various errands to assist the Senators.

Before the installation of the legislative buzzers and signal lights, pages raced through all the halls and committee rooms announcing impending votes as they ran. There were also riding pages before telephones were invented. They were mounted on horseback delivering urgent letters—also "telegraph pages" equipped with high seat bicycles to deliver telegrams.

The pages appointed by Democratic Senators sit on the steps to the presiding officer's desk on the right, and those appointed by

Republican Senators are seated on the left, waiting to be summoned by a snap of the finger from each Senator on their side of the middle aisle. They are on duty all the hours the Senate is in session so their days are long, sometimes extending into and through the nights.

One of the Senate pages' special duties occurs only every four years when they take part in the ceremony of counting the electoral ballots after a Presidential election. Two pages, one from each party, carry the wooden, inlaid with leather, boxes containing the ballots from the Senate chamber to the House chamber for the joint session when the votes are tallied, the final step in the Presidential election.

After unsatisfactory experimental educational arrangements starting in 1925, Congress included in the Legislative Reorganization Act of 1946 provisions for a tuition-free education of the pages in a school that would be part of the District of Columbia school system. In 1949 the Page School was moved from a subterranean location beneath the west wing of the Capitol building to more suitable quarters on the third floor of the Library of Congress.

Beginning with the 1983–84 school year, the House and Senate decided to have separate schools for their respective pages. Both met in the Thomas Jefferson building of the Library of Congress. They now offer a curriculum for only the junior year of high school.

When I was at the Senate, their studies for the ninth through the twelfth grades were covered. I attended graduation ceremonies that were inspiring and enjoyed a close relationship with all the Democratic pages who came and left during my years. Each time a bill was introduced, amendment offered, or a vote taken, they would rush the action to my assistants and me so we knew immediately what was occurring in the chamber. For example, during the various luncheons in progress in our private dining room, I was able to keep the Majority Leader and various Senators informed.

I remember the comment one of the pages, when asked what he wanted to be, said he "was studying to be a Senator." On many occasions after the pages left, they would come back to see me. I remember how shocked I was on one such day when a very good looking former page returned not too long after and he had lost all his curly black hair! He was bald! He had been so handsome!

One of my secretarial assistants on her late night turn (as our office always stayed open as long as the Senate remained in session) used to say she "sat up with the Senate." The page boys did that every night.

The pages are expected to maintain a "B" average in their school. Their report cards are issued not only to their parents but also their sponsoring Senators and the Senate Sergeant-at-Arms. The school year starts in September and runs through June, or as long through the year the Senate remains in session. The number of students at any one time may fluctuate since some pages are appointed for as little as two months and others remain for as long as a year. The college preparatory schedule includes courses in social studies, English, science, and mathematics, as well as tutoring in foreign languages.

The majority party appoints the majority of the twenty-one pages. In 1971, the tradition of "all boys" was brought to an end by Senator Jacob Javits of New York, who appointed the first female Senate page. He also appointed the first black page in 1965.

The pages were required to wear knickers until 1947 when the Republicans won a majority in the Senate for the first time in many years. One of their first acts was to change the pages' uniforms to a dark blue suit and tie. So when a girl page was appointed, she had no worry about wearing scratchy knickers. Prior to this time the House pages, who had switched to long pants years earlier, used to tease the knickered Senate pages unmercilessly.

In the early days, pages were paid $1.50 for each day the Senate was in session. This was raised to $2.00 in 1846. At the end of each session, after long hours and struggles in bad weather, the Senate usually voted to award the pages a bonus of $200 each.

Their current yearly rate is $9,090. Sometimes they would try to earn extra money to get Senators' autographs for tourists. The going rate in the 1850's was $.06 per name. Pages would trade names among themselves, trying to get a complete set, which might bring as much as $10.00. Most Senators cooperated with them until the demands became too frequent. Henry Clay and John C. Calhoun were particularly reluctant to give their autographs and to obtain them required strategic maneuvering by the pages. They also would profit from collecting orders for copies of Senators' speeches and selling them.

In later years, many of them retained the energy and enterprise, and rose to colorful careers.

One early page, Arthur P. Gorman, during a recess, carved his name in one of the stone columns of the old Senate chamber with his penknife. He must have planned to stick around as years later, in 1880, he was elected to the Senate and served for twenty years. He found the evidence of his youthful misdeed and never forgot his days as a page.

In the early days pages were responsible for making their own living arrangements, however, some of the boarding houses lacked bathing facilities. At one point, their appearances became so objectionable that officers of the House and Senate tried to enforce a rule that every page take two baths a week in one of the cold marble bathtubs in the Capitol basement. They tried every trick to avoid the baths and a ticket system was devised. But the clever boys took to selling their tickets to city boys who were eager to say they had had a Congressional ablution.

Edmund Alton became a page on December 2, 1872. On his first day he dutifully showed up in the required attire, dark blue knee breeches and jacket, long ribbed stockings, and white blouse shirt. In his history of the times, he recalled that when things were slow in the chamber, the boys would play marbles under the Vice President's chair—even with pages from the other political party.

Sometimes the page boys would dare one another to see who

was brave enough to sneak an exploding cap under the presiding officer's gavel. The next rap of the gavel brought a small explosion that would enliven the chamber and enrage many Senators.

Among the pages' tricks was mimicking the Senators they served. Some were so good that the ones they mimicked would come to watch. During the 1920s Vice President Charles Dawes gave some official status to these mock sessions when he presided at meetings of an organization the pages formed known as the "Little Senate."

Pages still find it advantageous to know the likes and dislikes of those they serve. Senator Harley Kilgore of West Virginia liked a certain cold drink, Senator McKeller of Tennessee preferred a special brand of mineral water and fruit-flavored chewing gum. Senator Carter Glass of Virginia liked a piece of apple pie with cheese at two o'clock in the afternoon. Senator Joseph O'Mahoney of Wyoming liked an unusual brand of cigarettes while Senator Charles Tobey of New Hampshire liked cigarettes with filters.

The fictitious "bill stretcher" was a favorite game. Skeeter Johnston was approached in our office by one of the new pages in search of a "bill stretcher." Senator Byrd, in his address to the Senate on this subject, admitted he had engaged in this initiation of new pages, but later had a luncheon and photo session with them to make amends. While Senators had fun at the pages' expense, they also had fun with them.

Senator McNary used to treat pages for a weekend of football, baseball, or theater going. Senator James Davis shared with pages candy he kept in his desk, and Senator Rufus Holman shared his comic books, almost as with their sons.

In 1913 Vice President Thomas Marshall began a custom for giving a Christmas dinner for the pages. Vice President Calvin Coolidge continued the tradition.

Since nine-year-old Grafton Hanson became the Senate's first page in the 1820's, there have been changes in the age limits. In 1854 the ages were between twelve through sixteen; in 1949, fourteen through seventeen; and at present they are required to be juniors in high school. There was an unwritten law in the nineteenth century that no page could be *taller* than the *shortest* Senator.

Senator Harold Hughes of Iowa once told a group of pages: "Actually, you probably know more about what is going on in the House and Senate chambers than we members do. You have heard virtually all of the speeches and parliamentary dueling that's going on, while we members, owing to committee hearings and other demands on our time, hear only part of the action."

When the graduating class went to the White House to meet President Lyndon Johnson, he described the chance to be a page as "a chance to see government without glamour—to learn that ideals alone don't make programs; that dreams do not automatically become reality." The pages seem to agree with these assessments of their job. As one described it: "It's having a chance to watch day by day what counts. It's fascinating to see how one thing balances against another, the compromises, the need to give way on this to get that. It's like a puzzle. When you look at just one piece one day it means nothing, but after a while, you discover how it all fits and locks together."

He reminisced about the Senate (where he spent twelve years) and complimented them on the nature and quality of their work. He said:

> *Woodrow Wilson said that the office of President requires the constitution of an athlete, the patience of a mother, and the endurance of an early Christian. Personally, I think he may have overstated the requirements of the Presidency. But from very long and close observation of thirty-four years, it seems to me that President Wilson may have been describing the requirements for a Congressional page.*

Among my friends at the Senate were former Senate pages who came up through the ranks to be elected as Secretary of the Senate. They were:

Carl A. Loeffler, appointed a page in 1889 and remained with the Senate for fifty-nine years, eventually being elected Secretary of the Senate before his retirement;

J. Mark Trice, whose Senate service of fifty years began and ended with his service as Secretary of the Senate;

Joseph Stewart, a former Senate page and one time editor of the page school's newspaper, was ultimately elected Secretary of the Senate.

Senator Byrd, former Majority Leader, observed in one of his addresses to the Senate that: "the Senate could not function very well without them. Moreover, the nation itself benefits from their labors, for, as Milton so wisely observed: 'They also serve who only stand and wait.'"

Senate Dining Room

Ours was the only official and private dining room in the Senate. Good food, good service, lovely surroundings and ambiance kept it well occupied. The luncheons served many purposes.

The most important were the Democratic Policy Committee meetings where the agenda for the consideration of legislation was scheduled.

Next in importance were the ones attended by Senate Committee Chairmen, another effort to streamline the Senate's programs.

Particular Senators were invited as guests at the request of the White House, at which conclaves the President's programs could be presented.

In addition, at times individual Senators requested use of our dining room and waiters for their personal functions.

Important national and international visitors were also guests at various times. Visiting celebrities also were invited, and finally the Secretary of the Senate could host his own affairs.

I gave a wedding luncheon for newlyweds Senator and Mrs.

George Aiken in our dining room and also a birthday surprise luncheon for Frank Valeo.

I was also honored during Skeeter Johnston's tenure with a birthday luncheon in our private dining room.

Vernon Talbertt and His Messengers

Under the jurisdiction of the Secretary of the Senate were many departments and approximately 150 employees. Of most importance was Vernon Talbertt, a black man, chief messenger in our immediate office for fifty years. He wasn't a black man; he wasn't a white man; he was Vernon. He personified the words "dignity" and "dedication." He had a sincere love for the Senate, his job and all the Senators thought highly of him. He had served many of the Senators. He served Sir Winston Churchill and yearly received Christmas cards from him. Everybody was as devoted to him as he was to them.

For his fiftieth anniversary we asked each of the sitting Senators to write a letter to him to mark the occasion. In addition to that, many of them volunteered to send money. We didn't ask for that, but all wanted to do it. It came to a nice sum.

The presentation of the book in our office was by Senator Lyndon Johnson and Senator Everett Dirksen, the two leaders. Mr. Johnston and the former Secretaries of the Senate were also there. It was very sentimental. Skeeter Johnston cried. To think! Fifty years he was here serving all those Senators. Vernon was invited into the Senate chamber to listen to speeches in his honor. The next day we ordered copies of the Congressional Record for him.

He was the chief messenger with a staff of nine. Two of the messengers were waiters, two were chauffeurs because we had official cars. There were errands to the State Department and other government departments and we had to take bills to the White House, etc.

Vernon was there to serve the Secretary and to serve all the Senators who came in. Of course he was there for the receptions before the luncheons and for the receptions for any foreign dignitaries, to keep things going smoothly, and keep all the messengers lined up. We had constant use of the boys in every way, to serve the Senators, to be there through the night sessions, and to perform miscellaneous duties.

It was Vernon's responsibility to close up our suite of offices each night; the outer office, the reception room, my office, Skeeter Johnston's office, and our conference room. Many times he had to stay late, as I did. For instance, on Saturdays when Senator Johnson and Senator Russell would come for late luncheons, he would have to stay as long as anything was going on. The office was considered open, and no matter how many hours would go by, Vernon was the last to lock up.

I went to his daughter's wedding, which was at his home. Everything was done very tastefully. His daughter looked lovely and the house was beautifully decorated. Large white satin bows and ribbons ascended the stairway and one room displayed gifts. Skeeter, Mrs. Johnston and I were the only white people there. We were so glad we were invited. It was a very dignified affair. The minister conducted the ceremony in front of the fireplace in the living room.

When Vernon retired, his assistant, Ellsworth Dozier, was given that job. Frank Valeo, when he was Secretary of the Senate, called him "Mr. Dozier," giving dignity, and Mr. Johnston, in his tenure, had done just the opposite, because he wanted to be friendly. He called him "Ellsworth." He was considerably younger than Vernon but he was very devoted and dignified. He was a different personality, but he had the same dedication to his work as Vernon.

All the boys were helpful in many ways, and I felt close to them all. On Christmas we exchanged gifts. On birthdays they would have flowers for me. One year, knowing so well my preferences, they found an umbrella with violets on it. They were very kind and devoted to me, and I felt the same toward them.

All my boys, of course, had their own personalities, but there was never any jealousy among them. Then Dozier became ill. This is so strange because Vernon, who had retired, died, and within one week Dozier died, although he was much younger. He was in the hospital when Vernon passed on, and he called me and said he was so sorry he couldn't go to the funeral. There's a strange thing about this; he had seen Frank, then his boss, just before he had gone down to Bethany Beach, as we were out of session. Frank told me Dozier had insisted on shaking hands as though it were "farewell." He passed on the day Frank had just arrived at Bethany Beach. I called him and he turned around and came right back. We could hardly believe they both had died within one week of each other.

The messengers were located in an outer office and we also had a sub-office for them on the lower level. They would come and spell each other and stay on duty as long as the sessions lasted, sometimes all night long. All were very devoted. When I retired, I had a party for all of them at my home. We used a gong in the entrance to the dining room when we needed more refreshments, such as the buzzers my girls and I used to summon them in our office.

Sometimes they would "moonlight." I had a party down at my cottage on Chesapeake Bay for thirty people from our office. The enrolling clerk, Harvey Carroll, played his violin strolling around the tables. Dozier tended bar in a white jacket and Jim Ketchum, the Curator of Arts and Antiquities in a chef's cap and apron, had a great time manning the barbecue.

There was another strange coincidence. I was vacationing in Palm Springs, California when Skeeter Johnston, who had retired, passed on. I had just arrived, so I didn't go back to Washington for the funeral. But I called his daughter. Within one week, Emery Frazier, also retired, died. This was so strange, the two former Secretaries of the Senate and two chief messengers of ours had died within a week of each other.

CHAPTER FIVE

Presidential Inaugurations

There is a Joint Inaugural Committee, composed of Senate and House members.

The Chairman is always a member of the party whose nominee is elected. All arrangements are made by that committee, and they are the ones who distribute tickets for the actual swearing-in of the President at the Capitol. These are like diamonds and very much treasured and sought after.

Our office always had all the members of the Supreme Court, which is a large body essential to the ceremony, use our conference room, to robe. The Chief Justice actually does the swearing in. Inauguration Day was usually cold and they would put their black robes over their coats so when they appeared on the inaugural platform they appeared in their robes. It was the Secretary of the Senate's duty to lead them onto the platform. We had the diagrams of each group. They would go out to the platform where they would sit. They would put on their robes and we would serve them coffee in our dining room prior to the ceremony.

On one of these occasions, Chief Justice Warren Burger, in 1972, had been on a bike and had broken his finger. I had a car hit my car and I had done the same, so we had a lot to commiserate about. Four years later, at the Carter inauguration, we were comparing fingers. "You're the most important person in the United States today because you're going to swear in the new President. Without you, it couldn't happen!" I said.

After the inaugural program, there is a luncheon for the President and his family and special guests. For President

Truman's, it was held in the Secretary of the Senate's office, when Leslie Biffle was Secretary. He and Truman had been best friends dating from his Senate days. At other times the luncheons are held in the formal Senate reception room. This is the same room made notable by the Chinese Ping Pong team competition. After lunch the President would lead the Inaugural Parade down to the White House, take his place in the reviewing stand (built every four years in front of the White House for the ceremony).

When President Carter was inaugurated he chose to serve a box luncheon en route for those who were going to be in the parade. Chief Justice Burger had wanted to host his own luncheon in the Supreme Court. But," he said, "we couldn't because the President wanted Mrs. Burger and me to ride in the parade." Mrs. Burger wasn't allowed to have any salt in her diet, so he had a sandwich in his pocket under his robe! His wife had asked him to carry it so when they'd be riding in the parade she wouldn't have to eat the box lunch. She was going to wear a fitted coat to the inauguration. She was afraid if she carried the sandwich in her inside pocket of the coat it would look like she was pregnant. So he was wearing it under his robe when he swore in President Carter.

The Carters upset protocol by jumping out of their limousine soon after it turned off the Capitol plaza onto Pennsylvania Avenue and walked in the procession! This had never been done before, and all the spectators were thrilled with a close-up look at the first family. Blasé Washington, of course, was aghast but charmed with this touch. There was more than the ordinary excitement, and it was a personal moment of acquaintance with the President and his lady. Just plain "Plains" people taking a walk!

President Clinton and his wife Hillary liked the warmth of this gesture and repeated it.

President Carter's daughter, Amy, and President Clinton's daughter, Chelsea, loved the exuberance and happily joined the "Walk to the White House" with their parents.

Both of these inauguration days will be remembered with feelings of good will and affection demonstrated by the inhabitants of the White House.

Another incident was during President Nixon's inauguration when Imelda Marcos, wife of President Ferdinand Marcos of the Philippines, came to town. Senator Mansfield and Frank Valeo were close to the Marcoses, having traveled to the Philippines frequently. Governor Remaldez, Imelda's brother, visited our office often. He graciously invited me to visit Manila, but I never made it. Imelda's uncle had served as Ambassador to the United States and her brother Remaldez later was Ambassador to China. The Marcos' two boys were pages in our Senate and their daughter worked for both the Senate Democratic Policy Committee and, later on the House side.

On this inauguration day, Mrs. Marcos called Senator Mansfield, who called Frank. She didn't have a ticket! Here she was, the wife of the head of a country and couldn't attend the inauguration.

This was a problem because, at the last minute, it was impossible to get tickets. We had used our supply and even had distributed step seat tickets. So when Senator Mansfield called we had to do something about it quickly. We finally managed one ticket. Of course, Inauguration Day is so hectic, it's just like the national political conventions. So we arranged for Darrell St. Claire, the Chief Clerk under our office, to deliver her ticket to the Madison Hotel. (Darrell was tall and handsome, so good-looking in fact that when, on one occasion when Elsie Brenkworth, the wife of the Senate financial clerk, told him so, he replied, "It's always been a problem!") So Darrell went downtown fussing and fuming, because the traffic was horrendous. Even to get back to the Capitol you had to have a special ticket to get on the plaza; a ticket to get into the building; a ticket to get up to our floor; a ticket for our office—all for naught. In the meantime, Mrs. Marcos had called the White House and they sent a ticket for her. Darrell came back, very angry, after going all through Washington on Inauguration Day and she didn't need it!

The Kennedy inauguration was almost paralyzing because the weather was so awful. It snowed all night inauguration eve. I had a $100 ticket for the gala at Constitution Hall. Vice President-Elect Senator Lyndon Johnson had a luncheon in our office with Mrs. Johnson and his daughters. Even after that was over, I had to keep the office open to accommodate Robert Hinckley, President of ABC, to have his inauguration ticket picked up. I didn't leave until around three o'clock, got stuck in the snow and had to abandon my car. Between rides with good samaritans, I arrived home at nine o'clock—six hours later and never had a chance to use my ticket.

The next day a friend of mine who worked in Washington and lived close to me in Silver Spring, gave me a ride. All the cars that had gotten stuck in the snow were hauled off the main roads and we found my car. The National Guard had shoveled snow all night long so the parade route would be open for the Inaugural Parade. How can I ever forget the Kennedy inauguration? A lot of the Senate employees stayed all night, some at the Carroll Arms Hotel, so as to be there the next day. One woman going to the gala that night at Constitution Hall hired a cab and must have gotten so upset she died in it. All kinds of situations and stories came out of that wild inauguration eve.

Nonetheless, the traditional inaugural balls were thrilling at all different hotels and even the National Guard Armory. The President and his family made the rounds to all of them and the color and glamour and excitement of attending them are wonderful memories. I enjoyed attending the balls for Presidents Truman, Kennedy, Johnson and Carter. I'll never forget Jackie Kennedy in her beautiful white inaugural gown, looking like a princess with her handsome prince, President Kennedy. That was, indeed, the beginning of Camelot in America. There was always a special glow and excitement when each first family would arrive for their inaugural ball, dance a few dances, then go on to the next party.

It made a long night for them but it was America's very special, historic and wonderful day and night so we were all up to it!

* * * * *

But before the inaugural excitement, glamour and pageantry of the official balls must come the tough, rough expensive campaigns which result in the conventions which choose and determine the peoples' choices.

CHAPTER SIX

A "Bird's Eye" View of Political Conventions

1948 Democratic National Convention
Philadelphia, Pennsylvania

Among the myriad of national political conventions that have taken place in America, I would like you to enjoy the pathos and excitement of some that I personally experienced when we produced the Democratic Platforms.

Skeeter Johnston, when he was Secretary for the Majority, was appointed secretary of the Platform Committee of the Democratic National Convention. Even though we completed a list of work in our Washington office in the Capitol, Mr. Johnston preceded me to the convention headquarters at the Bellevue Stratford Hotel in Philadelphia. I was scheduled to follow him in a few days, but the first night he was there he called me at home. It was a cry for help: "Miss Scott, you have to come up here right away!" So I took the train up the next day and entered the chaos. When I checked in, the best they could give me was a tiny, closet-sized room. It was really stark, had no telephone, but I stood it for one night and the next day was transferred to a nicer one. After dumping my suitcase, I went to Leslie Biffle's office at the hotel, where he was serving as Sergeant-at-Arms of the convention, hoping to find Skeeter there too. The office was closed as it was lunch time so back I dashed to the lobby where bedlam had broken out! It was alive with every sample of humanity—delegates checking in, suitcases all over, clerical types, members of the press, and inquisitive on-lookers, anxious not to miss any of the excitement. I ran into Henry Griffin, a photographer friend of mine with the Associated Press, who invited me to lunch. A few days later he took a picture of me on a ladder hanging a large poster of President Truman over the door of our office at the hotel. Before even catching my breath at lunch I had plunged into the writing of the Democratic Platform!

The mail was coming in and piling up like a snowstorm, the phones never stopped ringing and we were endeavoring to schedule sessions of the committee to hear the witnesses who would propose planks to the platform. The committee membership was made up of two delegates to the convention from each state while seventeen members of the Drafting Subcommittee held the hearings and completed the actual wording of the platform for presentation to the full committee for its approval. After the committee vote it would then be, in turn, voted on by the full convention and become the banner of the Democratic Party to be carried forth in the national election.

We held closed hearings in our rooms in a hotel away from the Bellevue Stratford morning and afternoon for a week. Private industry moguls, civil rights advocates, minority groups, and a cross section of American life were all represented. Finally we worked on the word-by-word construction of the platform, forgetting time completely. Members of the press were trying desperately to locate our working office to get a scoop. At one point Skeeter and one of our staff consultants were followed out of the Bellevue en-route to our secret location. They walked out one door, turned around and went around the block and came back in again, succeeding in giving them the slip. There were articles in the *Philadelphia Inquirer* wondering where the Drafting Subcommittee was holed up.

The hours our Drafting Subcommittee worked so intensely will always stay in my mind. There were heated discussions on all the proposed planks developed from the testimony of the witnesses at our hearings. The picture of Governor Pat Brown of California, a nice solid looking man with dark hair and glasses, possessing an ingratiating manner, remains vivid. The perspiration was pouring down his cheeks as he pleaded his positions in the heat of the hotel room. Mrs. Emma Guffey Miller, sister of Senator Miller from Pennsylvania, was quite a character. She resembled a slightly frumpy housewife, but stuck strongly to her convictions and was not to be out-talked by even Mayor Hubert Humphrey of Minneapolis. An old fashioned pair of long ladies' bloomers, large size, was later discovered in one of the bureau drawers of our hotel office, belonging to—you guessed it—Mrs. Miller!

It reminded me of Marlene Dietrich's song, "I Wonder What the Boys in the Back Room will Have." But these boys in the smoke-filled back room would have only grueling hours of debate, changing, improving, drafting and re-drafting the words to describe the important principles of the aims and ideals of the Democratic Party.

Biffle's office at the Bellevue Stratford was an extension of his gracious suite of offices at the Capitol back in Washington. The office was graced by his attractive assistants: Betty Euler, Betty Kraus, and Juliette Tucker. Many of the Senators in attendance at the convention were frequent visitors and I, too, enjoyed some visits there. One evening I had stopped by to pick up Juliette to go to dinner but we couldn't close the office because Senator McClellan, that studious and gentlemanly Senator with the gentle southern accent from Arkansas, was still there, in a talkative mood.

The two Bettys and I dined together another night downstairs in the hotel and although we were probably slap happy from the long hours and the exhausting pace of the preceding few days, it was a very enjoyable respite.

Betty Euler's wit and good humor were not diminished by the hard work in the world of the convention, and Betty Kraus, with her snapping dark eyes and dark hair was good company, her Irish love of stories and poetry combined to make her a very entertaining friend.

Then back I went to my hidden headquarters of the Drafting Subcommittee of the Democratic Platform.

Harold Beckley, the debonair, slim, and smooth Superintendent of the Senate Press Gallery, was in his element in charge of Washington press coverage of the convention. His premature baldness didn't detract from his charm. His friends ranged from Senate pages to Senators and Presidents, in addition to members of the media, and he was at home with them all.

"Beck's" office distributed credentials and facilitated the hectic pace of the reporters' participation in all phases of the convention proceedings. At one of our after-hour gatherings he invited me to dinner. We went to the famous "Bookbinders" restaurant where the first thing they served you was a large white napkin that the waiter carefully tied under your chin. Noted for their seafood specialties, this was a ritual. Our evening was delightful. I was so interested in the convention from the reporters' viewpoints and I was fascinated by Beck's entertaining conversation.

About an hour after I returned to my hotel room that night I was surprised and thrilled to receive a telegram which said:

> *How little one's concern for time,*
> *For in less than an hour*
> *I thought you were almost mine.*
> *But now, like a fading flower,*
> *A bud has died on the vine.*

This because he was a married man. Our friendship endured but the romance could never be.

In one of the other few hours when I could escape the tedium of our work I lunched at the Ritz Carlton with an interesting reporter friend, Frank McNaughton, formerly with the United Press and then on a leading news weekly. He was a vibrant person, caught up in the excitement of the city. He later wrote two books with Walter Hehmeyer, a staff member of the Senate committee which investigated the National Defense Program headed by then Senator Truman. The first book was *The Man Truman*, a study of President Truman's career prior to the Presidency, and the second, *Harry Truman, President*. This was described by critics as a "full and careful analysis of the whole Truman administration." It was written after his succession to the Presidency upon Franklin Roosevelt's death on April 12, 1945.

My attractive cousin Marilyn Arnold and her husband Murray, who was Vice President of Philadelphia radio station WPEN, lived in Radnor, a Philadelphia suburb. I only saw them at their home one evening for a short visit when I escaped from our working hideaway. They were vitally interested in my part in the proceedings and later attended a special convention television coverage reception at one of the downtown hotels.

Days became nights and Mr. Johnston insisted that I rest on one of the beds in an adjoining bedroom of our suite. Finally our work was completed, the full committee voted, and we made numerous copies of the platform on our duplicating machines with my boss' wife working just as hard as I.

I rushed back to our hotel, had room service send up a sandwich and twenty minutes later, clothes changed and lipstick applied, joined Mr. and Mrs. Johnston for the trip to Convention Hall. We went by limousine with a police escort, sirens screaming through downtown Philadelphia, on-lookers wondering who we were and what on earth was going on. They should have realized our flight was related to the convention. The entire city was "convention." You'd come out the doorway of the hotel and you'd hear the proceedings from Convention Hall from loud speakers everywhere. The whole thing just permeated the atmosphere. They had some coverage by television cameras, too, and our Platform Committee staff would go from one hotel to another, back and forth, trying to keep the whole thing secret until every word had been voted on and adopted. Friends back in Washington told me later they had seen me on television various times. It was all very exciting and I worked very hard those crazy long hours but it was intensely stimulating.

It was the fifth session of the convention and I thought as we rushed to the hall, "Now I will be present at last to see what I have been missing while being hidden away drafting the wording of the platform."

When we arrived at the hall, Senator Alben Barkley, temporary Chairman of the convention, was speaking. His references to various accomplishments during sixteen years of Democratic leadership, called *The New Deal* received many interruptions of applause. He went on to say, "The Republican nominee (Governor Thomas Dewey of New York) had announced with characteristic finality that he proposes to clean the cobwebs from the government at Washington as he cleaned the cobwebs from the government at Albany following long Democratic tenure. Well, I am not an expert in cobwebs but if my memory does not betray me, I recall that when the Democratic Party took over on March 3, 1933, the spiders were so weak from starvation even they could not weave a web in Washington." This resulted in a rising vote of applause.

Biffle's Sergeant-at-Arms' office there was one of the few places which was air conditioned. It was a haven from the suffocating heat of the convention floor, crowded as it was with Congressional members, state delegations and alternates, all of whom were waving banners and flags and wearing flag-bedecked and outlandish hats, the crazier the better. They were still milling around, knots of people, grouping and re-grouping, constantly talking and walking fanning themselves furiously, many totally oblivious to what was going on, who was speaking from the rostrum or what business of the convention was being carried on.

President Truman, looking cool and, as usual, well-groomed in his spic and span white suit, was waiting in the wings in Biffle's office. I was there for a while when Senator Olin Johnston of South Carolina invited me to take a ride with him to get away from the heat. It was a refreshing change from the furnace of the hall and in his air conditioned car, I finally relaxed.

The chauffeur helped me in and I felt very pampered to be riding around in an air conditioned car in the first place and with nice Senator Johnston. His Senate service had begun in 1945, just three years earlier. He was slightly portly with dark hair and had always been gentlemanly and friendly on his visits to our office. "Ah jus' thought you'd like a little air, Miz Scott," he said in his courtly southern manner. I replied with enthusiasm about attending the convention and being a part of the efforts of our Democratic party in this election year.

We returned in time for the presentation of the Democratic Platform by our Chairman, Senator Francis J. Myers of Pennsylvania. When I first met him, he only talked to me for a very few minutes before saying that he knew I, too, was from Philadelphia!

He was a big, friendly Irishman—what my Irish relatives would call "a broth of a boy." His dark hair, laughing blue eyes and natural friendliness belied a politically savvy and serious Senator. He had been kidding me during our hearings for making the Philadelphia papers so often with my photograph.

His words rang out as he addressed the convention. "We chart our future course as we charted our course under the leadership of Franklin D. Roosevelt and Harry S. Truman in the abiding belief that democracy—when dedicated to the service of all and not to a privileged few—proves its superiority over all other forms of government." As he went on to read our words with dramatic impact, I felt proud of my association with him and our committee in this historic undertaking. The Civil Rights plank stated: "We again state our belief that racial and religious minorities must have the right to live, the right to work, the right to vote, the full and equal protection of the laws, on a basis of equality with all citizens as guaranteed by the Constitution." Although this wording was greeted with applause, minority reports were presented by delegates from Texas, Tennessee and Mississippi.

The issue became States Rights as opposed to Civil Rights and the heated oratory reflected the extremely hot atmosphere of the hall.

During the debate, the permanent Chairman of the convention, Senator J. Howard McGrath of Rhode Island, said, "We want to get through with this thing so that we can recess for an hour or two and get out of this hot place."

After submission of several State delegations' minority reports amid a threatening walk-out by the Mississippi delegation, the minority report presented by former Governor Dan Moody of Texas substituting "States Rights" language for the "Civil Rights" plank was defeated by a roll call vote resulting in 309 yeas to 925 nays.

Former Mayor Hubert Humphrey of Minneapolis, a Platform Committee member, fired up the delegates in a powerful speech on behalf of the minority report offered by Delegate Andrew J. Biemiller from Wisconsin. His remarks included, "My friends, to those who say we were rushing this issue of Civil Rights, I say to them we are 172 years late. The time has arrived in America for the Democratic Party to get out of the shadows of States Rights and to walk forthrightly into the bright sunshine of human rights." The report was then adopted by roll call vote, 651 yeas to 582 nays, and the Civil Rights plank triumphed.

This was the first time I met Senator Humphrey. When he was first elected to the Senate, Senator Humphrey didn't adhere to the tradition of freshmen Senators, like children, who were to be seen and not heard. He started making speeches on the Senate floor immediately. What a vital man! He had so much pep and enthusiasm! Years later, when he was in the Senate and later when he was Vice President, he would kind of dance by my desk. He was always so full of life but he was very negligent about attending fund raising events, many times not showing up. I remember on one occasion I was at the White House and he came over and very cordially greeted my friend and me, making his visit memorable.

Years later, when seriously ill, he was returning from Minnesota and the Senate Staff Club members, realizing his situation was terminal, planned a big party to welcome him back after his medical treatments. It was held in the courtyard of the old Senate office building. A huge greeting card, about five feet wide by four feet high had been prepared. He was very well loved by all the different Senators' staffs and everyone was looking forward excitedly to seeing him. He couldn't make it so his sister made a speech in his place. It wasn't too long after that he passed on. That special evening, starting out so festively, left us all with very heavy hearts.

After routine business of the convention, the nominations of Harry Truman of Missouri for President and Alben Barkley of Kentucky for Vice President were voted on and agreed to.

Senator Barkley in his acceptance speech said, "I pledge to you my unremitting toil and my loyal support, not only to the head of our ticket but to the platform that has been adopted by this convention." He was greeted with sustained applause.

While listening to Senator Barkley I was seated on the rostrum with the handsome Governor G. Mennen Williams of Michigan sitting right in front of me. I was surprised to see him curl one foot under each of the two rungs of his chair. He tilted it, and all of a sudden, went over backwards! There he was, sprawled in front of me. The loud clatter interrupted Senator Barkley's speech momentarily and the Governor arose with an embarrassed smile as everyone broke up. Never a dull moment in the great hall!

When, after his nomination, President Truman strode to the rostrum to give his acceptance speech, I could not help but notice his cocky air and big grin across his face. His shoulders were back, his chest firm and his entrance was fast-paced. The whole picture was that of a strong man, straight-forward and confident. All of a sudden, hundreds of white doves were released over the platform and they flew up to the rafters of the great hall, surprising and delighting everyone.

In his speech he stated that he was going to call the Congress back into session. He had referred to the Republican-controlled 80th Congress as the "do-nothing Congress." He went on to say, "What that worst eightieth Congress does in this special session will be the test. In the record is the stark truth that the battle lines of 1948 are the same as they were in 1932 when the nation lay helpless and prostrate as a result of Republican inaction. I must have your help. You must get in and push and win this election. The country can't afford another Republican Congress." A standing vote of applause followed. He had taken the convention by surprise with his announcement to call a special session, calling the eightieth Congress' bluff, and the delegates went wild! President Truman's winning words were a fitting and provocative end to the convention.

The last day, after the convention was over, I was preparing our trunks for the trip back to Washington, actual carloads of letters and telegrams received prior to our hearings and during the long sessions. All the testimony had to be retained, our offices closed. I was in the Bellevue Stratford lobby, checking out of our rooms. I was approached by a representative of a local radio station. He wanted to interview me since I had been a part of the proceedings. I would have loved to have done it but I had to complete arrangements for our departure.

The convention was the kick-off of the 1948 campaign for the election that everyone thought Thomas Dewey was going to win when President Truman had the last laugh!

No one will ever forget the picture of victorious Harry Truman the day after the election, holding up a copy of *The Chicago Tribune* with a front-page banner headline proclaiming, "Dewey Wins!"

The editors really had red faces and the pollsters were confounded. Beck, who lived in Silver Spring, and I shared rides in a car pool taking turns driving to the Capitol. That morning as we drove in I was really tickled and he kept saying to me, "What happened?!"

My father and I were privileged to attend not only Truman's inauguration but also President Truman's inaugural ball.

1952 Democratic National Convention
International Amphitheater, Chicago, Illinois

Again . . . Skeeter and I were responsible for the creation of the Democratic Platform, the banner of the party and the campaign . . . having been again appointed secretary of the Platform Committee of the Democratic National Convention in 1952. It would be held in Chicago and would be my first visit to the Windy City. I took a train with a sky dome from my home in Silver Spring, Maryland, and became excited in anticipation of the prospect before me.

I checked in at the old Stevens Hotel (now the Hilton) in Chicago, already alive with convention fever. Our hearings were set to start a week before the convention. As in Philadelphia in 1948, we had national committeemen and women on the Platform Drafting Subcommittees. There were about fourteen people who would interview all the witnesses to get their ideas and suggestions. After the wording of the platform was worked up we had to have a meeting of all committeemen and women from each state to vote on and okay every word of it before it would be presented to the convention for adoption.

One thing I recall vividly about my convention experience was the odor as we approached Convention Hall, passing through the stockyards. I had to practically hold my nose every time. Out at Convention Hall Leslie Biffle, in his role as Sergeant-at-Arms, had an office located high above the speaker's rostrum. When our work on the wording of the Democratic Platform was completed back at our offices in the Hilton Hotel, we went out to the convention hall for its presentation and adoption by the convention delegates. There we attended the convention, looking down at the proceedings from Biffle's office.

The big news I heard on arrival was about Vice President Alben Barkley's walk, when he arrived in Chicago, from the railroad station to the Hilton Hotel. The beloved Vice President was endeavoring to convince the labor leaders how well and strong he was. Even though he was a Washington—as well as a national—institution, he was not endorsed for Vice President again.

When he addressed the convention some days later and said, "I am not here as a candidate for any office that this convention can confer," there were loud cries of "No!" He went on to say, "I am in somewhat the same situation as the country gentleman who, for many years, had gone to his county seat every Saturday in his farm wagon drawn by two mules. On all of these occasions he came home intoxicated. He had a gentle pair of mules—they knew the way home. They drove the wagon home—up to the locked gate and stopped in front of the house. Each night the boys would go on out, unhitch the team, take them to the barn and then take the old gentleman in and put him to bed. On one of these Saturday nights the boys unhitched the team, took them to the barn, but left the father in the wagon. As the sun came up over the horizon he aroused himself, rubbed his eyes and stood erect. He went to the front of the wagon and looked out over the tongue and saw no mules. He went to the rear and looked out over the wagon and behind the gate and saw no mules. He went again to the front and then said to himself, 'I have either lost a damn good pair of mules or I have found a damn good wagon.'" Laughter and applause greeted this great story teller but a wave of nostalgia washed over the hall as the delegates realized this was, indeed, the Veep's national swan song.

Later as the *junior* Senator from Kentucky, Barkley relished his new role, wearing youthful sporty clothes.

Chicago is a very stimulating city—a few of its charms intrigued me.

One evening, a group of us took a moonlight sail on the lake and it was fascinating to drift by on the water looking at the glamorous skyline of the city. The lights twinkled and Chicago seemed very modern and sophisticated, its urbane personality reflecting on the water. Of course, the fact that I'd been invited by Scotty Peek of the staff of Senator Smathers of Florida, made it most exciting. Senator Smathers was one of the most handsome members of the Senate and his Administrative Assistant was cut from the same cloth. Our group that night was very congenial and it was one of the highlights of the convention for me.

Another memorable evening was when I went to the Edgewater Beach Hotel for dinner and dancing. That was a beautiful spot and made the long hours at work fade into the background. I could even forget holding my nose against the odor passing through the stockyards en route to the convention hall.

Although the Hilton Hotel and Convention Hall were sites of frenzy and excitement where the convention had a life of its own, the city itself was not as completely saturated with it as

Philadelphia had been. Perhaps this was because Chicago was a more vibrant city and Convention Hall was out at the stockyards, away from the city.

We had three different sessions of hearings a day; morning, early afternoon, and evening. I visited with Mrs. Eleanor Roosevelt prior to her testimony and she was very gracious and dignified, a beautifully groomed lady whose outfit was quietly becoming. Surprisingly, while the public was used to her high-pitched voice, to me her voice was lowered and rich sounding, most impressive, with each word emphasized.

I had seen her earlier at the Mayflower Hotel in Washington, at one of the "March of Dimes" balls. She looked regal, standing at the top of a marble staircase, her beige satin gown with its magnificent train cascading down the steps.

These balls were held nationwide to fight infantile paralysis, appropriately inspired by President Roosevelt's personal battle with this dreaded disease. They were held on January 30 of each year, honoring his birthday.

In talking with Mrs. Roosevelt, I could understand why, with the depth of her devotion to our Democratic ideals and her ability to understand our problems, she was fitted singularly for her role of leadership and diplomacy on the world stage.

As is usually the case, life's really "big" people are the most down to earth. Mrs. Roosevelt was one of these and demonstrated her friendliness and caring when she gave a luncheon for the Senate pages. These young men were excited to have been appointed by their Senator to serve the August body of the Senate. Going to the Congressional Page School at 6:15 A.M. and reporting to duty in the Democratic and Republican cloakrooms adjacent to the Senate chamber at 9:15, they were on duty all the hours the Senate remained in session. My mentor, Betty Darling, was the guest of honor at Mrs. Roosevelt's luncheon and told me how cordial she was to the boys. Betty was assistant to the Secretary of the Senate, Leslie Biffle, and in that capacity was an informal supervisor of the pages.

In addition to testifying before the Platform Committee, Mrs. Roosevelt later spoke to the convention.

With these words, "Seventy million people are anxious to hear the first lady of the world," the temporary Chairman introduced Mrs. Roosevelt to the convention. Immediately great applause and cheers followed and a demonstration of flag waving delegates took place.

She stood, smiling, waiting for the applause to die down before beginning. "Mr. Chairman, ladies and gentlemen of the convention, you are very kind to me and I am glad to have been asked to talk to you about the United Nations, about its past, about what it is doing today and, more important, about its future." She described a meeting in her husband's study in the White House. He said to a friend: "When this war is over and we have won it, as we will, we must apply the hard lessons learned in the war and in the failure of the League of Nations to the task of building a society of nations dedicated to enduring peace. There will be sacrifices and discouragements, however, we must not fail for we may never have another chance."

Mrs. Roosevelt went on to say, "While the United Nations came into being under the present administration and President Truman has been steadfast in his support of the organization, it would not be in existence today if it were not for strong, bipartisan support in the very beginning."

She commented later in her address, "Some of you will probably be thinking that once upon a time the old lady speaking to you now did a tremendous amount of traveling around the United States. You may remember a cartoon showing two men down in a coal mine, one man saying to the other, 'Gosh, here comes Eleanor.'"

"In World War II when I visited so many hospitals in the Pacific I was glad I had traveled so much through my own country and could say to a lonely boy far away from home, 'You come from Lubbock, Texas?' The boy's face would light up. 'Yes, ma'am, I remember when you were there.'"

In closing, Mrs. Roosevelt read a speech which the President was preparing to deliver the day after his death, at a Jefferson Day dinner in Washington, April 13, 1945. "To you and to all Americans who dedicate themselves with us to the making of an abiding peace, I say: The only limit to our realization of tomorrow will be our doubts of today. Let us move forward with strong and active faith."

She said, "That was the last message that my husband wrote to deliver to you, the people of his party and of his country."

* * * * *

One of the touching aspects of the convention was when Senator Brien McMahon of Connecticut, who was ill, was honored to be nominated for President by his colleague, Senator Benton of Connecticut.

An excerpt from Benton's speech follows:

> *For months we free men of Connecticut have been looking forward to this moment, the moment when we could give you the name of the man we have supported for President. I am proud to speak for my delegation and the great Democratic Party of my state, as I present the name of this man to you.*
>
> *Our candidate is not in Chicago. He is watching us from his sick bed in Washington. I greet him now by radio and television, on behalf of this, our great convention here in Chicago. The hearts of this convention go out to him.*

Great applause ensued.

He then described Senator McMahon's leadership in seeing that the trusteeship of the atom bomb, after the first explosion at Hiroshima, should be placed in civilian hands. Again and again, Winston Churchill had said that one fact above all others kept Stalin from unleashing World War III—the terrible power of our atomic stockpile. Senator Benton went on to say that, "One man, above all others, is responsible for that stockpile, the man who wrote our atomic energy law and who sits as Chairman of the Joint Committee on Atomic Energy." He referred to Senator McMahon.

It saddened me to see large posters depicting McMahon's Senate career on display in his convention headquarters in Chicago. We were friends and he used to visit our office frequently. There was a big mystery as to why he would duck into our tiny, half-powder room (just a wash basin and mirror in our office, Room G-43 in the Capitol) and stay for several minutes at a time. I later learned it was to adjust his toupee!

Senator McMahon sent a letter to the Chairman of the Connecticut delegation withdrawing his name from nomination due to illness. After it was read to the convention, there was prolonged applause and cheers for, as Senator Benton described him, "A great son of Connecticut, a great Democrat, and a great American."

Members of his staff at the convention headquarters were endeavoring to be cheerful for their boss' sake.

When I was about to catch a train for my return to Washington at the end of the convention I ran into John Lane, the Senator's Administrative Assistant, who told me the Senator had just passed on. It was a sad ending to my trip as I climbed aboard the train.

John and the Senator's executive secretary, Bill Fey, were good friends of mine, both handsome and hard working men. Bill was later confirmed as a judge in the Washington D.C. District Court.

The Chairman of the Platform Committee was Congressman John W. McCormack. He was a tall, dignified man with graying hair and a serene manner. His New England accent, coming from Massachusetts, was distinctive. He was a loyal Democrat, politically savvy with a commanding presence. He and his wife had a close and warm relationship and despite the late hours which our committee labored, would wait until quite late to share the evening meal. Such devotion was memorable.

Congressman McCormack was very appreciative of my work on the committee. I have letters of appreciation from him following the convention.

At times some members of the Platform Committee would broadcast from our offices. Congressman Brooks Hays, when he came in to dictate some suggested wording, broadcast against a background of furious typing sounds, saying, "I am sitting here in the Platform Committee room of the national convention . . ." It was all very exciting.

Senator Theodore Francis Green of Rhode Island was a tight little packaged Senator, very dapper with pinched nose glasses and neat mustache. He had been elected to the Senate at age sixty-three. He was a member of our Platform Committee, as well as several other convention committees. His various credentials and scheduled appearances, as he attended one meeting after another, sometimes were confusing to him. Various times he would check with me as to where he was due next and have me check to see if he had the appropriate ribbons on.

Senator Green moved around quietly. He walked everywhere. Back in Washington he lived at the University Club on 16th Street and he used to walk back and forth from home to the Senate.

There was one night, a real cold winter night, when Kay Kenny and I were going down to the Statler Hotel on 16th Street to hear the singer Hildegarde. She drove her car and I drove mine. We decided to follow each other and then go home separately. There, outside of the old Senate office building was Senator Green waiting for a street car! I guess it was too cold for him to walk. So I stopped and said, "Oh, Senator, can I give you a ride? I'm going right downtown." He said, "Well, sure."

So he got in. I said, "My friend and I are going to hear Hildegarde. She's right back there," meaning in her car. He turned around and looked in the back seat of my car and said, "She's not here." So, of course, I had to explain that she was in the car in back of me.

Senator Green had a reputation as a "freeloader." The stories were that he would attend a lot of official cocktail parties and substitute the refreshments for his meals. He was also rumored to eat at the counter at People's Drug Store. It was interesting to picture him, the former Governor of Rhode Island, seated there.

In the closing hours of the convention after the nominating speeches and, finally, nomination by acclamation of Governor Adlai E. Stevenson of Illinois for President, President Harry S. Truman took the rostrum to applause, cheers and continued demonstrations.

Included in his remarks were: "You know, it's early in the morning and it's getting earlier. While I appreciate immensely this grand reception which you have given me, I will appreciate it a lot more, now, if you will be quiet and let me do my job and get the new Presidential nominee here so he can make his acceptance speech." He said, "We are going to win in 1952 the same way we won in 1948. And I pledge you now that I am going to take my coat off and do everything I can to help him win. Now, the Republicans can't understand why it is that the Democrats keep on winning elections. They think there's some kind of a trick in it, and they have just about gone crazy trying to find out what that trick is. You know, the real reason the Democrats win elections is a perfectly simple reason. It is because the Democratic Party gives the American people the kind of government they want."

President Truman then introduced Governor Stevenson at 2:10 A.M.

To cheers, Governor Stevenson stated, "I accept your nomination and your program. I should have preferred to hear those words uttered by a stronger, a wiser, a better man than myself." Shouts of "No!" followed. Thus started our country's acquaintance with the eloquence of Governor Stevenson.

His speeches lifted us up to his high level of intelligence, brilliance and inspiration. He was not a tall man, just medium height. He had a receding hairline but his dark hair and eyebrows punctuated the searching, forward-looking expression of his eyes.

Even though this well-to-do man was photographed with a hole in the sole of his shoe during the campaign, he was ever suave and never lost his vigor or vision.

Governor Stevenson ended his acceptance speech with these words. "Help me to do the job in this autumn of campaign and conflict; help me to do the job in these years of darkness, doubt and crisis that stretch beyond the horizon of tonight's happy vision, and we will justify our glorious past and the loyalty of silent millions who look to us for compassion, understanding and honest purpose. Thus, we will serve our great tradition greatly. In the staggering task that you have assigned me, President Truman would counsel me to say that I shall always try 'to do justly, to love mercy, and to walk humbly with my God.'" Cheers, applause, and a standing ovation greeted the Governor.

After Senator John J. Sparkman of Alabama had been nominated for Vice President, Governor Stevenson spoke again to the convention. He said, "Ladies and gentlemen of the convention, you have witnessed here in this hall for the past week, and inspected some of the finest political livestock in the United States." After the laughter ceased, he continued, "But of all the animals you have inspected, we have reserved until now the prize human animal for your approbation. I have the pleasure of presenting to you Senator Sparkman of Alabama, who will give me a little of the strength that I need and give you all of the heart that you need, and give America what we all need."

Senator Sparkman, in his acceptance speech, included these remarks. "I want to pledge to you my heartiest support in doing everything that I can to take the message of democracy to the people of this country, to the end that we shall be successful in November."

Speaker of the House of Representatives and Chairman of the convention, Honorable Sam Rayburn, then adjourned the convention *sine die*, and another campaign had begun.

1956 Democratic National Convention
Chicago, Illinois

Governor Adlai Stevenson was nominated for a second time at the 1956 Democratic National Convention. Although Skeeter Johnston was again appointed secretary of the Platform Committee for the 1956 Democratic National Convention, he declined because of his wife's illness. Wanda Johnston had had an operation for removal of a brain tumor.

During the long hours of the operation, many Democratic Senators sent letters of encouragement and best wishes to them. While he was with her in the hospital, I sent them to him, hand delivered by one of our chauffeurs. He was very deeply touched by their concern and support, and their thoughtfulness helped him bear this tragic ordeal.

In his place Mr. Johnston recommended that Bobby Baker, Secretary for the Majority of the Senate, substitute for him at the convention. I went along to work with Bobby doing the same job I had done at the conventions in Philadelphia in 1948 and Chicago in 1952. He also brought along his secretary, Margaret Tucker. Bobby turned things back to me because he knew I knew the job. The procedure was a little different. In 1948 and 1952, the witnesses actually were scheduled and appeared in person before the committee to make their suggestions for wording of the various planks of the platform. In 1956, some staff members of the National Democratic Committee traveled around to different cities months ahead of the convening of the convention. This streamlined the operation , and did not require everyone to come to the convention city.

Bobby Baker had difficulty getting some of our credentials for admittance to the convention floor. There was a little feud there. Bobby Kennedy was working for his brother, Jack Kennedy, and Bobby Baker's man of course was LBJ. Part of Bobby Baker's official functions was to get our badges and credentials. He spent one whole day at the head office waiting for the issuance of the proper authorizations for us, and felt the delay was due to interference by Bobby Kennedy.

There was also a rumor that the telephone lines in LBJ's convention headquarters were cut, by Bobby Kennedy. I don't know if this report was true. Both 'Bobbys' were loyal to their Senators, but it was felt that cooperation was lacking.

Biffle again served as Sergeant-at-Arms of the convention and brought his assistant and two secretaries with him. One of his personal secretaries, Betty Kraus, a lively, lovely, and hard working friend and I shared a hotel room. Our friend, Kay Kenny from Senator Douglas of Illinois' office joined us for the last two nights of the proceedings. Because of the crowded hotel conditions, we couldn't get an extra cot for our room. This resulted with all three of us sleeping in one bed for two nights! Needless to say, we didn't get much sleep, but kept going on excitement and nervous energy.

I'd been out to dinner a few times during the convention with some friends of Skeeter's, among them Jack Kane, a personable Washington lobbyist. On the last night of our subcommittee work to finalize the wording of the platform before presentation out at Convention Hall, after returning to our office from dinner, I told Jack to call me at two or three o'clock in the morning, and I'd still be working. He didn't believe me but did call at 2:00 A.M. and laughed when I answered, "Platform Committee."

We worked all night long. I remember the next day was a Holy Day of Obligation, and as I am a Catholic, I had to go to mass and didn't have time to go back to my hotel to change clothes. I went to church in the same clothes I had worn the previous day and all night long. Our hotel offices were being closed so I had to take personal things with me. I walked into church in my tired clothes clutching a big red fuzzy Democratic donkey someone had given me. I felt so out of place among all the bright-eyed and bushy-tailed rested and freshly groomed congregation members there. They were eyeing dilapidated me with my huge red donkey!

Then back to my hotel to change, and out to Convention Hall.

One late evening I ran into George Reedy waiting for the elevator at our hotel. He was a staff member of Senator Johnson's Policy Committee. I told George how I wished so much that LBJ would be nominated for President at the convention. He said, "I'd like to write that speech!" and I said, "I'd like to give it!" The next night Governor John Connally of Texas did address the convention, doing just that.

Governor Connally's speech began:

> *I am here to offer to you for the Presidency of the United States the name of a dedicated American, a winning Democrat and a forceful and persuasive leader of men.*

He continued:

> *Four years ago the Democrats of the Senate of the United States looked among their own ranks and unanimously chose this man to be their leader. They knew that here was a man for whom no apologies would ever need be made, a man to stand each day on the front line of battle and carry forward the fight for the people without fear or hesitation, a man to rely upon for fairness and justness and equality of treatment, and a man to prove by his personal conduct that a good Democrat places his country first, above all else. When he assumed that responsibility the Democratic Party was in the minority in Congress, but today our party is in the majority. The record on which that victory was won is a record this man could have claimed as his own.*
>
> *This man is a son of the hill country in Texas, where the sun is hot and the soil is meager and life itself is a never-easy challenge. He has known poverty. He knows people, and he loves them—and from that love burns an unquenched flame of trust*

*in their greatness and in the greatness of America.
Alongside the name of this man there must surely
be written: "This man works hardest of all."*

*Under his leadership, Democrats from all sections
of the country drew together in a common effort
for the nation's welfare.*

*Fellow Americans, fellow Democrats, with great joy,
with great pride, I offer you that son of the Texas
hills, that tested and effective servant of the people—
a real working leader in a time of crying for full-time
American leadership—Lyndon B. Johnson.*

Applause and a demonstration followed.

Senator J. Allen Frear, Jr., from Delaware seconded this nomination, ending with the words: "Love that Lyndon!"

Senator John C. Stennis from Mississippi also stated in his speech, seconding the nomination:

*As we face the future we can, with confidence, go
down the line and meet the future problems of the
decades with a man of the character and leadership
we find in Lyndon Johnson. My state and many
others join in the fine appreciation of those qualities, and it is an honor to present him to the convention as one of the world's foremost leaders and
one of the greatest leaders of our generation.*

These speeches were followed by continuing applause. During a recess of the convention sessions I encountered LBJ in the hall and told him how I had wanted so much for him to get the nomination. He said, "Well, if things had started earlier, I might have had a chance."

* * * * *

Most everyone expected that Governor Adlai Stevenson would again be the nominee for President.

Beginning his speech nominating Adlai E. Stevenson, former Governor of Illinois, for President, Senator John F. Kennedy, Senator from Massachusetts, stated:

> *We have come here today not merely to nominate a Democratic candidate, but to nominate a President of the United States.*

He went on to say:

> *We can offer to the nation today a man uniquely qualified by inheritance, by training and by conviction, to lead us out of this crisis of complacency, and into a new era of life and fulfillment. During the past four years his wise and perceptive analyses of the world crises have pierced through the vacillations and the contradictions of official Washington to give understanding and hope to people at home and abroad. And his eloquent, courageous, and experienced outlook on our problems here at home has stood in shining contrast to the collection of broken promises, neglected problems, and dangerous blunders that pave the road from Gettysburg to the White House. Let us be frank about the campaign that lies ahead. Our party will be up against two of the toughest, most skillful campaigners in its history—one who takes the high road, and one who takes the low.*
>
> *If we are to overcome that combination in November, this convention must nominate the candidate who can best carry our case to the American people—one who is by all odds and by all counts our most eloquent, our most forceful, our most*

appealing figure. We have an obligation to pick the man best qualified, not only to lead our party, but to lead our country. What we do here today affects the life and the way of life of all our fellow Americans.

The time is ripe. The hour has struck. The man is here; and he is ready. Let the word go forth that we have fulfilled our responsibility to the nation.

As he concluded by saying:

I give you the man from Libertyville, the next Democratic nominee and the next President of the United States, Adlai E. Stevenson.

Prolonged applause and an enthusiastic demonstration took place.

After Governor Stevenson was nominated by acclamation, he addressed the convention briefly to turn over to the convention the choice of a nominee for Vice President.

Senator Estes Kefauver from Tennessee was subsequently nominated for Vice President by acclamation. This followed several other nominations. Senator Kennedy, who has also been supported for nomination as Vice President had moved that the rules be suspended so that Senator Kefauver's nomination could be made unanimous.

In accepting his nomination for President, Governor Stevenson said:

I accept your nomination and your program. And I pledge to you every resource of mind and strength that I possess to make your deed today a good one for your country and for our party.

Four years ago I stood in this same place and uttered those same words to you. But four years ago, I did not seek the honor you bestowed on me. This time it was not entirely unsolicited. And there is another big difference. That time we lost. This time we will win!

He went on to say:

We can cross the threshold to the new America. What we need is a rebirth of leadership—leadership which will give us a glimpse of the nobility and vision without which peoples and nations perish. It is time to listen again to our hearts, to speak again our ideals, to be again our own great selves. Standing as we do here tonight at this great fork of history, may we never be silenced, may we never lose our faith in freedom and the better destiny of man.

Governor Stevenson's closing words were:

Goodbye and I hope we can meet again in every town and village of America.

Tumultuous applause and cheers greeted him as he waved and smiled a victory smile from the rostrum.

In accepting his nomination for Vice President, Senator Kefauver said:

A long time ago I went to the University of Tennessee, as I was on the track team. I have been in a lot of races, but I never have been in one like this. I have never been in a race with a finer, more wonderful contender. Senator John Kennedy is one of the fine young statesmen with an outstanding record already, and to be able to contend and finally win against him I appreciate very much. I want to express my appreciation to Senator Kennedy for his graciousness in moving that the nomination be unanimous, and I am very grateful to all of you who have supported me.

I can only say that as a member of the team, I shall try to do my utmost to hold up my part of the job, working the very best I can in all places where I may be able to go. In other words, to do what I can for the election of a man who, I am sure, will go down in history as one of the greatest Presidents of the United States, Adlai Stevenson.

Enthusiastic applause followed Senator Kefauver, as he descended from the rostrum waving to all.

He campaigned with his "coon skin" cap, his southern accent and dark rimmed glasses, seeming to fit the image of a "down home" candidate. In addition to the geographical mix—Governor Stevenson from Illinois and Senator Kefauver from Tennessee, the styles of the two were an interesting contrast. Adlai Stevenson's erudite and sophisticated personality was accentuated by Senator Kefauver's homespun charm.

At one point at Convention Hall, as we were watching the proceedings below from Biffle's office above the rostrum, Bobby Baker said to me, "Oh, Miss Scott, if only Senator Kennedy would be nominated, we'd really win!" Just as Bobby made this comment Senator Kefauver started to come up the steps. I was hoping he didn't hear Bobby's voice. It was interesting that despite his treatment by Bobby Kennedy, Bobby Baker had made that remark.

On another evening session at Convention Hall Betty Kraus of Biffle's staff, Bobby Baker and I were standing at the front of Biffle's Convention Hall box looking down at the speaker. Someone in the back of the office, watching the TV set, called, "You're on television!" We turned and saw our bodies with our heads turned around! Friends said they'd seen me on TV at some of the other conventions, in the hall and walking outside the headquarters hotels, but this was the first time I saw myself on TV—the back of my head, that is.

Later that year, Dottie McCarty (who was Chief Clerk in the office of the Senate Sergeant-at-Arms) and I made a trip to Boston.

While there we visited the office of Speaker John McCormack. We didn't have to wait at all, for as soon as we arrived and were announced he came out personally and greeted us, taking us into his private office, while numerous others continued to wait.

On leaving we stopped by Senator Jack Kennedy's office (in the same building).

We could hardly believe the contrast. One lone secretary was on duty and no one else was there. It was very quiet, really "dead as a doornail."

This was Adlai Stevenson's year—JFK's time had not yet come!

The Democratic Convention of 1960, however, would be a different story!

1960 Democratic National Convention
Los Angeles, California

I didn't attend the 1960 Los Angeles Democratic National Convention, at which Senator Kennedy, after being nominated for President, chose Lyndon B. Johnson to be his running mate for Vice President. Joe Kennedy, Sr., in 1956, suggested financing a campaign for LBJ to run for President with his son John Kennedy for Vice President.

I recall after the convention was over we had three of the nominees on the Senate floor when we were back in session in Washington. Richard Nixon was Vice President and Jack Kennedy and LBJ were Senators. It was exciting because crowds of people lined up in the outer corridor of the Senate gallery to see them. Some came carrying their lunches in paper bags. No matter how long they had to wait, they felt it was worth it to see three of the nominees in action on the Senate floor.

Shortly after the convention we had a luncheon to be attended by both Senator Johnson and Senator Kennedy. Every time LBJ attended luncheons in our private dining room, he was seated at the head of the table, being Majority Leader, Chairman of the

Democratic Policy Committee, etc. He was "it." Everyone wondered on this occasion when Senator Kennedy would come to the same luncheon following his nomination to be President, what would happen. Would the Democratic leader be bounced from his usual seat at the head of the table? The suspense was over when Senator Kennedy did not show up for the luncheon!

Ruth Watt, Chief Clerk of the Senate Investigating Committee, attended some meetings in Hyannisport. She had breakfast there with Senator Kennedy and his brother, Bob, chief counsel of her committee. Bob, as always, was very friendly but Jack read his newspaper through the meal, somewhat rude! He was a real loner and had a reputation for being cold to all, even his office staff.

After the exciting campaign, with the highlight being the Kennedy-Nixon televised debate, a formal dinner was given by Mr. and Mrs. Johnston at the elegant Metropolitan Club in Washington. It was for their 25th anniversary, and many of the Senators were among the large company of guests. As the debate took place during dinner, Mr. Johnston, fearing those attending wouldn't want to miss it, had the waiters bring a television set into the private dining room. We all watched the debate while eating, but Mrs. Johnston was furious. She thought it spoiled—really eliminated—conversation. She was right, but it had been a difficult decision for the boss!

Who does not remember the great contrast in the televised images of the candidates in that debate! The perspiring uncomfortable Richard Nixon and the youthful, self-assured Senator Kennedy. It was especially interesting to me to be watching it in the company of many members of the Senate.

1964 Democratic National Convention
Atlantic City, New Jersey

As luck would have it, I did not have to take part in the 1964 convention proceedings, but particularly enjoyed it as a spectator, accompanied by my aunt, cousin and her daughter from Philadelphia.

The location was really "old stomping grounds" for I lived in suburbs of Atlantic City, with my mother and grandparents when I was growing up. My mother and father had separated and were later divorced. I was so familiar with the famous boardwalk and the beautiful wide white beaches on the Atlantic Ocean, that it felt like I was coming home to attend the convention. I recalled dips in the ocean with my grandfather when he would stand at the water's edge donned in his swim suit and white sailor pork pie hat. He'd smoke exactly one cigar, then take a dip and leave. On the other hand my two cousins, Marilyn and Stanley Hughes, would spend all day at the beach. We'd build drip castles down close to the water, and a little further back it was large sand castles built to accommodate rolling balls in and out of the various tunnels and corridors of the construction. Stanley was the engineer and builder, and these were works not only of art, but of mysterious entries and exits for the paths of the balls. Stanley was a good sport and would let us climb up on his shoulders and dive off into the waves.

I remembered, too, luxurious rolling chair rides down the special center vertical tracks of the famous boardwalk. These were wooden chairs with wide arms, pushed by hand by the attendants. It was considered stylish for visitors to have their pictures taken sitting in the wicker chairs. A special time on the boardwalk was Easter Sunday when people would stroll in their finery past the beautiful hotels and elegant shops. "On the Boardwalk in Atlantic City" was the beginning of the song "Easter Parade."

Marilyn and I would take numerous walks with our grandparents on the boardwalk, always running ahead of them, and coming back to report something we saw which we wanted them to buy for us. They labeled us the "gimme and getme Girls"—give me this and get me that.

The "Miss America" contests made Atlantic City famous and my aunt who lived there served as a chaperone to the winner. Both my cousin and I at different times had been in the preliminaries. She had reached the finals in the Greater Philadelphia contest having been chosen "Miss Valley Forge, Pennsylvania."

I visited my grandmother in Atlantic City one summer. When we were on the boardwalk down in Ventnor, New Jersey, (a few blocks from Atlantic City proper) we were approached by two ladies who asked if I would like to be in the contest for "Miss Ventnor," one of the preliminaries for the "Miss America" pageant.

I explained that I was not a resident of Ventnor, was only visiting, and lived in Silver Spring, Maryland, a suburb of Washington, D.C.

They said there were to be two contests, one for beauty and one for talent. They asked if I sang and I told them I had been in some musical productions, both in high school, and as a member of the Columbia Light Opera company in Washington, D.C. They said I would be eligible to enter the talent contest. So I did and sang "Ah Sweet Mystery of Life" and "Smoke Gets In Your Eyes."

On the night of the contest, the winner of the beauty contest sang "Alexander's Ragtime Band." She was awarded both the beauty and talent contest prizes. When it was over, two of the judges came up to me and said it was not fair, that I should have won the separate talent contest.

After such reminiscences it seemed coming back to the convention in the "World's Playground," as Atlantic City was known, was a nostalgic visit for us.

* * * * *

When walking down the boardwalk in 1964 I was brought back to the reality of the Democratic Convention, especially when seeing a huge billboard with Senator Barry Goldwater's picture and the words: "I'd Rather Be Right!" on the beach.

Following President Johnson's nomination for President by acclamation, a film in memory of President Kennedy was shown. Following the screening his brother, Attorney General Robert Kennedy, addressed the convention, saying:

*I know that it was a source of the greatest strength
to my brother to know that there were thousands
of people all over the United States who were
together with him.*

In all efforts you were there—all of you.

*When there were difficulties, you sustained him.
When there were periods of crisis, you stood beside
him. And when there were periods of sorrow, you
comforted him.*

*When I think of President Kennedy, I think of
what Shakespeare said in Romeo and Juliet.
"When he shall die take him and cut him into stars
and he shall make the face of Heaven so fine that
all the world will be in love with the night and pay
no worship to the garish sun."*

After his eulogy there was a wave of emotion that went all
through the huge hall, lasting at least thirty minutes. It was like a
living force, going on and on. Bob Kennedy was choked up and
close to tears. After he concluded, it seemed a floodgate had broken, and the convention was awash with raw and tragic sadness.
I've never experienced anything like it. It was beyond description.
Certainly Bobby Kennedy had arrived as a figure in the
Democratic hierarchy.

When order was finally restored, President Johnson's time had
come to announce his choice for Vice President of the United States.

His statement:

*It is the traditional task of your Presidential nominee
to recommend for your deliberation a candidate for
Vice President of the United States. I have found
such a man. I want to say to you that I will feel*

strengthened knowing that he is at my side at all times in the great work of your country and your government.

Nothing has given me greater support in the past nine months than my knowledge of President Kennedy's confidence that I could continue the task that he began. I found a man I can trust in the same way.

He paused and there was quiet in the great hall as everyone waited.

The suspense was building in the silence. Finally, at the very last moment, President Johnson kind of curled his tongue around his mouth and said, with a huge grin: "I hope you will choose as the next Vice President of the United States my close, my long time, my trusted colleague, Senator Hubert Humphrey of Minnesota!" He had kept the air of excitement and anxiety up until the final moment. The hall erupted with cheers that crescendoed up to the top of the high vaulted roof.

That fall Lyndon Johnson and Hubert Humphrey were elected by sixty-one percent of all votes cast, the largest vote ever given to candidates in the history of our country!

1972 Democratic National Convention
Miami Beach, Florida

My next convention was in Miami Beach in 1972. I didn't go as an official, but was required to write a report. I interviewed many delegates and endeavored to report the tremendous contrast between the terrible chaos of the 1968 convention in Chicago and the respectable and wholesome American spirit in Miami Beach. In Chicago people were locked out, in Miami Beach they were all welcomed in.

Later, while considering that my report be sent to all Democratic national committee men and women, our office felt it was partisan and should not be distributed, even anonymously.

Senator George McGovern made his acceptance speech at a quarter of four in the morning! Senator Thomas Eagleton, first chosen as his running mate, was so appealing and enthusiastic that I was sorry he had to withdraw because of a medical condition.

It was at the end of the convention that I wrote:

Come Home, America

You would think that I, as an old line Democrat, steeped in the traditions of the Democratic party and its ways of functioning, in Congress, in National Committee, and in convention, would not have been easily persuaded to embrace the new look of our 1972 convention. Perhaps that is the very reason I can write objectively of what I saw in Miami Beach from July 9 through July 13.

I was used to a carnival feeling in "Convention Cities," when bands played constantly, when the whole city was one big circus, with the candidates' headquarters in different "tents." Loud speakers carried the speeches to the surrounding area from Convention Hall, as the sessions continued day and night. One's whole daily schedule was geared to the work and the sessions at Convention Hall. On occasion I had to be whisked, complete with motorcycle escort, from my hotel, when we finally completed the writing of the Democratic Platform, out to Convention Hall to meet schedule. One particular evening I had about fifteen minutes to change my clothes, dressed as I ate, and miraculously made it.

During the convention I remember the entire whole city vibrating with convention "sounds." Mad, mad worlds.

In rhythm with the sounds and pace of the proceedings at the hall, the wheeling and dealing went on in the smoke-filled rooms all over town—a thousand little conferences were taking place constantly–like the knotting and unknotting of separate groups of people at the same giant cocktail party. It was "show biz" at its most flamboyant, and each person had a role. I remember, too, the eloquence and inspiration of Governor Adlai Stevenson's acceptance speeches, both in 1952 and 1956. After some initial friction between the old pros and the local workers for Governor Stevenson, the machine was put into gear and Governor Stevenson's beautiful phrases, delivered from the depth of his heart, lifted us to both the unity and the team spirit which had been threatened.

And now, recalling the trauma and violence of the 1968 convention, I was a little nervous about the prospect of actually being in this convention city but having the opportunity to witness history in the making, and feeling that this would be an entirely different kind of convention, determined to be a part of it.

My first close-up glimpse of convention activity on Sunday, July 9, of the 1972 convention was a visit to Flamingo Park, the "Resurrection City" of the young. The kids had come in all earnestness to pitch their tents and be a part of the action. With their conforming to the non-conformist long hair and jeans uniform and their mono-personality community, this was their headquarters. It was in great contrast to the jet-set type luxury houseboats which sat imposingly along the water front at Collins Avenue, glistening and sparkling in the vacationland sunshine. They were anchored directly across from the lavishly beautiful hotels where many of the delegates, the staff of the Democratic headquarters, and press worked and lived so furiously this one week in July. As we made our visit to Flamingo Park, I wondered if, indeed, the presence of the "kids" would be heeded or ignored, and just what their individual thoughts were. They reminded me of a group of puppies, all gathered to frolic together, yet, despite the Sunday picnic atmosphere, they were reminding us of their purpose in coming, by their display of signs calling for a halt to the war, and advertising peace. This took the childish thrust of the gathering away for a moment. Beyond the fact that this was a lark for them—the "in" thing to do, these were America's future citizens, starting to develop their views on the way our country should be run, even before they were mature enough to grab the reins themselves. I wondered what each one would get out of this participation in one of the big "shows" of our democracy-in-action, or I wondered if it would be another exercise in frustration, or if they would be made to feel a part of the great party of the people. We now acknowledge they were a part of the body of voters to be reckoned with.

Their presence was evident in big and small ways. A "No Smoking" sign in Convention Hall was changed to read: "No Smoking Pot." The kids, a thousand or so in number, lived for a week as a city within a city, with a daily published Street Sheet, which contained a calendar of demonstration events. They attempted to build a dike outside the hall to protest the alleged bombing in Vietnam, but only got as far as bringing in some sand on which to base it. They did manage one "confrontation"— an audience with Senator McGovern in the lobby of his headquarters, the Doral Hotel. Against the advice of security personnel he came down from his suite to listen to them and answer their questions. He commented that, contrary to the tactics used in Chicago in 1968, he wanted to "hear them out" and not "drive them out." And so he did— and hearing them out, he brought them in—a part of America. As Sam Brightman, former publicity director for the Democratic National Committee, and a veteran convention worker, said: "This is the first convention where some of the delegates still have braces on their teeth!" (The youngest was seventeen!)

This was a new kind of convention. The old pros had for the most part been kicked upstairs or made to sit still and listen—to the people—all types and ages of those who were represented. Of the 5,114 delegates, eighty percent had never been to a convention before, thirteen percent were under twenty-five years of age, thirty-eight percent were women, and many were elderly. Strangely enough, without the "political bosses," without the pros, operating as before, the new vintage was so smoothly effective in its running of this convention that everyone was completely surprised and gratified.

As that old professional, Larry O'Brien, the Chairman of the Democratic National Committee and the permanent Chairman of the convention, said at the beginning of those special days, of the new rules: "We will see if we can make them work or whether they will self-destruct"—and work they did, in an open convention that gathered its strength from the open atmosphere where people could speak their minds honestly and air their views completely. It seemed that the to-and-from tugging of the threads of thought only proved the basic, gut strength of the party weaving a pattern of an ever-broadening spectrum of the colors of America, and providing the wide, strong base of our edifice.

Starting with the warm welcome by Florida's Governor Askew, the first night set the tone of the convention when the Credentials Committee ruling denying Senator McGovern the entire California delegation vote was rejected by vote of the convention. This was a crucial test not only of the strength of the new rules, but of the McGovern candidacy. From then on, this was Senator McGovern's convention.

The Platform Committee, which used to function by holding a week of hearings in convention city and then spend long days and nights working, through its Drafting Subcommittee, to come up with the thinking in pen and ink of the long thoughts and ideals of the party, now went instead to the people, crossing our great land to ask "the people" what they wanted. It did not just listen to the groups who could be represented by a well-paid lobbyists. The voices of the people were heard and their faces with down-to-earth emotion were shown in a film at the convention, expressing their discouragement and hopes and needs to their party. The Platform Committee was not just a gesture of the pros—the convention of the people was reflected in the composition of its members.

The whole convention, to me, seemed to ring true. It was just a packaging of a candidate like the packaging of a product to be sold to the public. The people were right there on the floor, (not protesting outside as in Chicago!), the old, the white, the black, the young, the women, the rich, the poor, people from all walks of life to work together and test whether it was all just idealistic talk or whether it could be done. Could we bring it all together? We could and we did—never before would you have heard the following comment: A Negro delegate said, "It was the first time in five conventions that I got on the floor. A complete stranger loaned me his binoculars and he asked if he could borrow my fan."—or, "When Kennedy was up there, did you close your eyes?"—or, "One vote for Archie Bunker, five-sixths for Martha Mitchell."

One night on the Democratic convention shuttle bus I sat with an elderly lady from Buffalo, New York, proudly sporting her "senior power" badge. She had only been "involved" in convention interests for a short few months but she had worked for some time with committees on the aging. She said she thought that one week in Miami had changed the world, that politics will never be the same again, and that it is the dawning of a new day for all Americans. She was filled with hope and enthusiasm, not just for now, for the future. This in itself was a wonderful contribution to the elderly—not just to make their twilight years bearable, but to make them look forward with enthusiasm to the future.

Part of the buoyant, contagious spirit of enthusiasm was expressed during this same bus trip when the delegates on our bus were all returning to their hotels from the hall. When we passed by the Doral Hotel, Senator McGovern's headquarters, one young delegate yelled out, "We did it, George!" and at that the whole busload of people let out a spontaneous cheer. It was like a football game, and a real thrill. It was in such contrast to my recollection of simulated demonstrations on the floor for candidates. This was the real America, made vocal in its excitement for our new kind of candidate in our newly refreshed party.

So we saw from all—the desire to come together. Senator McGovern had recognized the frustration and discouragements of our life and times. He wanted us to find all we have always loved in our great country. He wanted us to "change it so we could love it more." I, who feel that I may be a bit sophisticated politically, and not subject to being easily swayed by campaign oratory, was so touched that I cried when the Senator ended his acceptance speech with the words: "This land is your land. This land is my land. This land was made for you and me. May God grant us the wisdom to cherish this good land and to meet the great challenge that beckons us home."

Some people thought Senator McGovern's candidacy was stuck together with band-aids, paper clips and scotch tape. It was held together with the intangible strength of love, hope, and longing. Instead of being afraid that our party tried to promise too much, is too idealistic, we should have instead the vision of the young—and the old—the white and the black—the rich and the poor. We should think bigger and not look through opera glasses for a narrow view. We should turn and look around us—enlarge our sights to see—as Senator McGovern saw—our broad, beautiful land, and encompass all its hopes and dreams.

As I watched the principals play their roles, I felt we must all stop and take stock, and discover our own new roles. I felt this adjustment in the handling of the work of the convention by Larry O'Brien. He didn't wield a heavy gavel but, rather, a reasoning one with a velvet glove. He merely voiced the sentiment of all when he asked for order after allowing full participation in the matter at hand. It was amazing how a few quiet words from him resulted in a happy order, not a bitter one, being restored.

This was certainly the convention with a difference. Never before, for instance, had a Vice Presidential nominee seconded his own nomination—but Senator Gravel, one of the two Senators elected when Alaska became a state, did. This was a rather unorthodox move, not according to protocol. Never before had a former Vice President (Hubert Humphrey) who had nearly been elected President four years before, been denied the nomination after campaigning, again and again and again for it.

There is a remaining sadness in the picture of Senator Humphrey's face, which seems to reflect all shades of emotion so openly, when he announced that he would withdraw. He had the tired, resigned look of a man who no longer had the need to try and be young and energetic. His eyes were glazed with unshed tears, and all of us felt we wanted to do just what his wife, Muriel, did, bury our face close to him in understanding and wordless sympathy. Gone was the ebullience and left was heartbreak, for this was his last try.

And so I thought, as I left Miami Beach, that I took a memory of many emotions with me. I took thoughts of happiness and sadness, but over all a wonder at the wonderful deportment of all, and the spirit of great hope and enthusiasm.

From the bitterness of Chicago to the warm and corny, homespun feeling of Miami Beach, is a long way, and we've traveled so much further in too many diverse directions. Despite those ultra modern 1972 styles, the outlandish dress of delegates, demonstrators, and even spectators, all uninhibited, it is true that Americana shone through. The path had been lighted—the light in the window had been turned on—by George McGovern, who had the sincerity to grasp your hand and welcome you in. He called us by our first names and accepted our help. His personality was not the political appeal of other candidates, but was an appeal, trustworthy and true.

If the teenagers of those decades ago—1972—are still concerned, we need America returned to the life and land that we all love so proudly.

The Electoral College

I was considered the "registrar" of the Electoral College. I received all the actual votes of the electors from each state. This is very important, because this is it, this is the election of the President. No matter how people vote, if the electors (who are selected by state governments) do not carry out the wishes of their voters, the election would not be certified.

We have a joint session and the Senate walks over to the House chamber in session, led by two Senate pages carrying the votes. There are two large mahogany boxes inlaid with leather that we use. In each box we have half of the votes. Until the day of the joint session they are kept in our office safe. The Chief Clerk and I open and record them and make sure everything is proper, otherwise they have to be sent back to the states involved for the electors to submit them again. This is an important function every four years.

The photograph of the Senate walking over to the House chamber for the joint session to count the votes is typical of the historic processions of the Vice President and Senate members (according to protocol). This was when Nixon was Vice President and Senators Kennedy and Johnson are also in the procession. That particular joint session must have been embarrassing for Vice President Nixon as he presided jointly with the House Speaker when the votes were tallied, and he had lost to Senator Kennedy.

One time one envelope we received from Georgia had a mistake in it, because one of the electors did not vote for the candidate. Senator Richard Russell from Georgia at the time had to check into it. So as a result, we had to have a second joint session to count the electoral votes. That episode was unusual, and kind of historic.

> *If the electors do not give a majority to any of the candidates the election goes into the House of Representatives, and their votes would elect a President.*

When Alaska and Hawaii came into the union as two new states, each state elected two Senators at one time. Special boxes were constructed for this purpose. We didn't know which of the two would have the long six-year term, which the short two-year term, which would be considered the senior Senator and which the junior Senator, the determination of their terms and where we were going to seat them on the Senate floor. Skeeter Johnston devised a method for the Senators to make those determinations, indicating the length of their terms and whether they were junior or senior Senators. Thus, the problem was solved.

Clockwise:
Dorothye; Hanging President
Truman's photo at the Democratic
National Headquarters,
Philadelphia, PA, 1948; Home
away from home

Above: President Roosevelt and family; President Truman, Bess and daughter Margaret; President Truman holding up copy of the Chicago Tribune shocking and wrong headline "Dewey Wins"

Above: President Eisenhower and family
*Below: Alaska becoming our fiftieth state, Senators Ernest Gruening
and Robert Bartlett awaiting information from Senate Secretary
Felton Johnston determining their terms and seniority*

To Dorothy Scott
with best regards
John Kennedy

Clockwise:
President Kennedy; President
Kennedy meeting young, ambitious
future President Bill Clinton; The
Kennedy "Camelot" family

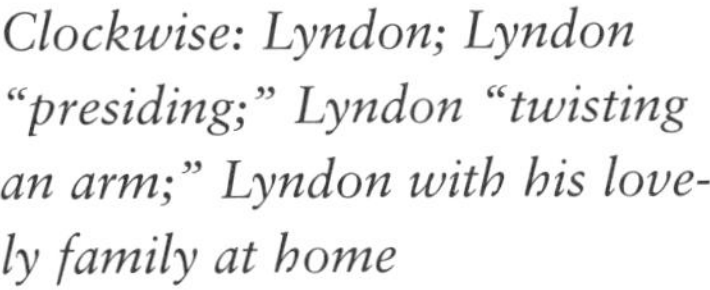

Clockwise: Lyndon; Lyndon
"presiding;" Lyndon "twisting
an arm;" Lyndon with his lovely family at home

Above: Three future Presidents, Nixon, Johnson and Kennedy, walking in a Senate body for a joint session of Congress held in the House of Representatives Chamber
Below: Astronaut John Glenn receiving a standing ovation in House Chamber during a joint session in his honor

Above: Nelson Rockefeller congratulating Ford on his appointment as Vice President, Rockefeller would soon succeed him Below: Senator Mansfield and Frank Valeo escorting Imelda Marcos in the Capitol

My pencil portraits of three Secretaries of the Senate: (upper left and right) Leslie Biffle, Skeeter Johnston; (lower left) Frank Valeo; (lower right) President Lyndon Johnson

Above: On March 1, 1954, a group of radicals from Puerto Rico gained admittance to the House gallery and started shooting House members, shouting "free Puerto Rico," felling five Congressman.
They were captured, served jail sentences and were freed from prison by President Clinton in September 1999.
Below: Donald Ritchie, US Senate Associate Historian who produced my oral history

*Above: Senator Mike Mansfield, Majority Leader of the Senate with Dorothye
Below: A Capitol guide with Dorothye at a party at the Capitol*

Above: Frank and Dorothye under our huge crystal chandelier
Below: Senator Robert Byrd of West Virginia with Dorothye at her retirement party

From above: President Nixon's family; The Senate walking over in a body to the joint session of Congress; held in the House Chamber to count the electoral votes. The Senators are led by two pages carrying the sealed boxes; Frank and I receive the electoral votes from each state, the Electoral College. We secure them in our safe until all are received. They are delivered to the joint session of Congress for the actual counting of the votes.

*Above: President Ford and family
Below: Vice President Ford and Frank Valeo (Ford holding the gavel he used to preside over the Senate)*

Above: President Carter's family
Below: Frank Valeo, Secretary of the Senate

To Ms. Dorothye G. Scott,
Your dedication to this presidency and the Democratic Party has been so very important this past year. We are grateful for your friendship and loyalty. With our very best wishes,

Hillary Rodham Clinton   Bill Clinton

President and Mrs. Clinton

Above: President Ford and Dorothye taken at his home in the desert
Below: Dorothye in front of the reflecting pool behind the Capitol building

CHAPTER SEVEN

The Magna Carta

In our bicentennial year, 1976, when the celebration of the Magna Carta was planned, it hadn't been determined if Congress was going to send its delegation over to England to formally receive it.

A member of the House of Representatives rose on the House floor and said, "It is inappropriate to spend money to send a Congressional delegation to England." Senator Mansfield saved the day because he spoke on the Senate floor, supporting the plan for a delegation to go to England. In that way we avoided an international incident! We were very close to England and they were trying to honor us for our bicentennial, and this Congressman was saying it wasn't worth the money!

I was so proud that Senator Mansfield answered him. Of course, he sold the Senate the idea. They passed a resolution for the delegation to go to England. In response, members of Parliament came back to America. Queen Elizabeth arrived for the ceremonies. Frank was working very closely with the office of the Speaker of our House of Representatives and we were conferring with them on the arrangements. In spite of a lack of cooperation with the office of the Speaker of the House of Representatives, plans did materialize after much negotiation.

The Magna Carta or Magna Charta, the most important instrument of English constitutional history, issued by King John at Runnymede, under compulsion by the barons in 1215. The purpose of original charter was to insure feudal rights and guarantees that the king could not encroach on baronial privileges. Provisions also guaranteed freedom of church and customs of towns; protections of rights of sub-jects and communities (which king could be com-pelled to observe); and words later to be interpret-ed as guarantees of trial by jury and habeas corpus. John repudiated charter as a grant made under coercion, was released from its observance by Pope, and civil war broke out. Later reissues of the charter had significant omissions; remaining claus-es came to be known as Great charter or charter of Liberties. Later it became the symbol of supremacy of law over king.

The Magna Carta helped establish the notion of constitutional democracy in the western world. America's foundation was, and is, based on it. Washington gave witness to its importance in the celebration in 1976.

Frank and I worked with Bill Ridgely, our Senate financial clerk, head of the Senate Disbursing Office, to get all the money needed for the whole delegation. This would include all the members of the Senate who went, as did Frank.

America's presence was appreciated and their ceremonies were impressive. In response, on the return of our delegation, many social, diplomatic, and festive events were held in honor of the Queen and the members of Parliament.

I attended most of the events, all very formal, even with strolling violinists from the Air Force. We did everything we could to make them feel welcome. There were many speeches and we answered "Hear! Hear!" as was the English custom for the Queen. We were doing it their way.

A special reception was held for Queen Elizabeth. (I envied her big lavender hat—my color!) We pulled out all the plugs and were very glamorous and hospitable.

The main event was the actual presentation of the Magna Carta, the transferal from them to us. This ceremony was held in the rotunda of the Capitol. We had great big, really huge, flags—one, the American flag, and one, the English flag, hanging side by side up in the rotunda ceiling. It was very dramatic.

Four English bobbies with great big plumed hats stood for the ceremony at each corner of the big glass case that held the Magna Carta. It was all jeweled and very beautiful. Just gorgeous! It remained there from the Fourth of July until the next Fourth of July, for a solid year, celebrating the bicentennial. When the bobbies left, we had a member of our four different armed forces stationed at each corner, twenty-four hours a day, for the following year until the Magna Carta was returned. We now have a copy that is still standing in the Rotunda.

Tourists, who come to the Capitol building from all over the world, are able to see English history as compared and shared by United States history. We felt both countries were cooperating with each other. It was a successful venture.

* * * * *

The celebration whetted my appetite to learn more about our mother country. Traveling to London with the Congressional Secretaries Club, we were taken to see Parliament. It was Easter Saturday and the woman who was Secretary of the House of Commons, was on holiday, but she came to London from her home to show us around. I think this position of hers was similar to that of Secretary of the US Senate although, of course, it was the House of Commons, not the House of Lords.

We went to her office in a building across the street from the Parliament building. It was large and comfortable and private. It was a great contrast to the offices of the members of Parliament, as so many of their desks were in one large room, with telephones in the back of the room, and not on each desk. They didn't even have separate booths. We couldn't understand this widely opposing contrast of accommodations.

It was interesting that her quarters were so elaborate in comparison to those of the members. The life-like statue of Sir Winston Churchill outside the chamber of the House of Commons pictured him very rugged, determined and energetic.

* * * * *

Speaking of the admiration we felt for the English, I remember the visit we had from Sir Anthony Eden. We had a separate session of the Senate to honor him. I wish I had had the same courage that Senator Howard Baker had, to take my camera. He used to run around taking pictures of many different celebrities. I wish I'd done that, but I didn't think it would be respectful. All tall and so handsome, Sir Anthony stopped by my desk and I was thinking, "Oh how I would like to have a picture!"

We had an informal reception for him in our dining room where the Senators could just come in and meet him before he went in to the Senate chamber to address the Senate. He was one of our most important visitors. (I was partial to the English long before our celebration of the Magna Carta!)

In addition to the ceremonies and celebrations in connection with the Magna Carta, Frank and I, with some of the Senators, went to Philadelphia for a Bicentennial dinner and entertainment, interesting to me because I was going back to my hometown. It was held at historic Independence Hall. It rained and rained, and the Marines came out with huge golf umbrellas to meet our train. Some of the interesting people in attendance were former Ambassador to Russia, Bob Strauss; Mrs. Lindy Boggs, widow of Congressman Hale Boggs and mother of newswoman Cokie Roberts. The trip was exciting. There was an accordion player entertaining through the cars. Very festive!

All of official Washington was represented, from the President on down, and it made me proud to be a part of the celebration of our country's great history.

Three Vice Presidents in Eighteen Months

Three Vice Presidents in eighteen months necessitated changing our records and files accordingly.

The first one was Spiro Agnew, elected with President Nixon. He was co-Chairman of the Joint Inaugural Committee. Senator Jordan, a Democrat of the Joint Inaugural Committee, accompanied Spiro and Judy to the Capitol. In my ear, Senator Jordan whispered "Judy is so cute. She was just like a little kitty."

*The Chairman was always from the winner's party
so if a Democrat was elected President it would be
a Democratic Senator, or a Republican President, a
Republican Senator.*

After Vice President Agnew had to resign because of shady financial dealings the second Vice President, Congressman Gerald Ford was sworn in, in the House chamber. I was there, seated in the gallery. That was the time he made the speech—the only time he could speak, other than to break a tie in a vote. He said, "I'm a Ford and not a Lincoln!"

Ford visited the Senate several times within two and a half weeks after President Nixon had resigned. He was then our President. He obviously was trying hard to cement relations with Congress. At a reception for Senator Mansfield, celebrating the fact that he had been Majority Leader for several years, longer than anyone else. I told Ford I admired the fact that he had pardoned Nixon and the fine job he was doing. He was trying hard to heal the wounds after Watergate.

As President, he appointed Nelson Rockefeller to the vice Presidency. The Twenty-Fifth Amendment to the Constitution provided for appointment of a Vice President in circumstances such as these as it also had in President's Ford's appointment. When he was sworn in, I was again watching from the Senate gallery. It was in the evening and Secretary of State Henry Kissinger was sitting across the aisle from me. I remember his wife, Nancy, was in the gallery on the other side of the chamber. She kept looking over and I felt she was thinking, "Why isn't he over here with me?" In the meantime, seated with her were Betty Ford, Happy Rockefeller, and the Averill Harrimans. When Vice President Rockefeller took his oath he turned around and threw a kiss up to Happy, but she had turned around to talk with Mrs. Harriman. Betty Ford nudged her. Everybody was waiting. I was holding my breath at this little scene. Some of the photographers were stationed in the row of seats behind me. Then, finally, she did look down over into the chamber and he threw her another kiss.

Afterward, our office signed the new Vice President in, as we always did all new members of the Senate, giving him the usual orientation regarding salary, office staff, etc. This included signing him in for his deductions and benefits. Considering his vast wealth, this was ironic, almost amusing. Frank said that when he met Rockefeller he commented, "Dorothye's prettier than you are," (endearing him to me!).

* * * * *

For three years Rockefeller was dedicated to his job as the Vice President, well-respected and popular until his death.

He died under unusual circumstances, suffering a heart attack at 10:15 P.M. on January 26, 1979. Emergency was not called until an hour later (at 11:16 P.M.). Sources said that Megan Marshack, a staff assistant, made a call at 10:15 P.M. or shortly afterward to Ponchita Pierce, a close friend of hers, a TV personality, who lived in the same nearby building as she did, and asked her to get help for Rockefeller. Ms. Pierce said that on the night he died she went to Rockefeller's town house at 13 West 59th Street, New York City, and Ms. Marshack was administering mouth to mouth resuscitation. It was Ms. Pierce who called 911 at 11:16 P.M.

Questions were raised as to why medical assistance wasn't summoned earlier, which might have saved his life. Different versions of Rockefeller's demise, location, circumstances and timing remain unsolved (publicly).

* * * * *

Presidents, dignitaries, statesmen and industry leaders were among the 2,000 people who attended his services. He was lauded for his patriotism, faith and efforts on behalf of America.

Rockefeller's four children said they were satisfied that Megan Marshack did her best to save him. It was said they accepted the opinion of Dr. Ernest R. Esakof, Rockefeller's personal physician, that their father died of a single massive heart attack.

Congressional Seminars

Congressional seminars (sponsored by the Civil Service Commission) were held monthly. Members of Congress and committee staff members were invited to address them. I also lectured to them for several years. Employees from all government departments attended as the audience, and there was often a waiting list. I also addressed the American University students and other groups on the operation of the Senate.

We distributed publications about the Electoral College, about the manner of selecting electors, delegates to national conventions, etc. and I used these in my seminars. I also spoke on the functions of the various offices of the Senate. Those attending would visit my office to obtain copies of our publications. At one time the gentleman who was in my same job on the House side, lectured, but later declined other appearances. He said that I covered everything and he wasn't needed.

These addresses were outside of my official duties and I was pleased when Frank Valeo said I was performing a service for the Senate, and I enjoyed them.

The Fourth Estate

Frequently I worked with members of the press. They were all hard-working, interesting personalities, many of whom wrote books, like Jack Bell's *The Agony of the Presidency,* Frank McNaughton's books about President Truman, William S. White's *The Citadel, The Professional* by William S. White, Helen Thomas' *Front Row at the White House,* and more.

The Senate Press Gallery was like the city room of a big newspaper. There were over 700 member reporters including representatives from Reuters, UPI, Associated Press and others, from around the world. We also had a periodicals gallery, and the radio and television galleries, all busy places, part of the media.

Many of the newspaperwomen were dynamic. Sarah McClendon, Mary McGrory, and Helen Thomas (the dean of women reporters, who still closes the President's press conferences) and May Craig, whom we called the "Flying Grandmother." She was an older reporter who had flown in glider planes.

You could always spot the Senate reporters, even away from the Press Gallery, rushing to telephone booths, to call in their stories.

After women were allowed to join the National Press Club in Washington, I was sponsored and became a member. Their meetings were important and I retained my membership after my retirement from the Senate.

I was included on a trip with President Truman on his private train when reporters covered his trip to Philadelphia to see the Army-Navy game. Truman was provided with a battery-operated stadium blanket for his use when he watched the game. Couldn't let the President get a cold!

My association with the press was always exciting. Skeeter Johnston had a close relationship with the newspaper people and was very perceptive in dealing with them. The only time we didn't cooperate with them was during the Democratic National Convention in Philadelphia, when they wanted a "scoop" on the wording of the Democratic Platform before we released it. Always, we appreciated their participation.

The media enriches the day-to-day life in the Senate halls and is relied on to properly report all its happenings to the public.

Congress of the United States

The legislative branch of Federal government, instituted in 1789 by Article 1 of US Constitution, prescribes its membership and defines its powers. Congress is composed of two houses, the Senate and the House of Representatives. The Senators, two from each state, have six-year terms and were chosen by the state legislatures until 1913, when the Seventeenth Amendment, providing for the direct popular election, went into force. The terms of one-third of the Senators expire every two years. A Senator must be at least thirty-years-old, not less than nine years a US citizen, and a resident of the state from which he is elected. The Vice President of the United States presides over the Senate, voting only in case of a tie. Representatives are apportioned to the states according to their populations in the federal census, every state being entitled to at least one representative. Representatives are chosen for two year terms and the entire body comes up for reelection every two years. A representative must be twenty-five or older, at least seven years a US citizen, and an inhabitant of the state in which he is elected. The presiding officer of the House, the Speaker, is elected by the members of the House. The two houses have an equal voice in legislation, though revenue bills must originate in the House of Representatives. The Senate, regarded as the more powerful body, must ratify all treaties and confirm important Presidential appointments. The proceedings of each house are recorded in the *Congressional Record*.

Traditions

While the Senate chamber was being restored in the late fifties, the Senate sessions were held in the "old Supreme Court Room," in the Capitol building. The court then moved into the imposing Supreme Court building, across the street from the Capitol building. The old Supreme Court room was then restored, and there was a colorful ceremony and reception to celebrate its renovation. Even the galleries above, looking down into the court, were restored. Admission was by ticket, and an elaborate buffet was served in the Senate hallway nearby. This now is one of the rooms featured in the guided tour of the Capitol. Frank Valeo took part in the ceremony, holding a quill pen in his dedication.

The wall coverings chosen were in gold, reflecting the "golden oratory" of the Senators' speeches.

As a contrast, the wall coverings in the House of Representatives chamber are blue, denoting the "blues" relating to the fact that all appropriations bills originate in the House.

* * * * *

It is an interesting tradition that "Senate Bean Soup" is on the menu in the Senate restaurant every day. The story was that one day, long ago, it was not listed and an old time representative got up on the House floor demanding it be served every day. Some food stores in the Washington still carry cans of "Senate Bean Soup" for sale. (I've since found it in California as well.)

Another specialty of the Senate restaurant is rum pie, which is served every Wednesday. When having lunch there we always ordered it, and the "mother" of our Senate family, Ruth Watt, in addition to having it for dessert, would always take another piece back to her office for the afternoon.

We had what we called our "family table" in the Senate restaurant. Often Senator Aiken of Vermont would come and sit with us, saying he got better service there than he did in the adjoining Senators' private dining room!

On Washington's birthday each year, the Senate does not celebrate with a day off. Instead, one particular Senator is chosen to read George Washington's Farewell Address to his troops in the Senate chamber. This is the only reason for the Senate to be in session on this day. It is felt to be an honor for the Senator chosen. A book with the signature of each Senator given this honor is kept by the Chief Clerk under the office of the Secretary of the Senate.

CHAPTER EIGHT

Capitol Headliners and Drama

President John Kennedy's Inauguration Speech
January 20, 1961

It made you want to cry—the picture of the young man appealing to his fellow citizens to join with him in solving the problems of today's world. It was an appeal to your heartstrings as well as your patriotic pride in being, on this most American of all days, an American citizen.

In sharp, firm outline the picture was seen. From the tedium of physical discomfort and dispirited and harried comings and goings in the snowbound Capitol, suddenly we were lifted out of ourselves, of the consciousness of practically frozen feet and fingers buffeted by icy winds on the historic Capitol Plaza. We were warmed and buoyed up to a feeling of being needed, of each of us being a vital part, to make our contribution to America's future in a very personal answer to today's challenge.

This evangelist of politics (even as the evangelist of religion, Billy Graham) was not just giving a speech—he was making an appeal. Kennedy's speech inspired all within hearing to shout out answers when he questioned us as to what we wanted for our future. This was not just a statement that the serious young President was making, it was an outstretching of his hands to ours . . . of his hopes and beliefs in what our country can do for itself and the world if we would all clasp hands and go forward together. It was, indeed, a call to join him in seeking a New Frontier. It was such a thrill to see the deeply sharp and contrasting change: from the old to the new—from the oldest President (Eisenhower) to the youngest. From the old order—of acceptance and "making the best of it" to shaping decisions in a definite and positive way, and not just reacting to events. It was in a way like the old English custom of "The

King is Dead—Long Live the King!" but with the thrilling realization that this was America's way. The new young leader did not inherit this job—he fought hard for it—against almost insurmountable odds—his youth and his religion. And, we ask ourselves, why would such a successful young man who literally had everything in a material way, including personal political success and fulfillment in his career as United States Senator, want to struggle so hard to become President? And, in answering this question we would be proud to agree that, as he said in his inaugural address— "sincerity is subject to proof." He certainly proved his sincerity to give all he had of inspiration and leadership and personal effort to bring this country back to greatness.

In watching that courageous, fine figure of dedicated American manhood, I was stirred to a feeling of a kinship with America's own proud history. Silhouetted against the cold blue sky, in the frame of the Presidential Inaugural Platform, white columns proudly rising to the sky, and with the beautiful white dome of our beloved Capitol above, it was an awesome sight. I had not had these feelings since President Roosevelt's reign. We should all feel this closeness and personal responsibility with our country, and never let a day go by without realizing that the way we personally live reflects on our country and its future. We need to all strive to make the world respect and admire us as a vital, alive nation.

Later in the afternoon, as I watched the last marching bands and horseback riders parading in the cold twilight of the winter's day . . . I looked over the nearly emptied stands which just a few hours earlier had been vibrant and alive with people and pageantry . . . as I looked up at our beautiful, inspiring Capitol, I was so proud of our democratic system which allows us to somehow, through all the maze of campaign and urgent influences, of emotional discussions, of all the thoughts and doubts and fears raised, elect a man who was equal to the task, his every thought set on a true course—straight ahead!

His historic words would live on: "Ask not what your country can do for you, ask what you can do for your country." It was hard to remember that just four years earlier, youthful Senator John F. Kennedy had stepped out in front of the ropes in front of those watching the inaugural parade for President Eisenhower to wave at some Massachusetts officials driving by in the parade. The Senate Sergeant-at-Arms gently ordered him back behind the ropes.

* * * * *

I had sent LBJ a yellow rose for his buttonhole that day and I proudly noticed it when he took his oath as Vice President. When he was elected Vice President he was also elected to another Senate term. He had to resign his Senate seat and the Governor of Texas sent us the necessary notice which had to be presented to the Senate by Skeeter Johnston. The papers were on Johnston's desk in our inner office. I had run into LBJ after just having seen the official document of his resignation from the Senate and I realized how much I would miss him after his twelve years at the Senate. Walking down the hall with him, I was feeling pretty badly about the prospect. Later on, at one of the White House receptions, Lady Bird Johnson said to me that those years had been the happiest twelve years of their lives. She sounded wistful with a reconciled smile, and I knew she missed their life in the Senate.

While he was Vice President he stayed around the Senate much more than other Vice Presidents had done. This was the "hands on" operation of LBJ.

As Vice President he continued to come to luncheons in our private dining room. After his election as Vice President, he attended the first Democratic Conference (of all Democratic Senators) of that Congress, at Senator Mansfield's invitation. A suggestion to have him preside over future such conferences was voted on and supported but he never attended another Democratic conference.

John Glenn, the second astronaut to address a joint session of Congress, came to the Capitol. After convening in the Senate chamber, members of the Senate always walk over to the House chamber in a body, to attend a joint session.

The Secretary of the Senate and the Senate Sergeant-at-Arms lead the procession, followed by the Vice President and the President Pro Tempore, the majority and Minority Leaders, then the other Senators. On this particular occasion, Vice President Johnson, as head of the Space Program, arranged to have Astronaut Glenn walk with him.

As I was watching the procession go by, LBJ apparently spoke to Joe Duke, the Sergeant-at-Arms, because all of a sudden the whole procession stopped. To my surprise, LBJ came directly to me, gave me a hug and then introduced me to John Glenn. I was quite elated that he had stopped the whole Senate to meet me. I followed them to the House chamber and attended the joint session with them. John Glenn was a very warm and gracious man. His mother, father and some officials from NASA were in the gallery and it was like "old home week." He waved to them all from the rostrum and there was a special air of honor and national pride which permeated the proceedings that day.

Later, when John Glenn was elected to the Senate from the state of Ohio, I spoke to him after the swearing in. I said, "This is a terrible question to ask because I'm sure you've heard it many times, but what were you thinking of when you blasted off to outer space?" He said, "Well, believe it or not—I had so much to do I couldn't think of anything else. I was just busy carrying out all my different duties." (At this writing, Senator Glenn completed another space trip at the age of 77. He is an inspiration to all generations.)

* * * * *

When Bobby Baker served as Secretary for the Majority he made some outside investments, among them the purchase of the Carousel Hotel in Ocean City, Maryland. He arranged for a grand opening of this hotel, providing buses and private cars to take the guests from Washington to Ocean City. The buses were complete with bars, and snacks and drinks were served en route. A reception went on all day at the hotel. There was a fashion show on the beach in front of the hotel and a dinner later, before the guests were driven back to Washington. The Vice President and Lady Bird were among the guests, as were many Senate members.

Bobby Baker's complicated financial investments led to his resignation. A trial ensued and he served a jail sentence, charged with conflict of interest. He had kept his position under Senator Mansfield who had succeeded LBJ as Majority Leader. A few days before the assassination of President Kennedy, LBJ talked to Skeeter Johnston for over two hours in our inner office about Bobby. Former Supreme Court Justice Abe Fortas, who was Bobby's lawyer, had told LBJ he could have no contact in any way with Bobby. I knew from Skeeter's report to me about that conversation that LBJ was very despondent about Bobby's situation and the fact that he could not help in any way. Within about three days President Kennedy was killed and LBJ was President and, still, he couldn't help him.

* * * * *

LBJ's touching speech, as President, to a joint session of Congress during the days of national heartbreak in our country after the assassination began the campaign for cooperation with the Congress to enact the Kennedy programs. I felt (from my seat in the House gallery on that day) it was his best speech. It was the real LBJ talking, straight from the heart, not the "cornpone" role he sometimes embraced for the TV cameras. Only sincere words of pleading for enactment by the Congress of the martyred young President's programs came from LBJ's lips. As we know, the Congress did carry out the Kennedy agenda. These were tough times to be a new President. It was a tribute to LBJ's relations with the Congress, and resulted in a very large victory for him when he ran for President on the Democratic ticket in 1964.

I remember Nancy Dickerson, the reporter who had traveled with Mrs. Johnson in the "Lady Bird Train" which was campaigning for LBJ's election. Nancy told me that once when Lady Bird was talking about their years at the Senate that she started to cry. Nancy said, "You know, it would have been good theater, but I wanted to stop interviewing her so she wouldn't be embarrassed. I stopped the interview immediately."

On one occasion when LBJ was President his personal secretary, Juanita Roberts, invited me to luncheon in the White House Mess and she took me on a little tour including the President's private room at the side of the oval office. One of our chauffeurs from the Secretary of the Senate's office called for me in our limo and picked me up at the East Portico entrance. I had been at the White House on other occasions but this was the first time I'd been a guest for lunch in the White House Mess. It was also the first time I'd had our office chauffeur call for me there. I felt thrilled and official coming out of that historic entrance. When I stepped into the car, the chauffeur had the radio turned to LBJ's speech from a meeting in New York City. That was exciting to me—the timing as I left the White House and his office, to ride back to the Capitol.

The Capitol building at Austin, Texas is red, and larger than the United States Capitol building in Washington—"Texas Style." It is significant because when LBJ became President he installed new red carpeting in his White House office (no doubt his favorite color).

One night when he was President, LBJ came to see Skeeter and me at our office across from the Senate chamber. It was during a night session and of course our office was open. He came in with just one secret service man. LBJ said, "I'm going to see Skeeter Johnston." Although he was heading for our office he ran into Senator Dirksen in the hall, who waylaid him and took him to his office for a visit.

I'm sure this was a "first" for a President to pop over to the Capitol at night to surprise the Secretary of the Senate with a visit. Usually Presidents arrive at the Capitol with formality and fanfare to address joint sessions of Congress.

* * * * *

Along this line again breaking precedent and in an unusual dramatic arrival, on June 1, 1972, President Nixon landed by helicopter on the East Front Plaza of the Capitol building following his return from Moscow, to address a joint session of Congress.

*　*　*　*　*

Another unique episode breaking tradition, featured President Harry Truman the day he took his oath of office following the death of President Franklin Roosevelt in 1945. He called the office of Honorable Leslie Biffle, then Secretary of the Senate, and asked his Administrative Assistant, Betty Euler, "What are you both doing for lunch?" He, of course, received an invitation to Biffle's private dining room adjoining his suite of offices. Even on the first day of his Presidency, he missed his Senate pals.

*　*　*　*　*

On another such occasion, President Truman, after again being a guest in Leslie Biffle's dining room, walked across the hall to the Senate chamber. Betty Euler had called and alerted me in my office to go to the Senate gallery and watch for a surprise. I did this and it was exciting to see the President stroll on the Senate floor and completely startle the members of the Senate. The expressions on their faces, as one by one they turned around to see him, were of amazement and delight. The session was immediately recessed so they could greet him. Subsequently, a Senate Resolution was passed extending the privilege of the Senate floor to any President or former President of the United States.

*　*　*　*　*

Jim Ketchum served as Curator of Arts and Antiquities of the Senate after nine years in the White House as curator. He and his wife Barbara were my neighbors and are still good friends.

When LBJ was President, Jim staged the unveiling of an official portrait by Peter Herd of President Johnson. Lady Bird Johnson, the two Johnson daughters, Linda Bird and Luci Baines, some of the newspapermen, Liz Carpenter of the President's staff, and many others attended. Everyone expected a serene, dignified portrait. However when the drape was removed, the painting turned out to be most uncomplimentary. On seeing it, LBJ called it the worst he'd ever seen.

It featured the Capitol building, lit up brightly at night, drawing attention away from President Johnson's face. I later saw it in the National Portrait Gallery, and I could understand the President's reaction. The Capitol building appeared to be the star with LBJ given second billing. It was really gross.

* * * * *

When the Vietnam War became the predominant issue, my reaction was to feel especially sorry for LBJ who had inherited this, and that is what brought him down. Of course it was also hard for Vice President Humphrey, who was caught in the middle, to be loyal to his President. In the meantime, Senator Bobby Kennedy was going great guns.

During his term of office in 1968, LBJ made a speech and ended (which was not included in the original text) with a statement that he would not run again. Watching it on TV, it was a real shock and totally unexpected. I think LBJ's heart was just broken because he was in such a bind, not only because of the Vietnam War but because he feared Senator Bobby Kennedy might be nominated for President.

After that decision came the assassination of Senator Bobby Kennedy.

His funeral mass in New York was, of course, covered by world news. The cameras revealed LBJ's reaction during Senator Ted Kennedy's eulogy for his brother. His feelings were written all over his face. He must have been thinking, "If I had known this was going to happen I would have run." It was actually Bobby Kennedy whom he was worried about. He would have been mortified had Bobby Kennedy gotten the nomination and would not have let himself be put in that position after Bobby Kennedy had rebelled against him. It was known that Bobby Kennedy didn't want his brother Jack to pick LBJ as his running mate. There had also been rumors of instances indicating lack of cooperation with LBJ with him. You could see the emotion on LBJ's face at the funeral service, and almost read his thoughts. Robert Galleck in his LBJ biography *Lone Star Rising*, commented that LBJ was the most outstanding Majority Leader in history.

One of the reporters, after LBJ's retirement to his ranch in Texas said that when he first went to visit with LBJ his face was gray and he was listless. He had been ill. However, when the reporter started to talk politics LBJ brightened considerably, the juices started flowing, and he seemed like his old dynamic self again.

I was very saddened to hear of LBJ's death not long after that. There were many wonderful tributes to his leadership and contributions to our country. After he died he didn't lie in state in the main rotunda of the Capitol underneath the big dome as was usually done. The rotunda had been closed at that time in connection with the building of the inaugural platform. So, they brought his body up the Senate steps of the Capitol, not the main steps, in the middle of the building as they had for President Kennedy's casket. When LBJ's casket was brought up the Senate steps, I felt as if he was coming home—as Lady Bird had once said to me—where he had spent his twelve happiest years.

Former President Nixon and Lady Bird Johnson and the procession went over to the Senate chapel with his casket. I watched from the same place where he had stopped the Senate's procession with the astronaut John Glenn. I stood there feeling very sad and nostalgic, remembering that much happier occasion. As there was still some work being done in the rotunda, his casket was placed in the Senate chapel. There was a continuous procession around it as there also had been when President Kennedy had lain in state in the rotunda. I was one of the first to walk around it and it was a very sad occasion for me. There were about 40,000 people—fifty a minute—who had paid their respects in this way. There was a line of people backed up for ten blocks outside the Capitol, waiting to join the procession. He had come home.

There was a memorial occasion on LBJ's birthday after his death to which I was invited. The memorial was given jointly by some members of his former staff and some members of the Texas State Society. It was the dedication of the LBJ Memorial Park in Virginia. Actually the memorial park had been purchased with donations from people who wanted to honor him. The entire area is a park. You reach it by walking over a small bridge into a wooded area off the highway. In a wall on the other side of the bridge is a button which, when pushed, plays an audio tape by Lady Bird. She tells how they had chosen this spot for his memorial park because whenever they would return to Washington from Texas they especially loved to take this route home to feel welcomed back. From this vantage point they could see the Washington Monument and all the government buildings which make up the Washington skyline.

The actual memorial itself is about nine feet high, made of pink marble, a huge, tall, beautiful imposing slab with hundreds of sparkling silver and white particles highlighting it. Below it in the concrete, the same as in the Kennedy gravesite in Arlington National Cemetery, are carved excerpts from some of President Johnson's speeches. The many trees had been donated, and the whole park had a majestic hushed and reverent air. I felt honored to be included to share our memories of LBJ with many friends on his staff and members of the Texas State Society. This evening recalled ever so vividly memories of other birthdays we had shared, including the one when we had a huge birthday cake and happy celebration with his staff members in our private dining room in the Capitol years before.

Along with all who worked with him I will always cherish our association and the inspiration of his leadership.

Lyndon B. Johnson
A Man to Remember

It is impossible to write about Lyndon Baines Johnson with brevity. This was a big man—big in status, big of nature, big on honor and tradition, big on friendships, and most importantly, a big "presence."

A positive "can do" Lyndon, for twenty-four years as Congressman, Senator, Vice President and President would appear, streaking under the arched doorway to my inner office in about seven long steps on his way to the Secretary of the Senate's private office—half the number of steps it took others to cover the same distance. In those seven steps, Johnson directed as many orders of people to call, papers to obtain and other things he wanted done.

You hear a lot about Lyndon Johnson still. He was a great influence in my Senate life. He has been the subject of television movies, stage plays and massive books about his life. Presidents and Presidential candidates talk about the continuing effect of LBJ's Great Society and of the war in Vietnam. He remains a tall presence on our national scene.

But somehow the Lyndon Johnson that I read about today isn't the man I knew when I worked for the United States Senate and watched him operate as Senate Majority Leader, and later as the nation's President.

LBJ was tall, handsome and dashing. An immaculate dresser, he looked the part of a Mississippi riverboat gambler. He didn't miss a trick—always knew what would appeal to everyone he had contact with, from Presidents to Senate page boys. His Texas drawl masked a sophisticated appeal as he towered over most other Senators, having to lean over and down to them and enveloping them in a most intimate caring way.

A large part of my Senate service was spent greatly admiring and working closely with LBJ. The boundless energy of this dynamic man was contagious. I always felt stimulated and energized when he came in, and felt that "a day without LBJ was like a day without sunshine." I, too, was a recipient of the Johnson "treatment," although in a different way from those used to his "pressing the flesh." That was done at political rallies, working the crowds, shaking hands, touching arms, always personal contact.

Occasionally, I had to interrupt his presiding over a luncheon meeting held in our private dining room. He knew I would interrupt him for only the most important matter, either action on the Senate floor that he had to know about immediately or some other pressing business of the Senate. When I approached him, he would turn completely around in his chair at the head of our long conference table, giving me his full, intimate and undivided attention, and I felt the bright spotlight of his gaze upon me alone. For a moment I was the only person in the room. It was this trusting gesture that made me feel important to his work and that I was an essential part of his endeavors. This same brand of successful persuasiveness was felt by many members of the Senate, resulting in his great record in passage of legislation.

All President Johnson's family were "LBJs:" Lyndon Baines Johnson, Lady Bird Johnson, Lynda Bird Johnson, Luci Baines Johnson and the dog—Little Beagle Johnson.

Mrs. Johnson was originally Claudia Taylor, but "Lady Bird Johnson" suited her.

Early in the years of my association with LBJ there was one afternoon when I was rushing along the hallway of the first floor of the Capitol to leave. Just as I sped past the Senate restaurant and made the right turn to go to the revolving doors at the exit I heard a loud crashing sound. Before I realized what had happened one shoe went one way, the other flew off in the opposite direction, and my handbag landed in the middle. The sound was me, falling down and sprawling! Who should come to my rescue but LBJ! He helped me up while I tried to gather my dignity as well as my scattered possessions. I was embarrassed but secretly pleased at his concern. When I related the happening to Skeeter Johnston the next day, he asked, "Did he recognize you?" in a tentative way, not knowing whether to be upset or grateful. "Of course he did," I indignantly replied.

That tumble I took was prophetic—working ever more closely with him I could say that, like everyone subjected to his energetic charm, "I fell for LBJ."

Of his friend, President Johnson said, "I discovered that any Senator could become a great Senator simply by listening to your advice, acting on it, and then taking the credit which you so generously allowed us to have . . . As I have said on many occasions, 'Thank God for Skeeter Johnston.'"

* * * * *

We worked together on a daily basis, sharing business and situations, both serious and humorous. LBJ brought former President Truman to my office one day and, although I had previously met him at the Senate, it was a special honor to have Lyndon bring the former President personally to see me.

I obtained a copy of the book *The Lyndon Johnson Story* that I asked LBJ to autograph for me. He wrote a very complimentary message, "To Dorothye G. Scott, With thanks, appreciation and understanding—of your cordial attitude and always high competence, from her friend, Lyndon B. Johnson." After I told him how much I appreciated it, as he stood by my desk, he turned, bent down and said warmly, "And I appreciate you." With the expression of such recognition, it made me vow to always please him even more.

I have a little memo of something LBJ once said to me—"I'm proud of the way you run the office, from Skeeter Johnston on down. It's a haven where the weary can relax and not a hangout for deadbeats." I was much touched by this. This statement was prophetic because after his severe heart attack, LBJ did find our office to be a "haven" where he could escape the pressures and rest for short periods.

When he suffered this major heart attack, it was shocking to see this vital, energetic man, white-faced and grimacing in pain, lying in his hospital bed. His words were, "I knew you would come, Skeeter. Thank you." His quick handshake and sad eyes brought moisture to Skeeter's own eyes. Lady Bird Johnson wordlessly smiled her gratitude. The darkened room seemed to be siphoning the energy from the fallen leader, despite the efforts at cheerfulness expended by Senator Clements, the Senate majority whip, also present.

After a short period of rest at the LBJ Ranch in Johnson City, Texas LBJ couldn't be kept down and returned to the Senate to work as hard as ever. He frequently would rest for short periods in our conference room, getting needed time away from the pressures of his own office in the Capitol. It fell to me to awaken him at the times he directed. I hated to disturb him and found his hectic pace never changed. Seeing this leader who moved, worked and rushed about constantly, lying asleep peacefully was a real novelty.

During the Democratic Platform Committee held in Chicago in 1956, I hoped so much that LBJ would be nominated for President, even though it was said that he would "always be a king-maker, and never a king," because he was from Texas. Tradition had it then that no one from a southern state could be elected President. At 2:00 A.M., after one of the sessions, while waiting for the elevator to return to my room at the Hilton Hotel, I was joined by George Reedy, later press secretary at the White House under LBJ. He was at that time on LBJ's staff at the Senate. I told him if he would write a nominating speech, I would deliver it! He said, "I'd like to write that speech!" and I said, "And I'd like to give it."

* * * * *

LBJ frequently would take turns having two of the secretaries from his Texas state office in the Senate office building, transfer to his leader's office in the Capitol. In this way, various secretaries were given the opportunity to work more closely with him.

In one of LBJ's letters to Skeeter Johnston on his birthday, along with presentation of a television set, he referred to him as the "ninety-seventh member of the Senate." The Senate was then composed of ninety-six Senators, two from each of the forty-eight states.

One day Skeeter was resting in our conference room. LBJ was standing in front of the fireplace in my office, looking in the gold gilt framed mirror, combing his hair. The Chief Clerk of the Senate, Emery Frazier, was working with Rose Ann Cosgrove, my third assistant secretary, at her desk. He said, "Senator, I'm always here in case you want anything." (Suggesting Skeeter wasn't.) I thought this was a rather obsequious remark and found it inappropriate. LBJ must have seen my look of surprise. He turned around to me and gave me a great big wink. It appeared to me that Emery was trying to butter him up in Skeeter's absence. I was there at my desk, facing LBJ. No words were spoken—just the wink which spoke volumes!

When LBJ was Majority Leader and Senator Everett Dirksen of Illinois was Minority Leader, both worked closely together on the Senate program. But LBJ was not above a little one-upmanship. There was a story after telephones were installed for the first time in the two leaders' cars. It was said that Senator Dirksen called LBJ from his car while both were en route home from the Capitol. When LBJ answered he said, "Wait just a minute, Ev, my other phone is ringing."

Speaking of telephone calls, the Capitol operators used to handle all calls personally. When a new Capitol switchboard was installed all calls had to be dialed. LBJ memorized all the numbers he frequently called at the Capitol.

Noted for restlessly pacing while issuing orders or dictating letters, this story made the rounds in the Capitol, that a psychiatrist died and went to heaven. When he arrived, Saint Peter said, "Oh, we really need you! God is striding up and down, He thinks he's Lyndon Johnson!"

The only selfish thing I ever heard of LBJ doing was when he got stuck in an elevator in the Capitol about midnight. He got so mad he insisted all elevator operators work until midnight every night from then on, even though when the Senate on occasion stayed in session late or all night long, all employees, including elevator operators, remained on duty. However, this particular instance occurred after the Senate was out of session and LBJ had to operate the elevator in the Capitol building himself. When it malfunctioned he got stuck—and mad.

* * * * *

We had a visit from the movie star, Jayne Mansfield, when she was in Washington to promote a movie. When we called the Senators' offices to invite them to meet her, they not only asked the time and date, they also asked for her measurements! When the Senators came in, they were like a lot of little boys, coming in to meet the star. She wore a light blue turtle neck sweater and a pink wool skirt on a hot summer day! Her ankle strap shoes were plastic. Her long blond hair was loose and flowing and I remember her make-up was very heavy and she had about forty people all around, brushing her hair and fussing over her. We only allowed them to take pictures out in the hall, none in our suite of offices. The page boys got very excited, too, and came to me for her autograph. So I got some for them—she dotted the "i" with a heart.

The Senator who did not come to our office to meet her was LBJ. She was originally from Texas so she went to his office for a private visit. The next thing she did was to pose for pictures out on the Senate steps. That was one of the most unusual times of my Senate service! I found it amusing to see how the Senators were like little boys following a Pied Piper in to our inner office to see her. Skeeter found the whole episode so embarrassing that he didn't come to the office that day. Bobby Baker and I officiated at the informal reception.

When she walked into my office she looked terrified. However, LBJ reported that during her private meeting with him in his office, she seemed very intelligent. So, his charisma, as usual, must have made her comfortable.

* * * * *

LBJ hosted a luncheon in our dining room for Arthur Godfrey and on their way in I felt I was greeting an old friend. He was very complimented that the Majority Leader would do this for him. He hung his cane on the edge of my desk and while chatting with me insisted on giving me his private telephone number to have for the leader. He told me how much he admired LBJ.

* * * * *

When Ralph Bellamy was in Washington playing the role of President Franklin Roosevelt in *Sunrise at Campabello*, he made a visit to our office. It was so interesting to see him walk in after having watched him as a cripple in the show. I took him to the Senate gallery and visited with him for a long while, explaining the action on the Senate floor, the duties of the Senate officials, the page boys, etc. When I took him out in the hall to get the elevator, we ran into LBJ. When I introduced them, LBJ said to him, "You are playing the part (of course FDR) of the man who was my mentor, the person who I respected over so many years. Ralph Bellamy replied in a charming manner how honored and pleased he was at the meeting. It was fascinating to me because I had seen the show and it was as if I was witnessing the meeting of FDR, the late President reincarnated, with LBJ.

* * * * *

After he retired, LBJ wrote his autobiography, *The Vantage Point*. He autographed my copy: "For Dorothye Scott, With the affection of her friend Lyndon B. Johnson." It is a cherished memento, and a good book!

I presented my oil portrait to LBJ when he and Governor Adlai Stevenson of Illinois were in my office. He accepted it but waited until Governor Stevenson had left to take time and really look it over thoroughly. Frequently after that his greeting to me would be, "How's my artist?"

* * * * *

During his years as Majority Leader and as Vice President, LBJ was in our office nearly every day. His reputation as a "can do" man, which he accomplished in many ways, some in courting votes with his charming personalized attention, invariably accompanied by a bit of arm twisting. He would present the same assignment to many different staff members, requesting their reactions and advice. In this way he received input from many employees and he would reach a consensus. His motto was from the Prophet Isiah, "Come, let us reason together."

When Dwight Eisenhower was President and LBJ Majority Leader of the Senate, he felt Ike was waffling as to his program. So before Ike gave his State of the Union address to Congress, LBJ gave a speech which official Washington termed his "State of the Union" address. At that time it seemed that LBJ and Speaker Rayburn were really running the country and Ike was only looking on.

Right after the 1960 national political conventions when Senator Kennedy had been nominated for President and LBJ for Vice President, it was an exciting time at the Senate. Counting Vice President Nixon, who had also been nominated for President, *three* of the nominees were present daily on the Senate floor. Tourists and political buffs carrying their lunches in paper bags waited in line in the hallways of the Senate gallery level to spend a few minutes watching "the show." These Senators were campaigning on the Senate floor where the national spotlight was on them.

The day before the Kennedy-Johnson inauguration, LBJ gave a luncheon in our dining room attended by Lady Bird Johnson and his two daughters. The lights in the crystal chandelier over the enormous dining room conference table added to the festive feeling and the logs crackling in the fireplace provided a home-like air.

This was a very special occasion—the last luncheon in our dining room while LBJ was still Majority Leader of the Senate. The next day he would be inaugurated as Vice President. Skeeter was feeling warm and welcoming to his revered leader and his family and cognizant of the historic overtones of the day.

Lady Bird Johnson, smiling as always, looked lovely in a bright red suit, cheerful in the cozy dining room with the outside of the

Capitol covered with snow. Her reflection in the gold leaf mirror over the marble fireplace, showing a large vase of gladiolus on the mantel brought a delightful dimension to the luncheon scene. She chatted vivaciously in her soft voice with its undeniable Texas accent, speaking of the wonderful adventure before her family. Lady Bird's dark hair was soft around her face and her makeup was fresh and bright. As she passed by me I got a whiff of her perfume, a slightly spicy, but feminine scent.

Lynda and Luci Johnson were typical smartly dressed young girls in attractive colorful woolen suits. Although this was before she started dating movie actor George Hamilton, who inspired a complete makeover for her, Lynda Bird was quietly attractive. Her long dark hair framed her cameo face, lighted up by dark, expressive eyes. She was poised and serene, the more serious of the two daughters. She frequently accompanied her father on campaign trips.

Luci Baines was round-faced and bouncy, with an irrepressible, fun-loving air. She was shorter and a little heavier than her sister, and her short and dark brown hairdo matched her personality— casual and perky. She was the less formal of the two girls. While a Senate daughter, she dated one of the Senate page boys.

The snow continued and grew heavier and thicker and the time dragged on. They were in no hurry to leave. The luncheon seemed to be lasting a very long time. I kept looking out the windows and couldn't believe how fast it was accumulating. I was growing nervous and getting worried about their drive home through the terrible storm—and mine!

After the luncheon was over and everyone had left, our waiters tried to clean up as quickly as possible. The blizzard (preceding the Kennedy Inauguration) propelled them into fast action.

Tickets to the actual inaugural ceremonies on the Capitol steps were like diamonds. They were distributed by the Joint Committee on the Inaugural (consisting of both House and Senate members) to members of Congress and Senate and House officials and honored guests.

All the reserved seats in the seating sections on the east front of the Capitol were filled. People were bundled up in warm clothes. Hundreds more stood on the grass leading across the street from the Capitol building to the grounds of the Supreme Court. Sharp shooters were stationed at many points on the roof of the Capitol building.

A special platform was erected over the front of the Capitol building to accommodate the President and Vice President-elect, members of the Supreme Court and Congress, the President's Cabinet, Officials of the Army, Navy, Air Force, Marines and Coast Guard, Ambassadors of foreign countries and honored guests.

Following a stirring Marine Band selection, Cardinal Cushing delivered the invocation and then the one and only Marion Anderson, the much loved black singer, sang.

After a prayer by Archbishop Iakovas, the oath of office was administered to the Vice President-elect Lyndon Johnson, by the Speaker of the House of Representatives, Honorable Sam Rayburn.

The beautiful American flag, waving proudly high above the platform in the crisp air was an inspiration to all of us gathered at the most important place in the world to be at that moment. As part of the inauguration ceremony, poet Robert Frost started reciting his poem. A small fire was suddenly ignited on the rostrum, seemingly punctuating his words. It was caused by a faulty microphone wire. LBJ quickly put it out with his high silk hat.

The oath of office was then administered to President-elect John Kennedy by Chief Justice Warren Burger of the United States Supreme Court.

None of us knew what would be in store—that our young President would be cut down in his prime by an assassin's fatal bullet and that Lyndon Johnson would pick up the reins of the Presidency. He was well suited by experience, ability, and heart to lead our great country.

LBJ stood for courage, devotion, and love of his family, his party, and his country.

Bobby Baker

I have known Bobby Baker from the time he was a page boy. He was from Pickens, South Carolina, and he had a slight southern accent and a lot of energy and ambition. He worked his way up to become the head of the Senate Democratic cloakroom in charge of the Democratic pages. Under Felton Johnston, who served as Secretary for the Majority, Bobby was appointed assistant Secretary for the Majority.

The then Majority Leader Senator Lyndon Johnson, told Mr. Johnston to keep an eye on Bobby's work to be sure he was doing a good job and really oversee his performance. So Johnston was doing time and a half at that point, as Secretary of the Senate, and watching Bobby's work.

Because of Mrs. Johnston's illness, Felton was obliged to refuse appointment to the Platform Committee at the Democratic Convention of 1956 in Chicago. Bobby went in his place and I performed the same chores for him in this capacity which I had for Johnston at the 1948 and 1952 conventions. Bobby also brought his secretary, Margaret Tucker, to work with us.

Bobby was a little flippant but quick-witted and an enthusiastic and hard worker, and I think the Senators liked him. He had his nose bobbed, and some said he tried to mimic LBJ's stance on the Senate floor.

Bobby invested in the Carousel Hotel in Ocean City, Maryland, and invited Skeeter Johnston and two of my assistants, Christine Johnson and Rose Ann Cosgrove, and me to attend. The opening day was to be an elaborate affair. Mr. Johnston refused to go. I think he just didn't feel right being associated with it. I think he was more perceptive about Bobby and he was right, because that was about the beginning of Bobby's financial troubles.

We were taken down on separate buses to the hotel. It was all done elegantly. On each bus was a bar and they served refreshments all the way. We stopped halfway for lunch. Pearl Mesta was there in a private limousine. She was with Bess Abell, Senator Clements' daughter, who later worked at the White House as secretary to Lady

Bird Johnson. We went on by bus after lunch and at the motel everyone could either go to a little cocktail party reception or go to the beach where there was a fashion show going on. President Johnson and Lady Bird came to the opening, which was festive and full of celebrities. It was fun to discover Lady Bird in the ladies room where some of the girls were changing into their bathing suits. Donald Dawson was at the opening with his wife, actress Ilona Massey. After dinner Bobby danced with his little girl, who looked very pretty, all dressed up, even with white gloves. She was about four-years-old at the time. Bobby's wife, Dottie, was ill and did not attend.

There was a group of people called "The Quorum Club" who used to frequent the Carroll Arms Hotel. Bobby Baker was a part of the group. He was very gregarious, and very "with it." We got along well and he was very cooperative and funny, too. I remember if he were ill, he'd say, "Boy I'd have to feel better to die." On one of the Congressional Secretaries Club trips that I took to Puerto Rico, he and his wife Dottie were along. He was master of ceremonies at one of the dinners, introducing the people from each Senator's office there. He introduced me as having one of the best jobs in Washington and being one of the most important women in Washington. Of course, that was Bobby, but it was complimentary. I had attended his wedding to Dottie Comstock at St. Patrick's, and their reception was held in the Senate District Committee. Not many Senators attended, as it was Thanksgiving, and many had left Washington. At one time there was a "Bobby Baker Day" down in Pickens, South Carolina like the "Skeeter Johnston Day" held for Mr. Johnston in Biloxi, Mississippi. I think had Bobby not been so ambitious he could either have been elected Governor of South Carolina or Secretary of the Senate.

When their first of six children was born he would bring the baby up to our office on a Saturday while his wife was having her hair done or something.

Bobby had asked me to try to find a new secretary for him after he had dismissed Margaret Tucker. One of the things I did unofficially was to keep a file of people interested in making a change in their jobs, with their qualifications and experience, etc. Mr. Johnston refused to let me help Bobby in this way. He hired Carole Tyler and asked me down to his office to meet her. When he had originally hired Margaret Tucker I had trained her.

Carole was always very cooperative. Then she started going down to Bobby's Carousel Hotel. Some people thought there was a relationship between Bobby and Carole, but I didn't think so. When Bobby got into a lot of trouble with his financial dealings said to constitute a conflict of interest, she testified on his behalf. Her picture was in *Life* magazine, and she looked very sophisticated, right down to her long black gloves.

When she was at the Carousel one weekend, a fellow who had been staying there had gotten together with her and several other people one evening. He had his own plane and wanted to give somebody a ride. She was the only one who accepted. On the flight the pilot started doing all kinds of stunts with the plane and it crashed. Both Carole and the pilot were killed. Joe Stewart, an assistant to Bobby, watched it crash.

There had been a weird and bizarre prophesy to this: the page boys who worked closely with Bobby thought it would be fun on her birthday to get Carole a special birthday cake. She had left early that day so they called her at home, and I guess she felt bad that they had gone to all this trouble, so she went back to the office for the celebration. It turned out to be a cake with black icing—with a tombstone on it, because she always said, "I don't want any more birthdays." She evidently was one of those people who thought they were growing too old, and humorously talked like that. The whole thing was kind of morbid in retrospect. She was only twenty-six.

There was another sad happening connected to Bobby. There was a girl, Trudy Novack, who worked for the Senate Small Business Committee. Her husband had been Bobby's law partner. Her husband was asphyxiated in their garage, and some thought it was possibly because of his association with Bobby that he had committed suicide. She had to testify and claimed it was an accident.

People felt that her husband had some of the same investments as Bobby and they tried to tie it together. It was very difficult for her.

Because of his many financial dealings Bobby was scheduled to appear before the Democratic Conference (a meeting of all Democratic Senators) for questioning. He didn't appear. He resigned instead because he knew they were going to call for his resignation. Since I had known him from his page boy days, we had been on trips and worked together, and I knew all of his good friends, I felt very bad. There was a fellow named Wayne Bromley, who had been a good friend of Bobby's, who testified against him. Most people thought Bobby was taking the blame for someone else.

* * * * *

When Bobby resigned, I was down at my cottage on Chesapeake Bay, and the telephone was cut off because it was a vacation place. When I heard he resigned I just couldn't believe it. I went to the hotel immediately and called Skeeter Johnston because Bobby had been his prodigy. He said, "Well, Miss Scott, I just got sick. I got sick to my stomach when I heard the news." He and Mrs. Johnston had season tickets for the shows at the Kennedy Center. He had his wife call Christine Johnson, one of my assistants, to accompany her because he couldn't stand to go to the theater that night. Frank Valeo was appointed to replace Bobby; and later was elected to the position of Secretary for the Majority. It was a very bad time because Bobby had worked so hard.

Sam Shaffer, head of the Washington Bureau of *Newsweek* magazine told me he was directed to write an article about Bobby and he refused to do it because he thought so highly of him.

LBJ was so sentimental and appreciative of people with whom he worked. He would go from one extreme to another in connection with his emotions. One time he got mad at Bobby and said he was going to send him over to the House side and, of course, after that they made up. In addition to the Carousel Hotel Bobby was financially into vending machines—other outside business interests.

When Bobby left, Majority Leader Mansfield issued an order that no one could talk to any of the pages or to the Secretary for the Majority until they identified themselves so as not to create further publicity. He was trying to cut off any contact with anyone who had worked with Bobby. Joe Stewart was the only one kept on and some of the pages were fired. Joe went over to the Appropriations Committee after that and, some years later, was elected Secretary of the Senate.

After Bobby served his eighteen-month sentence and was released from jail he was at Duke Ziebert's restaurant. Frank Valeo was there with a friend and his son, Jamie. Bobby came over to their table and said in a very loud voice, "There's Frank Valeo. He took my job." Jamie was incensed. Frank kept his cool and never answered him; never said a word. Frank's friend said evidently Bobby wanted to have the other customers, who are usually well-known people in Washington, hear this to help the sale of his book, *Wheeling and Dealing on Capitol Hill.* The last line of it refers to a place he owned down south (a motel of some sort). He invited the reader to "come down and bring money." In the book Bobby said some of his inmates in jail were out to get him and that one of Jimmy Hoffa's men protected him from being killed.

Later on there was word that there had been some new evidence and that Bobby might be retried and forgiven. This was based on the fact that he said that Senator Kerr of Oklahoma had helped finance his dealings. This was questionable because by that time Senator Kerr had died so nothing came of this effort.

Another footnote is that Johnston told me Senator Mansfield originally stated that unless Bobby stayed on as Secretary for the Majority, he wouldn't be interested in continuing as Majority Leader of the Senate. However, after Bobby resigned Mansfield was re-elected and continued to serve for a total of seventeen years. When Bobby resigned, Senator Mansfield praised his work. I was impressed at this because usually the Senator was rather taciturn. For instance, one time Johnston went to Senator Mansfield when he was leader to try to get more room for one of our offices, the Senate disbursing office. He said to Senator Mansfield, "I want to ask you about getting more room for the Senate disbursing office." The Senator was quiet for a minute, then said, "You asked me." He turned away and that was it!

Bobby's wife, Dottie, contributed to the payment of his fines every payday when she still worked at the Senate. Later, it was rumored she lived in California but returned to Bobby in Washington. Bobby also weathered another tragedy when his sixteen-year-old son was killed in an accident a few years ago. As one of the commentators used to say, "and so it goes."

Senator Joseph McCarthy

Senators came and went but Senator McCarthy stretched the boundaries of fairness and good taste in his Senate service. There was a spirit of fair play and non-partisanship in the Senate. Some of the Senators would really debate heatedly on the floor and they could come off the floor with their arms around each other. It was good because they worked together—despite the system of checks and balances.

I first met Senator McCarthy standing in line for lunch in the Senate office building cafeteria. He was Chairman of the Senate Investigating Subcommittee where Ruth Watt was the Chief Clerk. Some of us would go over to the Carroll Arms Hotel at times for lunch. McCarthy was very appreciative of Ruth's service and whenever he saw her, he would send drinks over to all of us. He was very friendly and cordial.

The hearings he was conducting showed him to be a bully, ruining the reputations of Defense Department and State Department employees, declaring they all were Communists. His manner and outlandish attacks sunk to a low that the Senate had never experienced. *Time* magazine carried a portrait of McCarthy on its front cover. His face was all black suggesting that all the mud he was throwing on suspected Communists was coming back to him. His remarks vilified members of the Defense Department to a point where their attorney, Joseph Welsh, was forced to say to him, "Senator, have you no decency?"

Everyone in the country was interested in these hearings including my cousin and aunt from Philadelphia. Ruth arranged tickets to the hearings for them. They wouldn't stay at our home in Silver Spring, preferring to stay at the Carroll Arms Hotel on Capitol Hill which Senator McCarthy and his staff frequented. They wanted to be "where the action was!" I was driving them around one night showing them scenes of Washington and when we passed the new State Department building Aunt Louise said to me, "Is that where all the Communists are?" It was sad to think that she had believed Senator McCarthy's ravings!

At the end, Senator McCarthy would stand there on the Senate floor with a blank piece of paper and he would wave it around. He would say, "I have here a list of Communists in the State Department." I think, finally, everybody got his number after the hearings. He continued unsuccessfully to get the news reporters' attention. He was really news for a while, but soon they lost interest.

Senator Millard Tydings from Maryland was running for re-election. Senator McCarthy dishonestly put pictures of him with Jimmy Hoffa. This was one of the reasons that Senator Tydings was defeated. I knew Tydings to be a dignified, fine gentleman. McCarthy and his force got to the point where it was just sickening.

Senator Margaret Chase Smith of Maine presented a "Declaration of Conscience" to the Senate condemning him. Later, her assistant Bill Lewis wrote a book with that title.

Not too long after this shameful debacle, I was at a party in the new Senate office building the night Senator McCarthy died. McCarthy had been in the hospital for liver problems due to his drinking. Certainly his broken heart and frustration contributed. I remember so well how the word about his death spread at the party.

The next day, Jean McCarthy, his wife, was allowed through one of the rules of the Senate, to have his casket placed on the floor—right in the Senate chamber. She did everything she could to seek revenge for him, because the Senate had officially censured him, and he was really condemned.

His casket was on the Senate floor and no one went near it. It was right across the hall from my office. Nobody! Nobody went in all day long. The *Time* magazine photo was a true prediction: a new word was coined, "McCarthyism" meaning mud slinging.

"The Three Kennedy Brothers"
Assassination of President Jack Kennedy
November 22, 1963

The day President Kennedy was assassinated I wasn't in my office. During adjournment my two assistants and I took turns having a little time off. I was at my townhouse painting the woodwork on my staircase. It was an old, historical townhouse and I was in the process of restoring it. I had removed the heavy mahogany banisters of the staircase and replaced them with a wrought iron railing which I had painted gold. The woodwork of the staircase and floor edgings I had also painted antique white and gold. This was my project on that tragic day when I heard the announcement over the radio of the shooting of our President in Dallas.

I called the office immediately and one of my girls, Christine Johnson, who was on duty, told me that all of the Senators had been coming into our office crying. They were in shock and couldn't believe it. Everyone, not only in the Capitol, but all over the world, was experiencing feelings of an unreal nightmare.

That night, back at my home in Silver Spring, my father, our housekeeper and I stayed glued to the television set. We saw the swearing in of the Vice President, Lyndon B. Johnson, by a woman, Judge Hughes, which took place on Air Force One, the President's plane. Jackie Kennedy had not changed her clothes, but stood in disbelief, along with Lady Bird Johnson and others to witness the ceremony. The Vice President had called the President's brother, Attorney General Robert Kennedy, to get the official wording for his oath of office. He was anxious to hurry the ceremony and get back to Washington, not knowing whether this could have been an act of violence from a foreign power.

When the bullet struck, Jackie tried to climb over the back of the convertible car to get the Secret Service agent who was walking behind the car. She was dressed in a rose two-piece suit with short jacket and a matching pillbox hat (her fashion signature).

Governor John Connally of Texas and his wife were in the front seat of the car and one bullet also hit him. During the fast and furious trip to the hospital spectators who had lined up on the sidewalk to greet the President's motorcade wailed and sobbed in shock.

The motorcade followed the President's car and complete panic took over as hospital attendants rushed the President into surgery. He died within minutes and the sad scene with its unreal drama of sadness and frustration, witnessed by innumerable members of the media, covered television screens everywhere.

Within minutes of his swearing in, the new President, LBJ, directed that the plane take off for Washington. Jackie Kennedy, still in her blood-splattered suit, sat beside her husband's body all the way back to the nation's Capitol.

As reported by United Press International, "House Speaker John McCormack, when he heard the news in Washington exclaimed, 'My god, what are we coming to?'" Texas Senator Yarborough, who had witnessed the assassination, cried as he tried to talk to reporters. In the Senate the chaplain said, "We gaze at a vacant place against the sky, as the President of the Republic goes down like a giant cedar."

The Stars and Stripes fluttered to half-staff across the nation and at American outposts across the world.

UPI reported that at Andrews Air Force base, with his wife at his side, President Johnson read his first public statement: "This is a sad time for all people. We have suffered a loss that cannot be weighed. For me, it is a deep personal tragedy. I know the world shares the sorrow that Mrs. Kennedy and her family bears. I will do my best. That is all I can do. I ask for your help . . . and God's."

Continuing, UPS reported: "America was in a state of suspension, and for a time the world seemed to stand silently still."

The new President's first act was a proclamation that set the following Monday, November 25, 1963, as a national day of mourning, which read as follows:

Proclamation

To the People of the United States:

John Fitzgerald Kennedy, thirty-fifth President of the United States, has been taken from us by an act which outrages decent men everywhere.

He upheld the faith of our fathers, which is freedom for all men. He broadened the frontiers of that faith, and backed it with the energy and the courage which are the mark of the nation he led.

A man of wisdom, strength and peace, he molded and moved the power of our nation in the service of a world of growing liberty and order. All who love freedom will mourn his death.

As he did not shrink from his responsibilities, but welcomed them, so he would not have us shrink from carrying on his work beyond this hour of national tragedy.

He said it himself: "The energy, the faith, the devotion which we bring to this endeavor will light our country and all who service it—and the glow from that fire can truly light the world."

Now, therefore, I, Lyndon B. Johnson, President of the United States of America, do appoint Monday next, November 25, the day of the funeral service of President Kennedy, to be a day of national mourning throughout the United States. I earnestly recommend the people to assemble on that day in their respective places of divine worship, there to bow down in submission to the will of Almighty God and to pay their homage of love and reverence to the memory of a great and good man. I invite the people of the world who share our grief to join us in this day of mourning and rededication.

IN WITNESS WHEREOF, I have hereunto set my hand and caused the Seal of the United States of America to be affixed.

DONE at the city of Washington this twenty-third day of November in the year of our Lord nineteen hundred and sixty-three, and of the Independence of the United States of America the one hundredth and eighty-eighth.

LYNDON B. JOHNSON

The President's body was taken to the White House as we all witnessed this tragic event on television that evening.

On the following day there was a viewing of the President's body at the White House. We all remember the next day's sad procession as heads of state from countries throughout the world joined the Kennedy family and members of official Washington in walking down historic Pennsylvania Avenue and over to St. Matthew's Cathedral for the late President's funeral mass conducted by Cardinal Cushing.

The picture of Jackie Kennedy with her heavy face veil, holding her son John-John's hand and that of her daughter Caroline while they were standing in the portico of the White House prior to leading the procession will always remain in our hearts. The tiny pathetic salute of John-John said it all.

A friend and I were at the cathedral during the mass and then walked back to the Capitol, following the procession taking the President's body to lie in state in the Capitol rotunda. Seeing the horse with the empty boots turned backwards will remain in my memory as a symbol of the emptiness felt by us all.

A short memorial service was held in the Capitol rotunda at which Jackie and her children knelt and kissed the President's coffin. At Senator Mansfield's request, Frank Valeo wrote with him this beautiful eulogy later adjudged a poem. These stirring words commemorating Jackie's placing her ring in his hands in his coffin, were translated into several languages and are to the right.

When standing on the Capitol plaza hearing this beautiful eulogy broadcast from inside the rotunda, next to me was a man with a small transistor radio which he had turned on. I heard the words that as Harvey Oswald, whom they had arrested as being the killer, was being led into the prison hallway, he was shot at point blank range by Jack Ruby. I couldn't believe my ears that, as the memorial services in the Capitol were proceeding, his assassin was being killed in Dallas!

That night the President's body lay in state in the Capitol rotunda, guarded by representatives of the four branches of our armed services. Members of the Senate started the sad trek around his casket, followed by Senate staff members. As I walked slowly around, memories returned of the times the young Senator visited our office. Before one of the luncheons in our private dining room which the Senator would be attending I had inquired of his personal secretary, Evelyn Lincoln, what he would like ordered for him. It turned out that Jackie sent over a covered basket with his meal being kept warm in a child's double broiler. This was a practice frequently used by her.

As the late President lay in state under the majestic dome of the Capitol, thousands of people climbed the Capitol steps to pay their respects. The procession was lined up for sixteen blocks on each side of Capitol Hill. I watched this historic moment on television. It continued all night.

It was heart-rending to see people of all ages dressed in warm clothes against the chill of the weather walking around the casket crying and silently grieving. Time stood still as many stopped to bless themselves and offer up prayers in sympathy. This long night

Senator Mike Mansfield's Tribute
to the Deceased President Kennedy

There was a sound of laughter; in a moment it was no more. And she took a ring from her finger and placed it in his hands. There was a wit in a man neither young nor old, but a wit full of an old man's wisdom, and of a child's wisdom, and then in a moment it was no more. And so she took a ring from her finger and placed it in his hands.

There was a father with a little boy, a little girl and a joy of each other. In a moment it was no more, and so she took a ring from her finger and placed it his hands.

There was a husband who asked much and gave much, and out of giving and the asking wove with a woman what could not be broken in life, and in a moment it was no more. And so she took a ring from her finger and placed it in his hands and kissed him and closed the lid of the coffin.

A piece of us died that moment. Yet, in death he gave himself to us. He gave us a good heart from which the laughter came. He gave us a profound wit, from which a great leadership emerged. He gave us a kindness and a strength fused into a human courage to seek peace without fear.

He gave us of his love that we, too, in turn, might give. He gave that we might give of ourselves, that we might give to one another until there would be no room, no room at all, for the bigotry, the hatred, prejudice, and the arrogance which converged in that moment of horror to strike him down.

In leaving us—these gifts, John Fitzgerald Kennedy, President of the United States, leaves with us. Will we take them Mr. President? Will we have, now, the sense and responsibility and the courage to take them?

I pray to God that we shall and under God we will.

must surely have been the most overwhelming, crushing, grief-sharing one witnessed through the Capitol's hallowed halls.

Jackie Kennedy and her brother-in-law, Bobby Kennedy, walked hand in hand through the Capitol grounds after walking around the President's casket.

I recalled, too, times he had rushed through my office to attend a meeting in our conference room, not looking left or right. I could still picture his handsome figure and quick, light step.

There was one occasion when Mr. Johnston was resting in our conference room. I had to turn Senator Kennedy away so as not to disturb him. The Senator turned on his heel and I think my two assistants were surprised, as I imagine I was one of the few people who ever turned him down.

As a young Congressman, President Kennedy had made an appointment to see Mr. Leslie Biffle, Secretary of the Senate. Betty, Biffle's assistant, had confirmed the appointment and when the Congressman arrived at her office and asked to see him, she said, "Oh, I'm sorry, you'll have to wait. He is expecting Congressman Kennedy." To her surprise this boyish looking young man with a "Skippy" haircut announced "I am the Congressman."

During President Eisenhower's inauguration Senator Kennedy was standing in front of the ropes on the Capitol plaza as the parade began, waving to some friends among the participants. He was chastised by Bill Wannall, the Sergeant-at-Arms of the Senate, and made to stand behind the ropes. Four years later he led the Inaugural Parade to the Presidential Reviewing Stand at the White House, as President himself!

The next day sixteen blocks on both sides of the Capitol building were strewn with chewing gum wrappers and all kinds of clutter, attesting to the crowds of people who bid our President goodbye that night.

Later that day I drove around downtown Washington with my movie camera to record a city in mourning. Large photographs draped in black with floral displays were in every store window on

F Street, and placards proclaimed sympathy. Everyone seemed to be clinging together in any way possible to bear the sorrow.

The days that followed were horrible and incredible. All kinds of stories and theories surfaced. Newsman Walter Cronkite and others broke down when reporting the tragedy and all over our great country there was unremitting grief.

After a trip I made to Mexico four years later with the Congressional Secretaries Club, a friend and I stopped overnight in Dallas on our way back to Washington. The next day en route to the airport we were driven by an experienced chauffeur of visiting VIPs who had been the driver of the second car in President Kennedy's motorcade the day he was assassinated.

It was exactly four years to the day of the assassination. Our driver told us of his sad trip to the hospital after the shooting, and described the unbearable grief of everyone in Dallas that fateful day. When we passed the Dallas Book Depository, scene of the tragedy, there was an informal memorial ceremony taking place on this anniversary.

On a bronze plaque marking the spot and date of the assassination offerings of roses had been laid. Vendors were selling pictures of Jack and Jackie in the open car with spectators lined up on the sidewalk. Somehow a picture of Harvey Oswald in the crowd had been added. As we drove by, our driver told us that the people of Dallas would never be the same. They were so heartbroken and ashamed that this had happened there. He said a secretary of his limousine company had been standing right in front of the book depository building and had seen two men running over the hill ahead after the shots rang out. He said when he went to the hospital the scene was one of uncontrollable grief and sadness.

Being right there at the scene of that horrible event brought all my feelings back to me. I remembered crying my heart out the day of the funeral, watching the sad procession go over the bridge to Arlington National Cemetery. When the eternal flame was lit on the President's grave by Jackie deep sobs practically choked me. This flame still flickers through the darkness, high on a hill above the city of Washington in reverent memory of our young martyred President.

In those days I couldn't stop repeating, "They killed our President!"

In the joint session of Congress on November 27, 1963 President Johnson said:

> *All I have I would have given gladly not to be standing here today.*
>
> *The greatest leader of our time has been struck down by the foulest deed of our time. Today, John Fitzgerald Kennedy lives on in the immortal words and works that he left behind. He lives on in the minds and memories of mankind. He lives on in the hearts of his countrymen.*
>
> *No words are sad enough to express our sense of loss. No words are strong enough to express our determination to continue the forward thrust of America that he began.*
>
> *For thirty-two years Capitol Hill has been my home. I have shared many moments of pride with you, pride in the ability of the Congress of the United States to act, to meet any crisis, to distill from our differences strong programs of national action.*
>
> *An assassin's bullet has thrust upon me the awesome burden of the Presidency. I am here today to say I need your help; I cannot bear this burden alone. I need the help of all Americans, and all America. This nation has experienced a profound shock, and in this critical moment, it is our duty, yours and mine, as the government of the United States, to do away with uncertainty and doubt and delay, and to show that we are capable of decisive action; that from the brutal loss of our leader we*

will derive not weakness, but strength; that we can and will act and act now.

On the twentieth day of January, in 1961, John F. Kennedy told his countrymen that our national work would not be finished "in the first thousand days, nor in the life of this administration, nor even perhaps in our lifetime on this planet. "But," he said, "let us begin."

Today, in this moment of new resolve, I say to all my fellow Americans, let us continue.

We met in grief, but let us also meet in renewed dedication and renewed vigor. Let us meet in action, in tolerance, and in mutual understanding. John Kennedy's death commands what his life conveyed—-that America must move forward. The time has come for Americans of all races and creeds and political beliefs to understand and to respect one another. So let us put an end to the teaching and the preaching of hate and evil and violence. Let us turn away from the fanatics of the far left and the far right, from the apostles of bitterness and bigotry, from those defiant of law, and those who pour venom into our nation's bloodstream.

I profoundly hope that the tragedy and the torment of these terrible days will bind us together in new fellowship, making us one people in our hour of sorrow. So let us here highly resolve that John Fitzgerald Kennedy did not live—or die—in vain. And on this Thanksgiving eve, as we gather together to ask the Lord's words.

America, America,
God shed His grace on thee,
And crown thy good
With brotherhood
From sea to shining sea.

* * * * *

I have studied a little about handwriting analysis. It was interesting to me to see the change in LBJ's signature from the time he was Majority Leader of the Senate to the time he was President. During his years as a Senator his signature was graceful and flowing. It seemed to indicate strong self-confidence and a relaxed feeling. After he became President his signature on documents delivered to my office by White House messengers—indicated a signature tightly controlled with all the letters pushed together. A tenseness, a feeling of being uptight and nervous—even the cramped letters suggested a "trapped" emotional mood. The Presidency changes all men.

Robert F. Kennedy
In Los Angeles

A beaming Bobby Kennedy, on the night of June 5, 1968, accepted the victory cheers from the jammed-in crowd in the Ambassador Hotel. According to author Margaret Burk's book, *Are The Stars Out Tonight*, about the hotel and the Cocoanut Grove, "On to Chicago," Kennedy said as he left the podium by way of the kitchen.

He was originally to have gone down a back stairway to another reception in the convention area of the lower casino level but his aides changed course so the writing newsmen who were pushing deadlines could see him.

Struggling through the crowds as he left were Mrs. Kennedy (pregnant with their eleventh child) and several aides who had been separated by the change of course. He turned to look for

Ethel while answering a question of Mutual Radio reporter Andrew West, when a single soft "pop," followed by a rapid volley of repeated "pops" sounded. Hotel employee Jesus Perez testified before the grand jury, "I was shaking hands with him and then he let go and fell to the floor."

Kennedy's hands went up toward his face. The impact threw his arms over his head, his feet were apart and he was lying about two feet from the side of the ice machine on the cold gray floor. He was mortally wounded by the gun of Jordanian immigrant Sirhan Sirhan. Several employees grabbed at the hand holding the gun while Rosey Grier and Rafer Johnson were reaching to pin Sirhan down.

Young kitchen worker Juan Romero knelt at the side of Kennedy, wrapped a rosary around Kennedy's left thumb and folded his hand over it. Kennedy brought it up to his chest while Romero cradled his head and whispered "Come on, Mr. Kennedy. You can make it."

Several minutes passed before Mrs. Kennedy, who had been held back when the gun fire broke out, was brought forward. Tenderly she took his hand. He turned his head and seemed to recognize her. She knelt there in her orange and white party dress, on both knees, stooped low, whispering to him on the cold concrete floor. His last words to her were "Am I alright?"

He was taken to Good Samaritan Hospital where his family and close supporters anguishly awaited him. He died at 1:44 A.M. on June 6, 1968, 25 1/2 hours after the shooting. He was forty-two-years-old.

The final chapter of Robert Kennedy's life, even a prediction, might be found in the poem by his favorite poet, Aeschylus, that he was fond of quoting:

> *In our sleep, pain which cannot forget*
> *Falls drop by drop upon the heart until,*
> *In our own despair . . . against our will . . .*
> *Comes wisdom through the awful grace of God.*

After Senator Robert Kennedy was shot, Senator Mansfield, then Senate Majority Leader, was notified immediately, and called Frank Valeo, who called me. It was about 5:00 A.M.. He told me the awful news and said: "Go over to the office right away." As my house was just eight blocks from the Capitol building, it didn't take me very long, and in minutes I arrived at the office. It was still dark outside and during my short drive, it seemed like a nightmare I would awaken from. It was the beginning of a long day, twenty-four hours of darkness engulfing us in a heavy brooding cloak of sadness. It was a scene frozen in time.

All day long members of the Senate were coming into the office, practically paralyzed by the tragic news. Our office took on the air of a funeral parlor, as though the Senators were waiting for the body to arrive. That is actually what they were doing, for the Senator's body was being brought to Washington on a funeral train after services in New York, for burial in Arlington National Cemetery that same night. One of my Senate "sisters," Angie Novella, who was Robert Kennedy's personal secretary, was working with Mrs. Ethel Kennedy on arrangements, and we were in contact with her in New York so we could notify the Senators who wished to go to the burial. We were ordering buses to leave from the Capitol building for the drive to Arlington National Cemetery.

The funeral train had proceeded very slowly. It was Ethel Kennedy's way, I felt, of duplicating the procession of world leaders who had walked down Pennsylvania Avenue from the White House to accompany Robert's brother and leading President John F. Kennedy's body to St. Matthew's Cathedral for his funeral mass.

Ruth Watt, Chief Clerk of the Senate Investigating Committee ("mother" of our Senate family), and her husband, Walter, former Senate doorman and Superintendent of the Senate folding room, had flown to New York to attend the funeral mass. Walter was a pall bearer, and they returned on the funeral train. They said afterward that adding to the tragedy, conditions on the train were terrible. It traveled ever so slowly and then ran out of food and the air conditioning broke down.

All along the tracks, crowds of people gathered to see the train go by. Two people were killed on the tracks, and the tragedy was acerbated.

All day long the Senators wandered into my office inquiring about the train's arrival. There was continuous radio and television news coverage. All throughout our country Americans lived each heartbreaking moment along with members of Senator Kennedy's family and his Senate colleagues. While awaiting the funeral train, the gloom deepened in our office. We felt as if in a funeral parlor attending a wake.

As the day turned into night the atmosphere grew heavier and sadder until the drama unfolding made it hard for all of us not to break down completely.

At about 8:30 that night the train finally arrived and we were able to accommodate all the Senators who wanted to attend the services out at Arlington National Cemetery on special buses.

Frank Valeo accompanied Senator Mansfield in his office limousine. After they left I was exhausted and remained at the office, to watch the services on television.

Then alone, I felt again the overwhelming and engulfing sadness I had experienced upon hearing of President Kennedy's assassination all those years before. I looked from the window to the left of my desk at the vista with only the view of the Washington Monument relieving the picture. It was another black night in a grief-stricken city, and waves of emotion were washing over all the land.

I went into Valeo's offices to watch the burial on television. Senator Kennedy was buried by candlelight in the pitch dark, near his brother Jack's grave, with its eternal flame burning. The flickering candlelight gave a surrealistic atmosphere to the scene. The faces of the Senators standing at the burial site were ashen and tragic. It was another nightmare, and all too familiar. How unreal and devastating were the circumstances! Two brothers in their prime, brought down mercilessly while trying to dedicate their lives, their strengths, and their patriotism to our country!

I had met Bobby Kennedy and his wife, Ethel, at a Christmas party given by the Senate Investigating Committee when he was counsel of the committee. Our headwaiter, Ellsworth Dozier, had been borrowed from our staff, and was serving. The party was given at the committee offices in the old Senate office building. Someone had given Bobby a little white pig for Christmas and there it was, walking around with its big red bow, gobbling up spilled potato chips on the office floor.

Ethel Kennedy was sitting on one of the conference tables, swinging her legs and laughing as she watched the pig. She was dressed very casually, her dark hair brushed back in an informal style, and wearing very little makeup. I had heard that she was a very active mother to their then six children, accompanying them and sharing in all their activities. It wasn't hard to picture her rough-housing with them and coming down the New England slopes on skis with them.

Ruth Watt was very devoted to the Senator and his wife, and each year she and her husband Walter received another dozen roses on their anniversary. As the years piled up, so did the roses! Each Christmas, too, they received another Christmas card with a picture of another new little Kennedy added to the family portrait. The final count was eleven.

It was especially difficult for me, remembering the light and happy moments at parties with them to witness the morbid and depressing hours after the Senator's assassination. Again Washington was devastated.

The Tragedy of Being Ted Kennedy

After the tragedy of the drowning of Mary Jo Kopechne, I received several strange postcards from Naticoke, Pennsylvania, the place where she was buried. The message was always written in green ink, containing sad, bizarre sentiments, *signed* MaryJo. They were so terrible I couldn't bear to file them so they were trashed.

According to a recent television program, *The Biography of Ted Kennedy,* he has redeemed himself.

Senator Ted Kennedy has served for two-thirds of his life in the Senate, the last of his three martyred brothers, the youngest son in a political dynasty.

Ted Kennedy was the ninth and last child of the senior Kennedys, born after his father's affair with Gloria Swanson. Following this, the senior Kennedys lived in opposite sides of their home. Joseph Kennedy served as Ambassador to Great Britain appointed by President Franklin Roosevelt, but was later recalled because of his support of Hitler.

Ted attended Harvard, and at the age of nineteen, entered the Army where he served for two years as a private. He went back to Harvard, did well and graduated, he also attended the University of Virginia Law School.

He was married in 1958, worked for his brother Jack in his campaign, and won his first Senate race for the seat vacated by President John Kennedy. He was sworn in at age thirty in 1963. He was considered a "most entertaining fellow," more so than his brothers.

On November 22, 1963, President John Kennedy was assassinated, and we all remember pictures of Bobby and Ted Kennedy walking on each side of Jackie, trying through their love to ease the heartbreak and give her strength and consolation.

Ted suffered a broken back in 1964, requiring six months of recovery, campaigned for re-election from his hospital bed, and was re-elected with more than seventy-five percent of the vote, becoming the senior Senator from his state.

In 1965 Ted campaigned for his brother, Bobby, who was running for the Presidential nomination of the Democratic party, in opposition to President Lyndon Johnson. Bobby was assassinated after a rousing speech in June 1968 at the Ambassador Hotel in Los Angeles.

Ted had now lost three brothers: His eldest brother, Joe, in a service related airplane accident; John and Bobby assassinated; and sister Kathleen, in an airplane accident, and sister Rosemary was institutionalized. At age thirty-six Ted was the only surviving son who then became a surrogate father to his brothers' children.

Another tragedy Ted Kennedy had to bear was in 1973 when one of his three children, his son, had to have his leg amputated. He was shattered by this experience and stayed the night in the hospital. On a visit to my office by the Senator around this time, Frank Valeo's mother was also visiting and commiserated with the Senator.

Ted and his wife, Joan, a charming lady, a concert pianist, both had alcohol problems and after separating and reunited, were divorced in 1983.

In 1976 he wanted to run for President, but lost in getting the nomination to later-elected President Jimmy Carter.

Ted had a good relationship with his nephew, William Kennedy Smith. However on one occasion over the Easter holiday in 1991 in Palm Beach, Florida, they went out drinking together. William became involved with a late night acquaintance at a nightclub whom he brought home. Charged with rape and sexual battery, he was brought to trial but was acquitted and released.

The big personal blow in Ted Kennedy's life occurred in July, 1969, when he attended a cookout honoring people who had worked on Bobby's campaign. They were referred to as "The Boiler Room Girls," attesting to their hard work. They were invited to a party and a sailing regatta the next day. A cottage was rented for this affair. This was held near Edgartown, Massachusetts. Upon leaving, Kennedy was driving Mary Jo Kopechne in his car to Edgartown, made a wrong turn going over Dykes Bridge and the car careened over into the water. Mary Jo drowned. According to court records in the Luzerne County Courthouse, Wilkes-Barre, Pennsylvania, he did not report the accident until the next morning, ten hours later. Mary Jo was fully clothed, had evidence of only a small amount of alcohol in her body, and there was no evidence of foul play. The petition for an autopsy was refused. There was conflicting evidence. A witness said a man and woman were both in the front seat of the car and a person, sweater, or purse in the back. The story in Washington was that Mary Jo had left the cottage and gone out to Ted's car and fallen asleep and he didn't know she was in the car. Another conflicting statement in the court petition was that he had returned to the cottage and some one drove him to Edgartown. In the inquest, it was stated that the report given by the driver to the Edgartown police varied from Ted Kennedy's television broadcast on July 25, 1969. The final agreement in the court case was that the prosecutors didn't bother to do their jobs.

After his statement on television I was filled with compassion, and wrote:

> *Once again our hearts went out to Ted Kennedy. When he called Mr. Kopechne to tell him the tragic news that his daughter had drowned in an automobile accident, he said he wished it were himself instead of Mary Jo. He was so broken up that Mr. Kopechne could hardly understand his words. We remembered the eulogy of his brother, Robert Kennedy, at the Atlantic City Democratic Convention in 1964 when his heart broke in front of the world on television. We all anguished along with him and our eyes overflowed with tears in the senseless emptiness and grim helplessness of the moment. Only in memory dimmed by the passage of time since the assassination of his brother, President Jack Kennedy, and with his feelings stirring close beneath the surface, do we remember him trying to be strong, walking on one side of Jackie Kennedy while his brother Bob gave him a lesson he had to learn well in bearing grief. He tried, for the Kennedy women, to be strong and provide a steady masculine shoulder to lean on. His was the younger, more boyish face—most eyes fell on his brother Bob who was then the grief-stricken closer brother. But Ted's feelings were as deep, the wound as raw in the tissues of his heart*

which had been torn open as his world was attacked by disaster. After he and his brother found the courage to face outward and gather strength while mustering up all they had within themselves to give their family—after the wound healed over a little, he and Bob moved closer together to try to fill the void. Ted found a place to bring his devotion and ambition—to his brother Bob who was endeavoring to obtain the Presidential nomination, and all his hopes then were centered in him. He worked to build a place with him in the American world of politics. They brought back a semblance of life again to show the world the upper layer of courage and determination which they had fashioned. The warmth of the reception of the American people gave life to their world. Bathed in their smiles and enthusiasm the sun was shining once again and the promise was growing green and blossoming. Just before it burst into full bloom, indeed, as the petals started to open with the warmth of the adoring eyes of Bob Kennedy's audiences, the lightening struck again—the thunder clapped and another long night of darkness descended upon the Kennedy clan. Bob was assassinated. A second beloved brother, who had leaned down and picked up the torch had lifted it high in the sky to light the way for his family and the world to see ahead through the darkness, was taken away. Bob was following his uncompromised win of the California primary election over Senator Eugene McCarthy at the Ambassador Hotel in Los Angeles.

*   *   *   *   *

*Once more Ted Kennedy had to pick up the shat-
tered bits and pieces of his life and this time bear
more of the grief of others loaded on top of his own.*

*As by love—which Kahlil Gibran says: "descends
to your roots and shakes them in their clinging to
the earth, threshes you to make you naked, sifts
you to force you from your husks, grinds you to
whiteness, kneads you until you are pliant and then
assigns you to his sacred fire."*

*The life of a lovely girl, devoted to his brother,
expending her energies and enthusiasm into fulfillment of the Kennedy dream—snuffed out in one
minute—after a little cheer of a relaxed evening
which brought together those with a single purpose
to unite them—the hardworking "boiler room
girls"—they had all worked together for Bob
Kennedy and were welded together by the fire of
their enthusiasm in his cause. By another thrust of
the cold blade of a cruel fate, another life was ended
in connection with the ideals of the Kennedy dream.*

*What was the effect of this tragedy on Senator Ted
Kennedy? Was God conditioning him as an athlete
is conditioned so he could be strengthened to stand
like a strong oak, to withstand all the storms of
life—to be a pillar of strength to others—to take
the place he was trying to reach?*

*This man somehow shy and unsophisticated,
reflected a much older image. As he walked in
Mary Jo's funeral he looked so lost and unsure, as
though overcome by this latest twist of fate.*

We are all a part of everyone we have ever met. We unconsciously absorb those qualities we admire in others. We treasure the things in others which bring us warmth and sunshine. We hold in our hands, as a child does a flower or a butterfly, those moments of joy which others sometimes give to us. We hope Ted Kennedy has stored all the good moments to help him stave off the unhappy ones which have crowded in.

Fate has not been kind.

Four months after this tragedy, Ted's father was dead. His son is a member of the House of Representatives and he and Ted are the only father-son family in Congress. Ted is very well thought of now for the fine job he is doing in the Senate, and to quote the late Barry Goldwater, "Ted Kennedy is the Senate's hardest working member." The saying is that his fingerprints are on every important piece of legislation today.

Tragedy Strikes Again with John Jr.

Boats searching; the family gathered to gain strength from each other; and the nation glued to their television screens awaiting the fate of the American Prince and his Princess.

John Fitzgerald Kennedy, Jr., son of the deceased President, his wife and her sister had crashed in John's single engine Piper Saratoga on their way from New York to the family estate in Hyannisport. They were to attend the wedding of his cousin Rory, the youngest daughter of Robert and Ethel Kennedy and her fiance Mark Bailey, the following day. The wedding was, of course, cancelled. The white tents and ordered food were used to accommodate the vast family as they waited, and waited, and waited, to hear the fate of the the pilot and his two passengers. The strengths of the Kennedy family were utilized and recharged with their familiar sailing, boating, bicycle riding, touch football, basketball and commiserating and comforting each other. As in many times past, Ted Kennedy took the reins of the family and sheparded them through another painful, excruciating disaster. Young Kennedy—handsome, witty, courageous and successful in his own right—was greatly admired by all. He was considered to combine the charismatic drive of his slain father and the enigmatic, charming dignity of his adored mother.

In his eulogy, patriarch Ted Kennedy read to the shell-shocked family, John's loving sister and friends at the wake, held at the Church of St. Thomas More in New York City, that "he and his bride have gone to be with his mother and father, where there will never be an end to love."

To those in attendance he tearfully said, "John Jr. had every gift but the length of years."

Martin Luther King
He had a Dream

A saddened, shocked and violent Washington, D.C. erupted into a devastating riot simultaneous with the Watt's Riots in Los Angeles, on the occasion of Martin Luther King's assassination. It was a wild time. People couldn't drive through Washington safely; one man was shot when he stopped for gas; stores were set on fire, broken into and looted.

I received a call inquiring if it was true the Capitol would be bombed. I left in a hurry! The Capitol police had also received the report. I wondered why they did not call the various offices in the Capitol and tell us to evacuate! There were National Guardsmen, Marines and metropolitan police, in addition to the Capitol police, stationed all around the Capitol grounds. Credentials were required to reach the Capitol. It was as though we were coming to work in an armed camp. I had to travel a circuitous route from my home on Eighth Street, which was only eight blocks from the Capitol building, because the police had closed off many of the streets in that area.

On leaving, I saw smoke from the fires downtown from the Capitol plaza when I went to get my car. Dr. Riddick, the Senate parliamentarian, had come out with me to get his car, also parked there. We shared the shock of what we saw.

On that first night, Dottie McCarty, Chief Clerk to the Senate Sergeant-at-Arms, wouldn't let me go to my home. Joe Duke, her boss, said he would have one of their chauffeurs drive me to her home, also on Capitol Hill, rather than allow me to drive my own car through the troubled city. Another friend wanted me to go out to Silver Spring, Maryland to stay at her house, but I didn't even try. The news was that you could not get anywhere that night in Washington.

At Dottie's, she, her sister, brother-in-law and I watched in tears the looting shown in downtown Washington on television. People were frenzied. The driver of a school bus filled with students, visitors from Philadelphia on their class trip, turned around and left the city immediately upon seeing the havoc.

Frank Valeo, in San Francisco, called me the next morning. He had heard reports of the riots and was worried about me because he knew I was living alone. It was a very frightening experience. The bridges from Annapolis and the Chesapeake Bay were closed. A curfew was in effect. Storefronts were boarded up and many of the businesses, particularly in the black districts, were burned out. This went on for days.

One of my assistants lived in Virginia in an apartment house high on a hill. She watched the fires burning throughout Washington. I was expecting a friend from Annapolis but when reaching the closed bridge, he gave up, turned around and returned home.

* * * * *

I attended mass at St. Dominick's Church on Capitol Hill the following Sunday after Dr. King was assassinated. President Johnson was there with his daughter Luci and her husband, Pat

Nugent. After the services they paused in front of the church and people formed a semi-circle facing them. We expected he might address the crowds, but he didn't. It was a quiet, emotional moment with all of us just standing there, in a way commiserating with each other in a mutual, mournful experience.

Another patriot had been killed.

The Astronauts

The beginning of our adventures in outer space, and the Senate role in the astronauts' accomplishments were also a part of my Senate career.

When our first astronaut, Alan Shepard, was set off in his capsule, the world watched on television with bated breath. We were all petrified—hoping he'd make it and return safely—so dangerous and so courageous.

Later on I had a radio at my desk and shared the excitement of another historic moment, the first voice transmission from outer space.

We watched in awe as Astronaut Armstrong was the first man on the moon and took "one small step for man and one giant step for mankind."

During a visit to Houston, Texas, I enjoyed going through the Lyndon B. Johnson Space Center. I was invited into the room where families of the astronauts on the Gemini flight were in communication with them. It was almost like being up in space with them.

I was in San Juan, Puerto Rico with the Congressional Secretaries Club and remember our excitement when Russia set off its first effort, "Sputnik."

Another "red letter day" for me in connection with the space program was when the Senate was presented with the "Moon Flag," which our astronauts had planted on the moon and returned. I locked it away carefully in one of our file cabinets and it brought me closer than ever to our "journey to the stars." The page boys got excited, too, and wanted to touch it, to see if any moon dust would rub off. We did have some moon rocks, too, which one of the Senate committees put on display. The Senate ordered a very large glass case to display the moon flag, and it was placed in the Capitol hallway just down from the Senate chamber. It was closely guarded during the day and at night locked up tightly in my office.

I took meticulous care of our American treasure.

Some Attacks in the Capitol

One day Senator Bricker was going over from the old Senate office building to the Capitol on the subway. One of the patronage employees whom he had appointed had lost his job and in revenge he shot at him. Senator Bricker quickly ducked down below the seat and yelled, "Start Off!" to the operator. He did immediately and saved the Senator's life. There were two holes in the walls of the old Senate office building, where the shots penetrated. The man was arrested and taken to St. Elizabeth's, a Washington mental institution

* * * * *

In 1965, when the Civil Rights legislation was being considered by the Senate, I received a letter with a rock in it addressed to the United States Senate. Who could be throwing a rock at the Senate?

* * * * *

In 1971 a bomb was planted in the ladies' room and exploded in the Capitol damaging the Senate disbursing office.

* * * * *

Another time a group of radicals from Puerto Rico gained admittance to the House gallery and started shooting House members from their seats. Because of this, security devices were installed at the entrances to the galleries on both the Senate and House sides of the Capitol. After the shooting, they came down the corridor passing my office where I was working, using our elevator to escape.

* * * * *

On one occasion, a man shot himself outside of the Senate Press Gallery. No explanations.

* * * * *

The suicide of one of President Clinton's staff, Mr. Foster, never knowing the reason for his action.

* * * * *

Howard Hughes was subpoenaed to appear before the Senate Investigating Committee relative to international airline routing, principally between Pan American and his airline TWA in July of 1947.

He had been his reclusive self, hiding in a Los Angeles hotel watching the hearings on television. His appointment to testify began on August 6th. His entrance (along with Noah Dietrich and other aides) caused a real stir with hundreds of would-be spectators and the committee as well. The atmosphere was circus-like as he defiantly answered questions indirectly, if at all. He wouldn't remove his hat, was not polite and showed an unmistakable low opinion of the Senate Subcommittee.

He said that he thought the investigation was illegitimate, and he was caught in the political cross-fire.

* * * * *

Recently two Capitol policemen were killed on the House side of the Capitol. They were on duty, protecting House members' offices. No explanation was forthcoming as to the reason for the mayhem.

CHAPTER NINE

My Senate Life

My Senate Family

Many of my friends in my Senate career became so close over the years that we constituted a warm "family."

Ruth Watt was a friendly New Englander from Yarmouth, Maine with a real sense of humor; tall, relaxed and loved by all. She was the Chief Clerk of the Senate Investigating Subcommittee (so-called the "McCarthy" committee when he served as Chairman). Bobby Kennedy was Chief Counsel of that committee. With her prematurely gray hair, we girls called her "mother." We called Walter Watt, her husband, "father." Walter served the Senate in different capacities.

One of our "family" rituals were Sunday breakfasts at their home in Silver Spring, Maryland where they served champagne and "Walt's wonderful waffles" (his own recipe with bacon in the middle of each waffle.) We always celebrated birthdays of each "sister" together, as well as Mother's and Father's Day. One year Ruth was away, but we had a Father's Day celebration at my cottage on Chesapeake Bay.

One of Ruth's official duties was to personally serve subpoenas on characters like Jimmy Hoffa and his associates.

Another one of our "sisters" was Rose Mary Woods, Executive Assistant to President Nixon. She first worked with him when he was a member of the House of Representatives and served on the House Un-American Activities Committee, and brought her with him after being elected to the Senate. She was a slim, lovely lady with pretty light reddish hair, a beautiful complexion, lovely eyes and impeccable in her manner and dress. She was warm and caring. Her outstanding quality was her sincerity. When President Nixon left the Senate she went with him to New York and worked in his law firm when he was associated with John Mitchell. She later traveled and campaigned with him when he was nominated for Vice President along with General Eisenhower for President. One of the trips was during the time of candidate Nixon's famous "Checkers" television speech when he defended himself against criticism relating to his expensive home and the financing of it and his lifestyle. He told of his wife's wearing of a "Republican cloth coat" and mentioned his little dog, "Checkers." This speech rewarded him with great emotional appeal and led to General Eisenhower's describing his companion nominee as being "clean as a hound's tooth." Reporters traveling with the campaign then formed a "Hound Tooth's Club" and wore the emblem on their key chains.

Even when Nixon was President, Rose always had time to attend with our other sisters and me at mother and father's election night parties. In fun, we seated ourselves on "both sides of the Senate aisle" which on the Senate floor divided the Democrats from the Republicans. She entertained the "family" at her Watergate apartment, coincidentally, the same complex of infamous "Watergate" fame. She was referred to as the "Fifth Nixon" and accompanied the President on all his foreign trips. A White House chauffeur called for her each morning and night to drive her to work. When she was out for the evening the car was stationed outside the Watergate until her return to assure her safety.

I recall sadly the front-page photograph of Rose clearly showing the agony on her face when President Nixon and his family climbed aboard their plane leaving Washington in disgrace. She went to San Clemente and worked for him there at his "Western White House."

My cousin, Marilyn Arnold, was invited with me to visit Rose there. It was a Saturday afternoon and we drove from Palm Springs. She had given me detailed instructions which seemed of no avail when we drove to a large forbidding-looking gate next to which was standing what looked like a tall gray trash can. We couldn't see any call boxes and thought the guards were gone, as it was a quiet Saturday afternoon. We got out of the car and tried kicking the gate. All of a sudden a deep male voice boomed, "Can I help you?" I gave my name and stated my appointment to see Rose. Immediately the gate opened. On the right as we drove into the spacious grounds was a long driveway leading to the mansion. Next to the stone pillars at the entrance was the former President's Rolls Royce golf cart, a specially designed one, a gift to him.

The office building to the left was low and white with offices and patios facing the Pacific Ocean. The President's office was right next to Rose's. While there we went out on the grass beyond the patio to take pictures. The President, sitting at his desk, flanked by a tall American flag, looked at us and waved. He was deeply concentrating on one of the books he was writing. It was a festive day because a party was in progress for daughter Patricia in the mansion. On a coffee table in Rose's office was an autographed picture of David Frost, who had conducted the televised "Nixon Interviews." Rose said the former President agreed to these interviews to help pay some of his expenses in connection with the Watergate tragedy and the lawsuits brought against him. However Frost edited the interviews, deleting some of the President's statements and adding comments of his own. At that time, Rose had been back in Washington for an operation; but perhaps if she had been present she might have kept this from happening. Rose turned down many requests for interviews but did conduct one with Barbara Walters.

I always visited Rose during my summer visits to Washington. On one occasion I took my camcorder to her condo and took a movie when she guided me through her apartment, pointing out her pictures of the Nixons as well as the many souvenirs she had brought back from her official trips with him. She had nearly missed one such trip when Bob Haldeman of the President's staff tried to keep her from going. The helicopter was ready on the White House lawn when the President said, "Where's Rose?" She had gone on every one of his trips prior to this. So he sent for her and she rushed out without any traveling clothes, foiling the continuing efforts of Messrs. Haldeman and Erlichman to drive a wedge between her and the President. Fortunately, the President's wife, Pat, and Rose were the same size and would frequently exchange clothes, particularly on this trip.

Speaking of clothes—years later I went with Rose in Washington to shop for her outfits to wear at the dedication of the Nixon Library in Yorba Linda, California.

Rose also described the sentimental visits of families of soldiers. They appreciated Nixon's efforts in bringing them home from Vietnam.

Another "sister" was Angie Novella, personal secretary to Attorney General and later Senator Robert Kennedy. She was tall, dark-haired, slim and attractive with a warm personality and sense of humor. In addition to working with Senator Kennedy when he was counsel to the Senate Investigating Subcommittee, she served as his secretary after he left the committee and wrote the book, *The Enemy Within.* Then she accompanied him to the Justice Department when he was appointed Attorney General, and returned with him when he was elected to the Senate. She attended all our "family" gatherings over the years. Angie's last sad duty for Senator Kennedy was in the handling of arrangements for his funeral when he was assassinated. She was our contact in New York when his wife Ethel had his body returned to Washington by train for burial in Arlington National Cemetery next to his brother, President Jack Kennedy. His grave is marked by a single cross.

Winnie DeWeese, former secretary to Republican Secretary of the Senate Carl Loeffler, and later a staff member of the Republican Policy Committee, although older than Ruth Watt, was still considered one of us "daughters." She was an interesting, attractive person with a beautiful figure and a husky voice, who chalked up three marriages.

Dottie McCarty, another "sister," Chief Clerk to three successive Sergeant-at-Arms of the Senate (who were elected by the Senate) was dark-haired with big brown eyes, vivacious, with a hearty laugh. In addition to attending all our "family" affairs she and I took many trips together as members of the Congressional Secretaries Club. She loved the Senate and was devoted to it.

Lola Pierotti was another of our "sisters." She was a wonderful addition to our "family." Senator George D. Aiken of Vermont was an honorary member of our Senate "family." This craggy, twinkle-eyed, New Englander attended, with "Sister" Lola Pierotti, his Administrative Assistant, all our functions. She had known him from the time he was Governor of Vermont and worked in the State House in Montpelier. He would frequently host private breakfasts for us in his Capitol conference room and would join us at picnics we had at lunch time at a little grotto on the Capitol grounds, where we would privately enjoy strong "iced tea." He was proud of Vermont's maple syrup and at one of the breakfasts when one guest didn't use it, he jumped up and poured the golden syrup on her pancakes. Two years after his first wife died Senator Aiken married Lola, and they became the "Sweethearts of the Senate." They were a great team politically, too. He was a typical Vermonter whose comments were always sparse, yet right to the point, and Lola lent her charm to their campaigning. She was petite with a sleek, smooth dark hairdo, beautiful figure, and a perky personality. Her quick smile and laughing eyes accompanied her witty comments. She and Senator Aiken had breakfast every morning in the Senators' dining room in the Capitol with Senator Mansfield, for many years the Senate Majority Leader. There was a saying, "If you want to know what Senator Mansfield is thinking, ask Senator Aiken; if you want to know what Senator Aiken is thinking, ask Senator Mansfield." When Lola and Senator Aiken were married (June 30, 1967), he took her off his payroll, but she continued working for him.

I was the first one to entertain them with a wedding luncheon the next day in our private dining room, complete with wedding cake and pictures. Many of the Senators and their wives wined and dined them also.

When asked about her age, Lola would reply, "Anyone who would tell that would tell anything!" She was quite a bit younger than the Senator. I always loved talking to him at parties. His views on world events and legislation were intensely interesting. He was an astute advisor to many Presidents, and many members of Congress and the media felt that his contributions should have led him to the White House. His was the first name alphabetically in the Senate to be called on to vote. One time he voted before flying to Vermont, and his was the only "nay" vote on a piece of legislation. He was an independent voter, who called it as he saw it.

After his retirement a "George D. Aiken" lecture series was instituted at the University of Vermont. He was living history and enjoyed his association with the students. I visited Montpelier several times, noticing the street names bearing his name and took a ride on the "Governor George D. Aiken Ferry" to a little town in Connecticut.

When other candidates would report large sums expended on their Senate races, his were usually about $20 *total*. He always said we should have declared victory in Vietnam and left. After a salary raise I received in a Senate appropriations bill, he said he should have proposed to me!

Carl Fogle, a jovial man in the office of the Architect of the Capitol was our "Cousin Buford." He was the entertainer of our group, having a never-ending wealth of jokes.

Elizabeth Voth, an exotic looking girl who had been born in India when her father was a missionary there also qualified as a "sister." She was personal secretary to Senator Schoeppel of Kansas.

"Uncle Bob" was an elderly Senate employee who had joined our "family." We all attended his wedding to a lovely older lady, and threw the traditional rice while the sweet couple beamed. We all frequently attended pool parties at a friend's, Jim Marks', home in Virginia. I took movies of Uncle Bob on the diving board, preparing to dive. After I panned back and forth several times he was still standing there. Finally he took the plunge!

Tempie Bailey, another "sister" was a beautiful girl who worked for the Joint Committee on Printing. Her husband was a policeman and they, too, added to the fun at our parties. She was so well endowed that one day at lunch at our family table in the Senate restaurant her beads broke and scattered to the far end of the large table. She stood for much kidding after that.

Kay Kenny worked for Senator Douglas of Illinois, also for Senator Byrd of West Virginia. As were we girls all fun loving, we made a happy group, loving Washington and our jobs.

Jim Ketchum, although not a member of my "Senate family" was a dear friend. He was a practical-joker even though serious in his position as Curator of Arts and Antiquities at the Senate. After Dottie McCarty and I had both retired, we went to the Capitol for a picnic on the Capitol grounds with Jim. Just as we got all set up under a big tree, a tractor came along and the tree was cut down! He denied planning it!

One of the reporters from the Senate Press Gallery wrote: "Everyone has noticed that this interesting group of young ladies is always exceptionally well-groomed and attractive. In addition to their devotion to their duties in the offices of the Senate, their appearance adds much to the Senate's image."

Little did they know that in our capacities we were privy to plans and policies and often effective in legislation enactments.

Light Moments

One day when Skeeter Johnston was hosting a luncheon exclusively for the reporters who covered the Senate, Beckley, head of the Senate Press Gallery, was standing by my desk, checking them in as they arrived. Senator Hayden of Arizona came walking in, and "Beck" said to him, "You can't go in there, you're a Senator!" Senator Hayden gave a funny smile and turned around and left. He was known as a "work horse" and not a "show horse" of the Senate. When Arizona came into the union in 1912, Senator

Hayden was the first member of Congress to be elected representing that state. After his term in the House of Representatives, he was elected to the Senate. He was a balance wheel when the biggest appropriation bill in history was enacted by the Congress.

* * * * *

One late night I was on the telephone to a friend in the House Press Gallery (our office remained on duty no matter how late the Senate was in session). He held the phone so I could hear the members of the House singing on the House floor as they waited for the Senate to adjourn! The cause to sing. It was the final adjournment of the year for both Houses of Congress.

* * * * *

It was the job of one of our chauffeurs to go to the Botanical Gardens twice a week to get flowers for our desks. A comedian, one day he announced that he was going to the "mechanical gardens," rather than the "Botanical Gardens" to get them. He also used to tell about the man going the wrong way on a one-way street, saying, "I must be late. Everybody has already been there, and is coming back!" This employee of ours was always coming out with something. One time it was, "People are dying who never died before."

* * * * *

We had an interesting Democratic Senator, Senator Young of Ohio, who would answer constituents' letters on occasion with one word—"no." Of course, he knew he only wanted to serve one term and wouldn't have to run for re-election!

* * * * *

I attended a party at the New Zealand Embassy with Frank, wearing a white lacy pant suit I had bought in Mexico. I was quite surprised when I was introduced to the Ambassador and he said, "How do you do, Chicken." When I asked what he meant, he said, "Your outfit is *lined*! You're too shy!"

* * * * *

One afternoon when J. Mark Trice was Secretary of the Senate and he was not in his office but on the Senate floor, one of his secretaries used the bathroom adjoining his private office. To her chagrin Mr. Trice returned to his inner office and Senator Joe McCarthy joined him.

She stayed, locked in the bathroom, until Senator McCarthy left. She had overheard their long conversation and feeling like an innocent eavesdropper, had to apologize to Mr. Trice as she stepped out of the bathroom!

* * * * *

When Senator Fulbright was Chairman of the Senate Foreign Relations Committee, he requested the Sergeant-at-Arms, who was in charge of Senate housekeeping, to get him a new chair. Joe Duke, the Sergeant-at-Arms, complied with this request. Joe asked if I would like Senator Fulbright's chair at my desk. As the Senator was known to have a brilliant reputation (being a Rhodes Scholar), Joe thought my using his chair might result in some of his brilliance rubbing off on me!

* * * * *

At one time there was quite a scandal when a secretary, Elizabeth Ray, employed in the office of Congressman Wayne Hays, couldn't type! Everyone was talking about the inferences regarding her duties and she even wrote a book about it. Many of the Senators started asking all the secretaries in all the offices they visited if they could type. They thought this was funny. Lois Schering, our number three girl in our outer office, was tired of the question, as she'd heard it so many times. So when Senator Quentin Burdick said to her, "Can you type?" she was ready for him and answered, "Yes, I can type, *too!*"

Sad Moments

Although many of the days of my Senate career were filled with cheer and exhilaration, there were also some very sad ones. For instance, Senator Lester Hunt of Wyoming committed suicide in his Senate office. The movie, *Advise and Consent*, contained a role purported to be that of Senator Hunt. It was rumored he had discovered his son was a homosexual and that was the reason he took his own life.

Senator Robert LaFollette committed suicide, too. Mr. Johnston used to drive in to the Capitol occasionally with him, and he always said Senator LaFollette was very quiet on their trips. His father, Robert LaFollette, Sr. was one of only five Senators whose portraits were commissioned for the Senate Reception Room in the Capitol.

* * * * *

Mary Ann Parsons was a member of the Senate staff of the office of *The Daily Digest*, under the Secretary of the Senate. The office maintained a joint House-Senate staff and covered for the daily congressional record a summary of all floor proceedings and committee hearings. It was printed in the back of each day's congressional record.

Mary Ann married our Ambassador to Afghanistan, Adolph "Spike" Dubbs. She went to Kabul with him.

A short time after their marriage, Ambassador Dubbs was assassinated. I will never forget the photograph in the newspaper of President Carter trying to console her at the memorial service. Her head was on his shoulder, and they both looked heartbroken. Later she was appointed as an assistant to Ambassador John Gavin in Mexico.

* * * * *

Senator Margaret Chase Smith, after a hip operation, couldn't walk very well. She wouldn't be held down though, and traveled around the Senate on a little electric scooter. I admired her gumption. A group of us used to go over to Mike Palm's on Capitol Hill occasionally after work and stop there and have a drink before we went home. One spring evening Senator Smith came by alone. She waved at us and you could practically read her mind. I think she wanted to come in and join us. She seemed lonesome.

Senator Smith had a wonderful record in the Senate. She was there, even night after night when necessary, and never missed a roll call vote. Senator Aiken of Vermont nominated her for President at one of the Republican National Conventions. America wasn't yet ready for a female President.

* * * * *

Another sad moment was when Senator Russell died on the first day of a session in Congress. He, too, had physical problems and came into our office often on his electric scooter.

He was a pillar of strength to the entire Senate, a treasured advisor to President Johnson when he was Majority Leader, and a respected and admired man by all. Many people felt he should have gone much further in his political career. On the day he died, Frank said to me, "I guess Senator Russell just couldn't start another session of the Senate."

* * * * *

Another nostalgic moment was when Senator Biden from Delaware was sworn in. It was a bittersweet experience, and very touching. After the Senator was elected, his wife with their two sons and daughter drove to Washington. On the way home they had an accident and Mrs. Biden and their little girl were killed. The little boys survived but they suffered injuries.

The Senator didn't want to come to the Capitol to be sworn in because his little boy was still in the hospital. So we passed a resolution enabling Frank to go over to Wilmington, Delaware and swear him in in the hospital.

We went into the room where the little boy was, with his leg elevated. Though she was gone, Mrs. Biden's handbag was on the floor near the little boy's bed. It was a very touching scene.

Senator Biden's mother and father were there, as well as Mrs. Biden's parents. Frank swore the Senator in, and it was an experience to be remembered.

Senator Biden made the statement that, "I'm going to be a father first, and a Senator second. And if being a United States Senator interferes with my being a good father, then I'm going to resign from the Senate." He was very sincere, and the tears of his parents were proud ones.

* * * * *

There was a very dramatic joint session when General Douglas MacArthur, who had been fired by President Truman because he wanted to go too far after our victories following the attack on Pearl Harbor, made his address.

The general was like an actor! He had a most dramatic air. During the war he had everybody feeling he could "walk on water," which they say he practically did. President Truman had stepped in and did not let him get any further because he didn't want the war to escalate. President Truman was not popular with that decision at all, but he had the guts to shoot the general down. General MacArthur was a commanding figure. Some of the soldiers under him were resentful, though, because through the engagements he had his wife and son with him and they could not.

MacArthur held the members of Congress spellbound during his speech. Here was this handsome warrior, who had just been removed from the service following an inspiring tour of duty, giving his farewell speech! Del Malkie, who then worked in the House Press Gallery, taped it and gave me a copy. Later a record of it was produced.

He ended with: "Old soldiers never die. They just fade away. Goodbye." It was really quite a nostalgic experience to feel the passion and the drama in the air.

Upon his death, his casket was permitted to lie in state in the Capital rotunda. In many ways the Capitol is sort of like a big theater noting the series of events, interesting and intense, which take place under its majestic dome.

Investigations

And then there was Watergate

In my quiet, dignified office next to Frank Valeo's office, was a magnificent circular window that contained the Seal of the Senate in colorful stained glass. It was seen from both sides while coming up the winding marble Senate steps. *Life* magazine featured it in one issue.

I brought in a small television to watch the Watergate hearings and placed it on the window ledge.

The calm of our daily activities was shattered at the mention of "The Nixon Tapes." Alexander Butterfield had dropped the bomb of their existence and I flew into Frank's office to inform him. This development was the beginning of the end, for then the President was really going to be tried by the House Judiciary Committee for impeachment.

We all suffered through the heartbreaking hearings conducted by Congressman Peter Rodino, Chairman of that committee, hoping against hope that the charges could be proven untrue. The Supreme Court had upheld Judge Sirica's order to the President to produce the taped recordings of his private conversations in the White House and to turn them over to the Judiciary Committee. After the unbelievable course of events and President Nixon's refusals to release the tapes finally took place, the "smoking gun" tape was released to the committee on August 5, 1974.

After the emotion-filled hearings, when we watched the raw sadness and disbelief reflected in the faces of the committee members and heard the deep sobs of grown, dignified men, our hearts were touched and the Articles of Impeachment were adopted. They were submitted to the House of Representatives on August 20, 1974.

The Senate would, after adoption by the full House, sit as a court and provide the second step of impeachment.

The Articles were:

Article I   Obstruction of Justice
Article II   Abuse of Power
Article III   Defiance of Committee Subpoenas

The President's Executive Assistant, Rose Mary Woods, was called upon to appear at Nixon's trial before Judge Sirica. She was questioned about the existence of the missing "eighteen minutes of tape" crucial to the outcome. She revealed it had been destroyed.

This was a trying time in her life. She made many court appearances and was constantly hounded by the press. She bravely defended the President. Her devotion and sincerity were know to all and she was a pillar of strength to him and his family. She used to be called the "Fifth Nixon" and indeed demonstrated her support.

One evening Rose read a newspaper article that quoted a comment by Judge Sirica. She showed it to him in court the next day, feeling that it was a breach of the proceedings. Rose conferred with the judge alone as her attorney was not allowed to be present. It was ignored. There were some light moments. Rose told me that during the trial a girl who was an assistant attorney for the prosecution wore very short skirts in the courtroom. Rose told her lawyer "My legs are better than hers and I am going to shorten my skirts, too." He disagreed and insisted she continue with her lady-like attire.

We all shared the tragedy of the President's resignation but felt it was the "lesser evil" of his facing an impeachment trial in the Senate. Also our country's national prestige and relations with countries throughout the world would suffer.

Rose and I were good friends and close "Senate sisters." She described her feelings to me when she was present for the President's resignation speech. It was a sad time for all Americans but especially for her. The President asked Rose to break the news to his wife Pat. This took all her compassion and sympathy. It may have been because he was suffering so much anguish and Rose and Pat were so close, the blow could be softened coming from her.

Before we knew that the President's resignation had been determined, Frank conferred with the Senate Sergeant-at-Arms, Bill Wannall, on the arrangements that were in order for a trial on the Senate floor. We ordered official Senate identification pins for the members of the Senate to wear on the Senate floor during the trial in the Senate chamber, but because of the President's resignation, these were not distributed. We also had our office checked to see that it was not bugged.

In announcing his decision, the President said:

> *I would have preferred to carry through to the finish whatever personal agony it would have involved, and my family unanimously urged me to do so. But the interests of the nation must always come before any personal considerations. To leave office before my term is completed is abhorrent to every instinct in my body. But, as President, I must put the interest of America first.*

I knew my "sister" Rose was suffering and I wouldn't be able to reach her on the White House telephone at that time. So I sent a telegram, just to let her know I was thinking of her and was standing by. She wrote a lovely letter in acknowledgment.

When Rose was initially interviewed for her job with then freshman Congressman Richard Nixon, a member of the House Committee on Un-American Activities she announced to him, "First of all I'm a Democrat, and secondly, I'm a Catholic."

He was undeterred. Impressed with her brisk efficiency and their appreciation of their mutual tidiness, precision handling of his expense account, and the orderliness of the office.

Their impenetrable alliance was set . . . and for almost three decades she was his right hand. Rose stood by Richard Nixon through a slush fund scandal; saved his career by short-stopping his impulsive letter of resignation from the ticket; stood by with

THE WHITE HOUSE

WASHINGTON

November 13, 1973

Dear Scottie:

How dear of you to take a moment just to let me know you
"understood!" Really, friends such as yourself have made
these recent trying days memorable. As I am sure you will
appreciate, it is far more difficult to watch helpless, as those
close to you endure unjust criticism, than to accept it personally and return the fire. The truly frustrating thing was knowing
there was so little any of us could do to ease the hurt for our
great President.

So -- as you must have guessed -- I did just as you did. My
prayers were (and are) constant that the President remain
strong until his final vindication. It does seem to me now that
we are receiving slightly fairer news coverage and hopefully
we will soon be free to direct our efforts as they should be --
in the pursuit of President Nixon's great programs for our
nation and that which we all desire so much -- world peace.
Therefore, it is most reassuring to know we continue in your
thoughts and your prayers.

With very best personal regards,

Love,

Rose Mary Woods
Executive Assistant
to the President

Miss Dorothye G. Scott
103 Eighth Street, S. E.
Washington, D. C. 20003

P.S. I hope we will have a chance to get together one of these days!

his defeat in his 1960 Presidential bid (due to criticism by the press regarding his expensive home.)

She travelled with him to China and went along on all his other official trips, serving his many needs.

Rose's loyalty and deep respect for President Nixon never wavered. In a town where this commodity is not a priority, her sincere feelings were unique and appreciated.

On the occasion of the 1982 reunion on the anniversary of his 1972 landslide election, Nixon's cabinet, staff members and friends attending at the Washington Marriott Hotel, in his presence, she said, "Richard Nixon is the most honorable man this country has ever produced." A standing ovation followed.

Now living in Ohio near her sister, not in the greatest health, Rose Mary is enjoying the resurgence of respect for Richard Nixon. He had become America's "elder statesman," sharing his knowledge and leadership with Presidents and politicos, and giving much back to the American people. His wife Pat's death, not long before his own, was another blow in his life.

*****

As a devout Catholic, Rose attends mass every day and of course her faith sustained her through his terrible ordeal.

Not All Work, Some Play

I had time for fun and dates, despite my long working hours under the Capitol dome, at many of Washington's social events and glamorous night spots. Included was Michael's, where the gypsy violinist was a favorite of one of my special dates and mine. The Shoreham Hotel, where the famous (in Washington) Barnie Breeskin's Orchestra played, was another. Barnie and his wife accompanied some of us on one of our Congressional Secretaries trips to Puerto Rico. The Congressional Country Club, Georgetown night spots and luncheon favorites like Clyde's, provide nice memories.

Often, our sisters patronized the Wardman Park Hotel, the Washington Hotel, the Washington Hilton, the Hyatt on Capitol Hill, and our close Carroll Arms Hotel on Capitol Hill where that well-known comedian Mark Russell got his start. He entertained all the politicians with marvelous original songs about their activities. He is still going strong now, nationally.

Attendance at many of the formal party fund-raising dinners, receptions at local hotels, Administrative Assistants Association affairs, in addition to dating some of the embassy officials on some of my trips, kept me busy. Some personal romances are among my Washington memories . . . and are *private*!

And of course I loved giving parties, playing bridge, boating on Chesapeake Bay, water skiing there and entertaining at my cottage on the bay. I enjoyed visiting Annapolis, the Naval Academy and Annapolis Yacht Club. On vacations I made some trips to Louisville, Kentucky for the Kentucky Derby; New York City for shows; New Orleans, Louisiana, Biloxi, Mississippi, Dallas, Texas and the LBJ Space Center at Houston, Texas.

More exciting were exotic trips to Puerto Rico, Bermuda, Mexico, Canada, England, Ireland, Germany, Austria, France (where I ate escargot!), Italy, Switzerland and Egypt. Seeing the world!

White House Visits

I invited my cousin and some of her friends who were in Washington from Philadelphia, to visit the White House.

President Nixon's personal Executive Assistant, Rose Mary Woods, showed us around and presented us a silver seal of the President, encased in glass. It was a lovely souvenir of our visit.

We enjoyed chatting with Secretary of State Dean Rusk and other notables.

* * * * *

I also visited the White House as a guest of President Johnson. He had invited the Administrative Assistants to each member of the Senate.

It was a lovely evening and the first thrill was in using my invitation and pass to park in front of the White House on historic 1600 Pennsylvania Avenue. Since that evening whenever I drive by, I remember that reception and feel again like a "VIP."

When I went through the receiving line to greet the President I told him how much I missed him at the Senate. He shook hands as he had with the other guests in line before me, and started to walk on, then turned around and came back to me saying, "How good it is to see you."

* * * * *

On another occasion, I attended a ceremony held by President Johnson for the signing of a bill passed by both Houses of Congress. The President arrived amid great fanfare. The signing by the President of an important piece of legislation is always an occasion for a ceremony.

On entering, it was a thrill to hear the playing of "Ruffles and Flourishes" as the President joined us in the West Wing reception room. To me, his presence, self-confident, and in command as he always was on his daily visits to my office, made me feel at home. The Democratic and Republican leaders of the House and Senate were there as were members who had sponsored this particular legislation.

I missed the days of Johnson's electrifying presence in my office which changed to pride in his new role as President of the United States! I was delighted to witness this historic ceremony.

* * * * *

During President Johnson's term I was showing a friend through the White House and bouncy, ebullient Vice President Humphrey spotted me and rushed over and warmly greeted us. (Needless to say, as my guest was a man I was dating at that time, he was greatly impressed!). Senator Humphrey was a friendly man, a real "people" person; congenial, with a warm personality. He once suggested establishing an outdoor branch of the Senate restaurant on the terrace outside our offices. We had full-length windows in our outer office; one was actually a door which was covered with drapes, and never used as such. It didn't happen then, but not long ago I saw on television a shot of House Speaker Gingrich sitting on the terrace outside of his office.

The Senator was ahead of his time!

Senate Portraits

I am an artist and enjoy painting likenesses as well as expressing the characters of each of my subjects.

I did a pencil portrait and an oil painting of President Johnson when he was Majority Leader of the Senate. The oil hangs at his ranch in Johnson City, Texas.

One night Senator Jordan from North Carolina asked me to do a pencil portrait of him. And so I did. His wife said it looked more like him than any photograph he'd ever had taken.

Mrs. Johnston hung my portrait of Skeeter Johnston in their den. She said the eyes seemed to follow her all around the room.

I also did a "pencil portrait" of him, which I had made into a little ashtray (not realizing that he might be insulted when smokers put their cigarettes out on his face!)

Others I painted were Senator Aiken, Senator Symington, and one of a young Senator Jack Kennedy with his Skippy-like hairdo. Also, Senator Mansfield, and Senator Lausche of Ohio were two of my models, as were Leslie Biffle, Frank Valeo (for his birthday), Joe Duke, Emery Frazier. Others included Mr. Huskey, head of the Cabinet Shop in the Senate and Ruth and Walter Watt.

I tried to portray my regard for each of these people in my portraits.

CHAPTER TEN

A Special Association

When Frank Valeo was elected Secretary of the Senate, he decided that I retain my position and responsibilities. It proved to be a significant working relationship.

Valeo had served as a speech writer in the Library of Congress, later joining Senator Mike Mansfield, as a member of his staff. In addition to writing the Senator's speeches, he also accompanied Mansfield to foreign countries and the United Nations on formal government business.

Following the forced resignation of Bobby Baker, Secretary for the Majority, due to outside financial activities, Frank was appointed, then subsequently elected to that position.

Following Skeeter Johnston's retirement, it was known that Frank Valeo would be elected Secretary of the Senate when Senator Mansfield, Democratic whip, would succeed Senator Lyndon Johnson as Majority Leader.

In the meantime, Emery Frazier, former member of the Kentucky State Legislature, who had served as Chief Clerk of the US Senate in the secretary's office, was elected Secretary of the Senate.

Upon Emery Frazier's retirement, Frank Valeo met individually with the heads of all departments under his office, thereby solidifying their association with him. When Frank came into his new position he seemed quiet and serious, something of an introvert.

Frank was going through an emotional upheaval due to a divorce at the same time he was learning his new job. He asked me for ideas about his manner of carrying out his duties. I suggested he cultivate the other Democratic Senators, as in his position he was working for them as well as for the entire Senate.

We worked very closely together and our relationship became a personal as well as an official one. He was invited to many formal affairs befitting his new position and invited me to accompany him. We attended many embassy functions and other official affairs at which I was able to acquaint him with the head staff members of each of the Senators' offices. While his forte was the written word, I'm just the opposite, so with my talkative nature, we were a good social team.

As a matter of fact, we were "on the same beam" and my feeling was that I helped him pick up the pieces of his life after his divorce.

Socially, I met his friends and he met mine. He and his son, Jamie, came down to my cottage on the Chesapeake Bay frequently, one time bringing their bicycles and their dog, "Vicky." As soon as they arrived the "pooper scooper" came in handy for their affectionate police dog. My father and I entertained them and I was hostess to his closest friends, the Fosters, and others. We had a favorite place for dinner on the bay. It was close by, "Pirates' Cove," and Jamie loved walking on the piers looking at the boats moored there. We even went down in the winter and I remember the chilly weather, the season for our "hot buttered rum." During one visit, Jamie slipped and called me "Mommy," and my heart went out to him.

Frank had many dinner parties at his condo, with his Spanish maid, Sixta, preparing gourmet meals. Friends of his from Hong Kong sent him birds' nests and shark fins, for his Chinese dinners. Vicky would attend each dinner party.

At the first dinner I was invited to with just Frank and Jamie, they sent Vicky out to the back yard. I could tell Jamie was upset at their abandonment of her and asked if I minded having her under the table. Of course I acceded and Jamie rushed out to bring her in.

Frank's mother became a special friend of mine and I had a little dinner for her, Frank and my father. Frank said it was the first "date" his mother had since his father's death fourteen years before. I took her on a White House tour and to breakfast on the Washington Hotel Roof, among other places. We were very close and often she would visit and supervise Sixta in preparing tasty Italian dinners at Frank's condo, which he referred to as the "best restaurant in Washington." I acted as hostess at many of them, with some of the Senators as his guests. I vividly remember Senator Jordon, of North Carolina, instructing me on how to eat escargot.

Later I took three plane trips in one day to bring her back from New York for a visit and on one occasion I had her as a surprise guest at a luncheon for Frank' birthday in our private dining room at the office. She stayed overnight at my Capitol Hill townhouse and just before the luncheon I sent one of our office cars to pick her up. She hid in the hallway and on cue came in the back door of our dining room. Senator Mansfield and the other guests had been spirited in and Frank nearly fainted when Senator Mansfield's assistant gave him a shove into the dining room and he discovered his mother there. We corresponded frequently and she called me her "darling daughter Dorothye." When she decided to move to Washington, Frank's son, Jamie, and I drove her to inspect retirement homes and she became happily ensconced in one we chose. Frank and I visited her often and she made a special friend there who accompanied her to more of Frank's dinners. She gave me a beautiful lavender cameo which I still treasure. I remember her dearly as a warm and lovely lady.

When I went to Paris with my friend, Betty Kraus, Frank was also there with Senator Mansfield and Ken Calloway from the State Department. Frank wanted to arrange for the four of us to have dinner but Senator Mansfield "pulled rank" on us and he took Ken and Frank for dinner. Later Frank and I had lunch in Paris. I was delighted as he showed off his French (one of the five languages he spoke.) It was a memorable day. (We had escargot, and I remembered Senator Jordon's instructions.)

When I had a short hospital stay, Frank had my father to dinner at his place, which was especially nice.

At one point our chief messenger, Ellsworth Dozier, confided in me that Frank had asked him if he thought I would be interested in marriage. One evening after Frank and I returned from a party he lingered a little while at my place. He brought up the subject of marriage and I replied, "But, you're my boss!" Down deep inside I was thinking of the religious angle, my being a Catholic and not allowed to marry a divorced man. During our romantic discussion, a timed lamp in my living room went out unexpectedly and we were in the dark. It was quite a timely moment, causing a laugh and relieving the tension. We did have a wonderful relationship and always had so much to say to each other—our stimulating conversations never ended. Some associates in the Senate noticed our appearances at affairs together and thought we were an "item," as did some of my friends. I think my father thought (hoped) Frank and I would end up together.

Packed in his briefcase on his various foreign trips with Senator Mansfield was my Scottie dog as a good luck charm. (Everyone from Senators on down called me "Scottie.") Frank had a Scottie dog carved in ivory in Hong Kong for me, so they both graced my desk. On a later trip I didn't put it in his briefcase and he told me when he returned he had missed it. For one of his trips I typed up postcards with multiple choice comments for him to send us; comments about the trip. I was chagrined when he came back and said the countries he visited preferred to have their own postage used! Of course I had put American stamps on them!

Frank had a good friend from New York, Major Holthusen, who had been our Ambassador to Belgium. I always thought of him as an American version of Maurice Chevalier. He had an electric, interesting personality. He and his charming wife were frequent guests at Frank's dinner parties, and we would sit for hours at the dinner table in stimulating discussions.

Major Holthusen was appointed by the Inspector General's office to visit the homes of many of our Ambassadors in a number of countries to grade them and their families on how well they represented our country. I had a little dinner in my home so Frank and I could launch him on this trip. Frank, in a charming way, served the wine with the usual napkin over his arm. Some time later, on another visit to Washington, Major Holthusen took me to lunch and said he was so grateful that Frank, since his divorce, had another woman in his life, "one with *joie de vivre.*"

I admired Frank's business, political and creative qualities and was happy with his comments when he remarked to me, "When you talk you say something," and he told others, "Dorothye's worth twice what she's paid." Whee!!

A Shocking Political Move

I will never forget receiving a call from Frank one evening as I was cuddled in a warm hostess gown and feeling cozy, content and relaxed. I could hardly believe what he was saying, that in the organizational meeting of all Democratic Senators the next day two of the Democratic Senators would be campaigning for Stan Kimmett, the Secretary for the Majority, to succeed Frank as Secretary of the Senate. Senator Mansfield was retiring, and after having served as majority whip under Senator Mansfield, Senator Robert Byrd would be elected Senate Majority Leader. Previously Byrd had come to our office and conferred at length with Frank. The outcome of their meeting was a letter Frank sent to Senator Byrd confirming his duties and the manner in which he would assist him as Majority Leader. We thought it was all set. Not so.

The next day he and I called many of the Democratic Senators from his private office to elicit their votes. Many of the Senators were shocked and pledged their support in the upcoming election.

At the conference of all Democratic Senators the next day, Frank was defeated and Stan Kimmett was elected. Rumor had it that if Senator Byrd had not gone along with this development he would not have been elected Majority Leader. He subsequently asked Frank to join his staff as a speech writer, and I didn't hesitate to tell Frank I thought that would be a terrible comedown from his former position as an officer of the Senate. The Senators' lack of support, I felt, was because Frank had taken a third trip to China with Senator Mansfield and was away when the Congress adjourned sine die that year. Frank had studied Mandarin Chinese on his first trip there with Senator Mansfield and had been able to make dinner table conversation only, but on his final trip he made two speeches in Chinese, which was very complimentary to his attendance there with the Senator. Upon his retirement, Senator Mansfield was appointed Ambassador to Japan. After Frank's defeat Senator Mansfield vacationed in Florida and never contacted him with any regret or sympathy. Every day I would ask Frank if he'd heard from the Senator to whom he had been so devoted and I got madder and madder when he had not. Frank commented that I was madder about it than he was! He declined Senator Byrd's offer and retired. I also tendered my resignation. This was a sad time.

* * * * *

At one of the parties we had attended some time before, a friend of Frank's was very vocal in demeaning the post of Secretary of the Senate. I got mad and Frank said I was like a mother hen, with my feathers all ruffled! I think my reaction was the same this time.

After our retirement Frank wanted me to serve as a partner with him in a consulting business, which he would run in the winter, and I could run in the summer, but I declined. He said it would only be if I were bored when I returned from my California home to Washington in the summers, but I was busy and happy with my life.

Recently Frank said he was writing a book and would send me some of the manuscript, asking for any suggestions I might have. I told him I was writing one too, just a color story of my Senate days. It will be fun to compare our versions, whether divergent or in agreement.

All in all, he remains a good friend in addition to having been a kind and thoughtful "boss."

Attached is a copy of the Senate resolution adopted at the time of his retirement, in appreciation of his Senate service.

Resolution Commending Honorable
Francis R. Valeo Upon His Retirement as Secretary
Of the Senate
April 1, 1977
(Congressional Record, Page S5407)

Mr. Robert C. Byrd: Mr. President, I send to the desk a resolution, joined in by my friend the Minority Leader, and ask for its immediate consideration. The resolution (S. Res. 133) was considered and agreed to as follows:

Whereas, upon retirement of its secretary, Francis R. Valeo, the Senate wishes to express its appreciation for his 19 years of service as an employee of the Senate and his over 10 years as Secretary of the Senate;

Whereas the said Francis R. Valeo at all times has discharged the difficult duties and responsibilities of his office with high efficiency and abiding devotion; and

Whereas his unsurpassed service and his unfailing dedication to duty have earned for him our affection and our esteem; Now, therefore, be it

Resolved, that Francis R. Valeo be hereby commended for his long, faithful and exemplary service.

Sec. 2. The Secretary of the Senate is directed to transmit a copy of this resolution to Francis R. Valeo.

(signed)

Robert C. Byrd

Statement of Francis R. Valeo, Secretary of the Senate
To the Democratic Majority Conference

January 5, 1977

Over the years, I have found that the value of a Senate official is usually calculable in direct ratio to the infrequency with which he opens his mouth. Since the leadership has invited me to address the caucus, however, I will say in these farewell remarks that I have been associated with the Senate and the Democratic side in particular, for two decades. The experience is deep and abiding. The give and take of that experience, its pleasures and pain, its achievements and frustrations are forever interwoven with whatever meaning attaches to my life. I leave as the friend of every member of the Senate, and with deep respect for what Senators do for the country. I leave with no regrets. I leave with the hope that whatever I may have touched in the Senate's house is a little better rather than worse than it was before and with every expectation that my successor will do the same. I leave with full confidence that Democrats united under a new leadership and in concert with Republicans will add another illustrious chapter to the history of the Senate's contribution to the nation.

CHAPTER ELEVEN

My Retirement

After thirty-one-plus years in the service of the Senate, I was given a retirement party. It was held in the huge Senate Reception room, the largest room in the Capitol building. Very beautiful and impressive!

One hundred and forty people attended. A buffet table and bar were set up, and waiters from my office officiated, as well as some of my close friends. I was presented with a gold charm bracelet, with the Capitol and a gold disc engraved with the dates of my service.

My remarks were straight from the heart. I was given other celebrations, but this party is among my fondest memories.

After Frank Valeo's heartwarming tribute (see introduction), I answered:

> *This party is just like my Senate service. I'm having such a good time I hate for it to be over.*
>
> *Frank Valeo told me I was a pack rat. So I'm not going to leave the Senate, I'm going to take it with me.*
>
> *I'm going to take memories of all my friends over the years who have meant so much to me. Skeeter Johnston was my "boss" for twenty years. Frank is my friend and my "boss." I think he makes all of us feel we are working with him and not for him.*
>
> *I've had some soaring moments and some sad moments, but this is the nicest moment of all, my very own. I'll always cherish it. Thank you from the bottom of my heart for giving it to me.*

On My Retirement

Dear Dorothye,

None of your friends would consider it appropriate to say farewell to you today. Rather, as the network announcer would say, "It's time for station identification."

You've given so much energy towards making the Senate a better institution and have worked hand-in-glove with its most vital element, the people. From Senators to messengers (yes, and even curators) you've shared with all, your sympathetic understanding of this body politic. Such a contribution is impossible to measure, let alone appreciate fully.

On this special occasion, I take pleasure in telling you of the very special tablecloth we used for your luncheon. Its brief history follows:

In the summer of 1963, President Kennedy traveled to Europe, stopping at various capitols, including London, Rome, Bonn, and Dublin. Those who accompanied him said later that the journey through Ireland was by far the highlight for JFK. While the President's time on the "Emerald Isle" was spent in the Irish Republic, he did accept some gestures of friendship from the Northern Irish, including a banquet-size linen tablecloth, bearing the Great Seal of the United States and the shield of Northern Ireland.

One morning in the Fall of 1963, Mrs. Kennedy dropped by the White House curator's office with a large package under her arm and an even bigger smile on her face. (She had recently recovered from the loss of her third child and was in good spirits, preparing for a trip to Texas with President Kennedy.) It seems that she and the President were going through the gifts received during his summer travels and the tablecloth was "rediscovered." While his heart was always in Ireland, it was definitely in the South, not the North. Thus, I assume he suggested that Mrs. Kennedy make a gift of the cloth to someone not quite so prejudiced in favor of the South of Ireland. When Mrs. Kennedy asked if Barbara would care to accept such a gift, I nodded yes, not realizing that a tablecloth eighteen feet in length was not your ordinary, everyday size. Well, Scotty, fourteen years were to pass before an occasion appropriate to its use would arise. Happily for us, President Kennedy's banquet cloth made its first appearance on the evening of January 25, 1977, as your many friends gathered in your honor. It could not have had a more fitting debut!

With greatest affection,
Fondly,
James Roe Ketchum
Curator of the US Senate
31 January 1977

"Thank you for all you meant to us."
(Senator Talmadge of Georgia)

"I'm going to shoot myself—the Capitol without you?
(Darrell St.Claire)

"There's no one like you. I don't know what I'm going to do tomorrow. I can't say goodbye. It's been a pleasure to work with you."
(Charles, one of our
dignified messengers)
Also from Charles:
"I think you'll write a book. Like Mr. Valeo said, you deserve to get out and do other things."

"I hope you can stay"
(Senator Robert Byrd)

"Hope you will enjoy your retirement as much as I do. You are as lovely as a rose."
(Kay Martin, formerly Kay Kenny)

"Aren't you coming back? I hate to see you leave."
(Darrell St.Claire)

"Are you going forever?"
(Senator Quentin Burdick)

CHAPTER TWELVE

Epilogue
Then and Now

Secretary of the Senate Frank Valeo, my "partner" for the last eleven years of my Senate career, used to say "You have a wonderful feel for the Senate." I think it was an awareness that I had of the quality of life in the Senate. The inspiration and pride at that time of each individual Senator was reflected in the overall spirit of responsibility and dedication in the "greatest deliberative body in the world."

When you realize what a member of the Senate goes through to be elected, the endless campaigning, raising of funds and sacrifice of his or her personal life, stop and think how dedicated this person must be to our country. Once elected, he is then responsible for fashioning the laws of our land, the pattern of every phase of our lives in this great citadel of freedom.

Statesmen of special caliber were Senators Barkley, Hayden, Gore, Vandenberg, Taft, Aiken, Kennedy, Inouye, and Johnson who served in the Senate of my day, and from them I recognized the high calling to which they had responded. I cherish these memories, even the long hours I was at my desk to serve the Senators' needs while the Senate was in session.

There were times when I would leave my office in the wee hours, drive home, sleep a few hours, and arrive back at my desk at 9:00 A.M. the same morning.

One morning Skeeter Johnston called me at home before I left for work to tell me not to go to my office, as one of the Senators was sleeping there. They had been in session all night during a filibuster and were taking turns grabbing naps to keep going.

I have an inspiring memory of watching the fireworks on the night of the Fourth of July from my office window. The Senate was still in a night session, and as the beautiful display lit up the sky over the Washington Monument, I realized why I was there. It was a national holiday celebrating our independence, and the upper body of our national legislature, which was helping to preserve the freedoms and our way of life, was still working in the Senate chamber. Patriotism was a great motivator for me and the appreciation of the Senators for my work gave me pride in being a part of their endeavors.

After long and sometimes frantic debates on the Senate floor, two of the most vocal opponents would be seen coming out of the chamber arm in arm. True friendly dedication.

My friend, Harold Beckley, Superintendent of the Senate Press Gallery, was visiting with Skeeter in my office. They were both claiming that each had the best job in Washington. I thought while hearing this that their claims were certainly interesting. Here was Johnston, serving as he termed the Senators, "100 prima donnas," and Beckley, supervising 700 plus newspapermen who covered the Senate. They, even as I, valued their roles in the service of the Senate. Harold Beckley always said he wanted to die with his boots on—and he did, while still active in his position.

At a reception in Puerto Rico during a trip with the Congressional Secretaries Club, Bobby Baker, who was then Secretary for the Majority, introduced me in a speech to the group as a woman who had the best job in Washington—and so I felt!

In our common endeavors, inspired by the purposeful work of the Members of the Senate, I found a warm family of fellow workers. We reflected in our positions the determination to do the same good job that we witnessed on the part of the Senators. They worked, argued, debated, and fought for their ideals in finely crafting legislation worthy of our great country.

Why is ours the greatest democracy in the world? It is because there is democracy in action in the United States Congress.

Recently in a dentist's office in Palm Springs, when hearing I had worked at the Capitol in Washington, one of the dentist's assistants asked, "Is it as bad as they say?" I hastened to correct her implication and hotly expressed my view that despite the unworthiness of some of our legislators at *this* time, there still exists a calling to inspired patriots to serve their country in the United States Congress.

The halls are still there, enriched by the spirits of the great statesmen in our history who walked them. Those who would walk them now and in the future must strive to be worthy of such a treasured heritage.

CHAPTER THIRTEEN

Presidents In My Time

President Franklin D. Roosevelt
1933–1945

Franklin D. Roosevelt, thirty-second President, Democrat, was born on Jan. 30, 1882, near Hyde Park, New York, the son of James and Sara Delano Roosevelt. He graduated from Harvard University in 1904. He attended Columbia University Law School without taking a degree and was admitted to the New York State bar in 1907. His political career began when he was elected to the New York State Senate in 1910. In 1913 President Wilson appointed him Assistant Secretary of the Navy, a post he held during World War I.

In August 1921, he was stricken with poliomyelitis, which left his legs paralyzed. As a result of therapy he was able to stand, or walk a few steps, with the aid of leg braces. Roosevelt served two terms as Governor of New York (1929–1933). In 1932, W.G. McAdoo, pledged to John N. Garner, threw his votes to Roosevelt, who was nominated for President. The depression and the promise to repeal Prohibition ensured his election. He asked for emergency powers, proclaimed the New Deal, and put into effect a vast number of administrative changes. Foremost was the use of public funds for relief and public works, resulting in deficit financing. He greatly expanded the federal government's regulation of business and by an excess profits tax and progressive income taxes produced a redistribution of earnings on an unprecedented scale. The Wagner Act gave labor many advantages in organizing and collective bargaining. He promoted legislation establishing the Social Security system. He was the last President inaugurated on March 4, 1933, and the first inaugurated on January 20, 1937.

Roosevelt was the first President to break the "no third term" tradition (1940) and was elected to a fourth term in 1944, despite failing health. Roosevelt was openly hostile to fascist governments before World War II and launched a lend-lease program on behalf of the Allies. With British Prime Minister Winston Churchill he wrote a declaration of principles to be followed after Nazi defeat (the Atlantic Charter of August 14, 1941) and urged the Four Freedoms (freedom of speech, of worship, from want, from fear) January 6, 1941. When Japan attacked Pearl Harbor on December 7, 1941, the US entered the war. Roosevelt conferred with allied heads of state at Casablanca (January 1943), Quebec (August 1943), Tehran (November–December 1943) Cairo (November and December 1943), and Yalta (February 1945). He did not, however, see the end of the war. He died of a cerebral hemorrhage in Warm Springs, Georgia on April 12, 1945.

* * * * *

President Roosevelt was elected after running against President Herbert Hoover and brought us out of the Great Depression with all new programs to stimulate our economy and our American way of life. We remember him for initiating our Social Security Administration and "New Deal" via his radio "Fireside Chats." He governed long and well and gave his heart to our winning in World War II. After his election to an unprecedented fourth term, it seemed he would go on forever leading our country despite his physical weakness, with his big heart and unbelievable charisma. That cajoling voice was silenced. That grace and jovial enthusiasm were gone. Citizens of our country in every walk of life, young and old, rich and poor, suffered a moment of paralyzing shock when his life stopped. Years later, people would compare stories of where they were and exactly what they were doing in great detail when they learned that this momentous figure in our history had died.

I listened to the sad words. I recalled the many conversations I had had with my father about this man. During his Presidency we enjoyed discussing his many accomplishments and experiences, always with admiration. I felt greatly privileged to be able to attend the memorial service.

Harry S. Truman
1945–1953

Harry S. Truman, thirty-third President, Democrat, was born on May 8, 1884, in Lamar, Missouri, the son of John Anderson and Martha Ellen Young Truman. A family disagreement on whether his middle name should be Shippe or Solomon, after names of two grandfathers, resulted in his using only the middle initial "S." After graduating from high school in Independence, Missouri, he worked (1901) for the *Kansas City Star*, as a railroad timekeeper, and as a clerk in Kansas City banks until about 1905. He ran his family's farm from 1906 to 1917. He served in France during World War I. After the war he opened a haberdashery shop, was a judge on the Jackson County Court (1922–24), and attended Kansas City School of Law (1923–25). Truman was elected to the US Senate in 1934 and reelected in 1940. In 1944, with Roosevelt's backing, he was nominated for Vice President and elected. On Roosevelt's death in 1945, Truman became President. In 1948, in a famous upset victory, he defeated Republican Thomas F. Dewey to win election to a new term.

Truman authorized the first uses of the atomic bomb (Hiroshima and Nagasaki, August 6 and 9, 1945), bringing World War II to a rapid end. He was responsible for what came to be called the Truman Doctrine (to aid nations such as Greece and Turkey, threatened by Communist takeover), and his strong commitment to NATO and to the Marshall Plan helped bring them about. In 1948–49, he broke a Soviet blockage of West Berlin with a massive airlift. When communist North Korea invaded South Korea (June 1950), he won UN approval for a "police action" and sent in forces under General Douglas MacArthur. When MacArthur opposed his policy of limited objectives, Truman removed him.

Truman was responsible for a higher minimum-wage, increased Social Security, and aid-for-housing laws. He died in Kansas City, Missouri on December 26, 1972.

* * * * *

Upon President Roosevelt's death, Betty Darling, assistant to Leslie Biffle, Secretary of the Senate at that time, received the call announcing his death. She rushed into Biffle's office to tell him and he told her to call Vice President Truman's office. She did and was told he was on his way to the Speaker's office. Betty called and told the Speaker the President was dead and to have Vice President Truman come to the Secretary of the Senate's office immediately.

The Vice President appeared at her desk in a few minutes, out of breath. Biffle sent him down to the White House in one of the Secretary of the Senate's official cars. It was at the White House he immediately took his oath of office as President of the United States.

In appreciation, Truman gave Betty his first autographed photograph as President. The next day Betty's phone rang and it was President Truman saying: "What are you doing for lunch?" (He often had lunch in the Secretary's private dining room.) But this time several secret service men appeared at her desk before the President's arrival.

The President's family life with wife Bess and daughter Margaret was true Americana. After his term, President Truman returned to Independence, Missouri, there to live out his life quietly, playing his piano and mowing his lawn. Daughter Margaret who was married to the late Clifton Daniel, was the apple of Truman's eye. She has become a recognized author, writing mystery novels featuring settings in Washington and in the White House.

Dwight David Eisenhower
1953–1961

Dwight D. Eisenhower, thirty-fourth President, Republican, was born on October 14, 1890, in Denison, Texas, the son of David Jacob and Ida Elizabeth Stover Eisenhower. He grew up on a small farm in Abilene, Kansas and graduated form West Point in 1915. He was on the staff of General Douglas MacArthur in the Philippines from 1935 to 1939. In 1942, he was made commander of Allied forces landing in North Africa; the next year he was made full general. He became supreme Allied commander in Europe that same year and as such led the Normandy invasion (June 6, 1944). He was given the rank of general of the army on December 20, 1944, which was made permanent in 1946. On May 7, 1945, Eisenhower received the surrender of Germany at Rheims. He returned to the US to serve as chief of staff (1945–48). His war memoir, *Crusade in Europe* (1948), was a best-seller. In 1948 he became President of Columbia University; in 1950 he became commander of NATO forces.

Eisenhower resigned from the Army and was nominated for President by the Republicans in 1952. He defeated Adlai E. Stevenson in the 1952 election and again in 1956. Eisenhower called himself a moderate, favored the "free market system" vs. government price and wage controls, kept government out of labor disputes, reorganized the defense establishment, and promoted missile programs. He continued foreign aid, sped the end of the Korean War, endorsed Taiwan and Southeast Asia defense treaties, backed the UN in condemning the Anglo-French raid on Egypt, and advocated the "open skies" policy of mutual inspection with the USSR. He sent US troops into Little Rock, Arkansas in September 1957, during the segregation crisis.

Eisenhower died on March 28, 1969, in Washington, D.C.

* * * * *

President, and former General Eisenhower, served after having been our national hero in World War II. With Mamie and his family by his side, he served two terms. His death was a great loss. He served valiantly for his country in many capacities.

Eisenhower's grandson, David, married Richard Nixon's daughter, Julie.

John Fitzgerald Kennedy
1961–1963

John F. Kennedy, thirty-fifth President, Democrat, was born on May 29, 1917, in Brookline, Massachusetts, the son of Joseph P. and Rose Fitzgerald Kennedy. He graduated from Harvard University in 1940. While serving in the navy (1941–1945), he commanded a PT boat in the Solomons and won the Navy and Marine Corps Medal. In 1956, while recovering from spinal surgery, he wrote *Profiles in Courage*, which won a Pulitzer Prize in 1957. He served in the House of Representatives from 1947 to 1953 and was elected to the Senate in 1952 and again in 1958. In 1960, Kennedy won the Democratic nomination for President and narrowly defeated Republican Vice President Richard M. Nixon. Kennedy was the youngest President ever elected and the first Roman Catholic.

In April 1961, the new Kennedy administration suffered a severe setback when an invasion force of anti-Castro Cubans, trained and directed by the US Central Intelligence Agency, failed to establish a beachhead at the Bay of Pigs in Cuba. By the same token, one of Kennedy's most important acts as President was his successful demand on October 22, 1962, that the Soviet Union dismantle its missile bases in Cuba. Kennedy also defied Soviet attempts to force the Allies out of Berlin. He started the Peace Corps, and he backed civil rights and expanded medical care for the aged. Space exploration was greatly developed during his administration.

On November 22, 1963, Kennedy was assassinated by Lee Harvey Oswald as he was riding with Mrs. Kennedy in a motorcade through Dallas, Texas.

* * * * *

President Kennedy's short tenure in the White House, one thousand days, took us all to "Camelot." He had a glamorous service, even with the "Bay of Pigs" confrontation with Cuba. His assassination at such a young age brought us all to our knees with shock and compassion for his young widow, Jackie, and his two children, Caroline and John-John.

Mrs. Kennedy later married shipping and business magnate Aristotle Onassis, divorcing him a few years later. She died of cancer on May 19, 1994. Millions mourned her death.

Lyndon Baines Johnson
1963–1969

Lyndon B. Johnson, thirty-sixth President, Democrat, was born on August 27, 1908, near Stonewall, Texas, the son of Sam Ealy and Rebekah Baines Johnson. He graduated from Southwest Texas State Teachers College in 1930 and attended Georgetown University Law School. He taught public speaking in Houston (1930–31) and then served as secretary to Representative R. M. Kleberg (1931–35). In 1937 Johnson won an election to fill the vacancy caused by the death of a US representative and in 1938 was elected to the full term, after which he returned for 4 terms. During 1941 and 1942 he also served in the Navy in the Pacific, earning a Silver Star for bravery. He was elected US Senator in 1948 and reelected in 1954. He became Democratic Leader of the Senate in 1953. Johnson had strong support for the Democratic Presidential nomination at the 1960 convention, where the nominee, John F. Kennedy, asked him to run for Vice President. His campaigning helped overcome religious bias against Kennedy in the South.

Johnson became President when Kennedy was assassinated. He was elected to a full term in 1964. Johnson's domestic program was of considerable importance. He won passage of major Civil Rights, anti-poverty, aid to education, and health-care (Medicare, Medicaid) legislation—the "Great Society" program. However, his escalation of the war in Vietnam came to over-shadow the achievements of his administration. In the face of increasing division in the nation and in his own party over his handling of the war, Johnson declined to seek another term.

Johnson died on January 22, 1973, in San Antonio, Texas.

* * * * *

Upon President Kennedy's death, President Lyndon B. Johnson considered that "can do" man from his outstanding leadership of the Democratic Party in the United States Senate, and his short vice Presidency, assumed the Presidency. He put the Kennedy

United States Senate
Office of the Democratic Leader
Washington, D. C.

September 5, 1958

Dear Dorothye:

Your sweet thoughts brought extra happiness and
joy to my birthday celebration. What could be
a more perfect gift than a beautiful golden rose
and handsome vase to commemorate a Golden
Anniversary? Lady Bird says to tell you that you
have given her a wonderful idea that she intends
to use for the fiftieth birthdays of some of our
friends.

It has never been difficult to assess why Skeeter
relies upon you so strongly. I might add, too, that
your efficiency and friendly cooperation make my
job easier and more pleasant.

I hope you enjoy a wonderful relief this Fall from
the hectic days of the session. I'll be looking forward
to seeing you come next January.

With warmest good wishes.

Sincerely,

Lyndon B. Johnson

Miss Dorothye Scott
Secretary to the Secretary of the Senate
The Capitol
Washington, D. C.

LYNDON B. JOHNSON
SENATE DEMOCRATIC LEADER

August 28, 1957

My Fair Lady:

One of the nicest things that
happened to me on my birthday was
late yesterday afternoon when I received
that "Yellow Rose of Texas" from you to
wear in my lapel.

I felt mighty debonair all during
the evening with my yellow rose and everybody wondering where I got it.

We were both pretty wilted when
I got to bed after eleven last night, but it
was a wonderful day and you did much to
make it so.

With best wishes, I am

Sincerely

Lyndon B. Johnson

Miss Dorothye G. Scott
Office of the Secretary
United States Senate
Washington, D. C.

United States Senate
Office of the Democratic Leader
Washington, D. C.

July 25, 1955

Dear Miss Scott:

Lyndon was very pleased when I read your
nice letter to him and he told me to send you his warmest
regards. He added that he knows you are taking good
care of Skeeter and will have everything in good shape
when he returns to the Senate.

Sincerely yours,

Lady Bird Johnson

Mrs. Lyndon B. Johnson

Miss Dorothye Scott
Office of the Secretary
of the Senate
Washington, D. C.

THE WHITE HOUSE
WASHINGTON

December 28, 1963

Dear Dorothye:

To be remembered at Christmastime by friends like
you is what means most to me! Thank you so much
for the handy desk item that you sent to me.

I am grateful, too, for the words of confidence and
support conveyed in your accompanying letter.

With every good wish to you for much happiness in
1964,

Sincerely,

Miss Dorothye Scott
Secretary to Hon. Felton M. Johnston
United States Senate
Washington, D. C.

Program through Congress. In the next election he was elevated by approximately sixty-two percent of the popular vote, surpassing the Franklin D. Roosevelt sweep in 1936. His lead was estimated as fifteen million despite an expected Republican surge in the South, largely a result of the Civil Rights issues. President Johnson, while Majority Leader in the Senate, was responsible for the passage of the first Civil Rights bill in sixty years.

President Johnson gave us the Great Society, instituted Medicare and always worked hard. He inherited the Vietnam War, which was his downfall. He did not run for re-election, as Senator Bob Kennedy was campaigning hard until his assassination. Watching the President at Kennedy's funeral mass, he appeared to be thinking: "If I'd known this would happen, I would have run."

He returned to his ranch in Johnson City, Texas. He had a heart attack some years before and was in declining health. One of the newspapermen who interviewed him commented that his paleness disappeared and the juices started flowing when he talked politics. He died en route to Brooke General Hospital, San Antonio, on January 22, 1973. Funeral services were held in the United States Capital, the National City Christian Church in Washington, D.C. and the LBJ Ranch in Johnson City, Texas. His wife, Lady Bird, survives him.

Richard Milhous Nixon
1969–1974

Richard M. Nixon, thirty-seventh President, Republican, was born on January 9, 1913 in Yorba Linda, California, the son of Francis Anthony and Hannah Milhous Nixon. He graduated from Whittier College in 1934 and from Duke University Law School in 1937. After practicing law in Whittier and serving briefly in the office of Price Administration in 1942, he entered the Navy and served in the South Pacific. Nixon was elected to the House of Representatives in 1946 and 1948. He achieved prominence as the House Un-American Activities Committee member who forced the showdown leading to the Alger Hiss perjury conviction. In 1950 he was elected to the Senate.

Nixon was elected Vice President in the Eisenhower landslides of 1952 and 1956. He won the Republican nomination for President in 1960 but was narrowly defeated by John F. Kennedy. He ran unsuccessfully for Governor of California in 1962. In 1968 he again won the GOP Presidential nomination then defeated Hubert Humphrey for the Presidency.

Nixon appointed four Supreme Court Justices, including the Chief Justice, moving the court to the right, and as a "new federalist" sought to shift responsibility to state and local governments. He dramatically altered relations with China, which he visited in 1972—the first President to do so. With foreign affairs adviser Henry Kissinger he pursued détente with the Soviet Union. He began a gradual withdrawal from Vietnam, but US troops remained there through his first term. He ordered an incursion into Cambodia (1970) and the bombing of Hanoi and mining of Haiphong Harbor (1972). Reelected by a large majority in November 1972, he secured a Vietnam cease-fire.

Nixon's second term was cut short by scandal, after disclosures relating to a June 1972 burglary of Democratic Party headquarters in the Watergate office complex. After it emerged that most of Nixon's office conversations and calls had been taped, the courts and Congress sought the tapes for criminal proceedings against former White House aides and for a House inquiry into possible impeachment. Nixon claimed executive privilege to keep the tapes secret, but the Supreme Court ruled against him. In late July the House Judiciary Committee recommended adoption of three impeachment articles charging him with obstruction of justice, abuse of power, and contempt of Congress. On August 5, he released transcripts of conversations that linked him to cover-up activities. He resigned on August 9 becoming the first President ever to do so.

Nixon died April 22, 1994 in New York City.

* * * * *

President Nixon was elected twice after having served in the House, Senate and as Vice President. He rose from his birthplace in Whittier, California to prominence with his wife, Pat, and daughters Patricia and Julie. He opened the door to China and was responsible for getting our troops returned from Vietnam. He loved the coziness of books, friends and fireplaces and even in summer, with air conditioning on, he would put on some logs.

President Nixon was always friendly and cordial to me when he was Vice President and when he visited our office in the Capitol. I was invited to a special reception he gave at the White House, also attended by then Senator Lyndon Johnson, Senate Majority Leader, and his family.

President Nixon was brought down by the Watergate scandal. He resigned rather than face an impeachment trial in the Senate.

Nixon's life-long friend, Adela Rogers St. Johns, the eminent author, columnist and world-renowned figure, was the world's first woman reporter. Hired by William Randolph Hearst, she figured in the press corps of the White House, wrote national columns, and presided over radio and television programs. She had known Richard Nixon as a boy delivering her groceries from his father's store, and they continued a relationship up to and during his Presidency. She wrote many of his speeches, was a trusted advisor, and as he stated, pressured him into writing his first book, *"Six Crises."*

Would that he had taken her advice early in "Watergate" and called in all of the news media to announce, "I have made mistakes, I am sorry, please forgive them and let us get on with the business and the governing of this great country."

After his death, he was honored at his funeral in Yorba Linda, California, his birthplace, where his library is located. While living in San Clemente he wrote several important books, contributed greatly, advising subsequent elected officials on domestic and foreign policy, redeeming his stature. He earned recognition as an elder statesman. Nixon was preceded in death by his wife, Patricia.

Gerald Rudolph Ford
1974–1977

Gerald R. Ford, thirty-eighth President, Republican, was born on July 14, 1913, in Omaha, Nebraska, the son of Leslie and Dorothy Gardner King, and was named Leslie Jr. When he was two his parents were divorced and his mother moved with the boy to Grand Rapids, Michigan. There she met and married Gerald R. Ford, who formally adopted him and gave him his own name. Ford graduated from the University of Michigan in 1935 and from Yale Law School in 1941. He began practicing law in Grand Rapids, but in 1942 joined the navy and served in the Pacific, leaving the service in 1946 as a lieutenant commander. He entered the House of Representatives in 1949 and spent twenty-five years in the House, eight of them as Republican Leader.

On October 12, 1973, after Vice President Spiro T. Agnew resigned, Ford was nominated by President Nixon to replace him. It was the first use of the procedures set out in the Twenty-Fifth Amendment. When Nixon resigned, August 9, 1974, Ford became President; he was the only President who was never elected either to the Presidency or to the vice Presidency. On September 8, in a controversial move, he pardoned Nixon for any federal crimes he might have committed as President.

Ford vetoed forty-eight bills in his first twenty-one months in office, mostly in the interest of fighting high inflation; he was less successful in curbing high unemployment. In foreign policy, Ford continued to pursue détente. He was narrowly defeated in the 1976 election by Democrat Jimmy Carter.

* * * * *

I have taken a particular interest in the role of President Gerald Ford. He assumed the Presidency after President Nixon's resignation and had to call on all his strength and courage to heal our country in this sad time.

President Ford assumed the Presidency and became a strong pillar to insure the country's values.

Considering advice from his associates and Washington politicos, his own national and moral obligations, and adhering to his prayers for guidance, Ford opted to pardon former President Nixon. He began his public announcement with, "My fellow Americans, our long national nightmare is over." Ending a sad chapter in our history. It was generally accepted that Richard Nixon relied too heavily on his staff, delegating too much to them while he was focusing on foreign affairs.

I had the opportunity in Washington to tell Ford that I admired him for issuing the pardon because it saved our country the agony which could have followed. I repeated this recently while visiting his home (he's my neighbor in the desert) of my admiration for his action. President Ford suggested through a letter to the *New York Times* a lesser rebuke than impeachment for President Clinton.

At the time of the call for impeachment of President Clinton, he "broke ranks" and weighed in on the side of the Democrats in calling for a censure rather than impeachment. His stand was heralded as statesmanlike and a voice of reason amid rancor. He received wide praise in the media for his courage and sincerity in stating that "America must rise to the occasion and keep from sinking in the mud."

Ford is uniquely qualified to understand and feel the sadness which has settled over our nation and he was inspired as he said, "To rescue it from further turmoil." Many people felt that he was not re-elected because of his pardon of President Nixon, but his action was of inestimable value to our country. Ford quoted Abraham Lincoln in the midst of a far graver national crisis, saying "The occasion is piled high with difficulty and we must rise to the occasion." He added that we should be guided by Lincoln's words.

Upon President Ford's retirement to California's golf capitol, Palm Springs, he has become very active in many worthy causes. One of these is his loyal and strong support to his "first lady's" dedication to the Betty Ford Foundation. He is Chairman of "The Valley's Promise," championing the challenge of providing children access to the fundamental resources they need for happy, healthy, and productive lives. This is the local affiliate of General

Colin Powell's "America's Promise," established in 1977 at a Presidential summit. Recently his star was placed with an official unveiling ceremony on the Palm Springs "Walk of Stars" in front of the Desert Museum. He received the Victory of Freedom award from the Nixon Foundation. It coincided with the fifty-ninth anniversary of his election to Congress. Ford vetoed sixty-seven pieces of legislation and had his vetoes over-ridden only eight or nine times, saying "I had a pretty good scorecard or batting average." He also stated that when he served in Congress there was much more civility and less bitterness and the result was a more efficient legislative process. An editorial in the Palm Springs *Desert Sun* stated, "We should recognize the unselfishness of former President Ford, a great man who consistently has served his country in a way that deserves tribute from Americans of all political persuasions." My sentiments exactly and it came to pass.

"I could sprout wings and fly to the top of the rotunda," said Betty Ford on receiving her Congressional Gold Medal in Washington, for dedicated public service and humanitarian contributions.

The former First Lady and her husband, President Gerald Ford, both received their awards, Congress's highest expression of appreciation, from President Clinton who said, "The world would have been a poorer place if not for the Fords."

Mrs. Ford has been praised for raising the awareness of breast cancer and for her work on substance abuse, which ultimately was the beginning of the Betty Ford Center.

Gerald Ford's reputation for integrity and openness made him popular during his twenty-five years in Congress, nine of which he served as House Minority Leader.

He dealt with the aftermath of Watergate and President Nixon's resignation, succeeded him and faced the challenges of ensuring world peace, reviving a flagging economy and solving chronic energy shortages.

"He was just what America needed at that point in history," Senator Trent Lott said, "He did right by his country."

Jimmy (James Earl) Carter
1977–1981

Jimmy (James Earl) Carter, thirty-ninth President, Democrat, was the first President from the deep South since before the Civil War. He was born on October 1, 1924, in Plains, Georgia, the son of James and Lillian Gordy Carter.

Carter graduated from the US Naval Academy in 1946 and in 1952 entered the Navy's Nuclear Submarine Program as an aide to Captain (later Admiral) Hyman Rickover. He studied nuclear physics at Union College. Carter's father died in 1953, and he left the navy to take over the family businesses. He served in the Georgia State Senate (1963–1967) and as Governor of Georgia (1971–1975). In 1976, Carter won the Democratic nomination and defeated President Gerald R. Ford.

On his first full day in office, Carter pardoned all Vietnam draft evaders. He played a major role in the peace negotiations between Israel and Egypt. However, in November 1979, Iranian student militants attacked the US embassy in Tehran and held members of the embassy staff hostage. Efforts to obtain release of the hostages were a major preoccupation during the rest of his term. He reacted to the Soviet invasion of Afghanistan by imposing a grain embargo and boycotting the Moscow Olympic Games.

Carter was defeated by Ronald Reagan in the 1980 election. Carter administration efforts finally resulted in the release of the hostages on Inauguration Day, 1981, just after Reagan officially became President. After leaving office, Carter was hailed for his humanitarian efforts and took a prominent role in mediating international disputes.

* * * * *

Little known when Jimmy Carter began campaigning for the 1976 Democratic Presidential nomination, his first press conference produced not one member of the press. When his remark "I'll never lie to you," his honesty caught the attention of the public.

He followed it with "I'll never mislead you." With these statements, he garnered the necessary votes to claim the Presidency.

President Carter was not a member of the "Washington establishment," having been a former farmer from Plains, Georgia and not imbued with the D.C. social activity. He and his wife made history by *walking* in the inaugural parade. He also was "down to earth" enough to be seen carrying his coat informally over his shoulder on occasion.

I was sorry for President Carter in connection with the Tehran hostage situation. He worked long and hard for their release. The last night of his Presidency he worked all night long trying to achieve it. The day President Reagan took his oath of office, the hostages were released. Ironic. They were released on Day 444, just thirty-three minutes after Carter left office and Reagan was sworn in as the new President. Carter had won their freedom and lost his job.

After his retirement he initiated a program of "Habitat for Humanity," a non-profit volunteer organization that builds houses for low-income people. He hammers in the nails himself, gives of his own personal efforts, and works hard for this program.

Carter keeps extremely busy writing books, teaching at his University, and inspiring in people patriotism and service to America. He came out for censure rather than impeachment of President Clinton.

The *Virtues of Aging* and *Living Faith* are Carter's recent books. Throughout what Carter calls "wonderful accomplishments" and "devastating setbacks" of life, he says a deeply rooted Christian faith has been a constant source of strength, stability and courage for him. Since leaving public office, the Carters have founded the Carter Center in Atlanta, an institution devoted to peace, democracy, and health around the world.

He looms larger on the American scene now than he did when he was President.

Ronald Wilson Reagan
1981–1989

Ronald Wilson Reagan, fortieth President, Republican, was born on February 6, 1911 in Tampico, Illinois, the son of John Edward and Nellie Wilson Reagan. Reagan graduated from Eureka College in 1932 after which he worked as a sports announcer in Des Moines, Iowa. He began a successful career as an actor in 1937, starring in numerous movies, and later in television, until the 1960s. He served as President of the Screen Actors Guild from 1947 to 1952 and in 1959–60. Reagan was elected Governor of California in 1966 and reelected in 1970.

In 1980, Reagan gained the Republican Presidential nomination and won a landslide victory over Jimmy Carter. He was easily reelected in 1984. Reagan successfully forged a bipartisan coalition in Congress, which led to enactment of his program of large-scale tax cuts, cutbacks in many government programs, and a major defense buildup. He signed a Social Security reform bill designed to provide for the long-term solvency of the system. In 1986 he signed into law a major tax reform bill. He was shot and wounded in an assassination attempt in 1981.

In 1982 the US joined France and Italy in maintaining a peace-keeping force in Beirut, Lebanon, and the next year Reagan sent a task force to invade the island of Grenada after two Marxist coups there. Reagan's opposition to international terrorism led to the US bombing of Libyan military installations in 1986. He strongly supported El Salvador, the Nicaraguan contras, and other anticommunist governments and forces throughout the world. He also held four summit meetings with Soviet leader Mikhail Gorbachev. At the 1987 meeting in Washington, D.C., a historic treaty eliminating short- and medium-range missiles from Europe was signed.

Reagan faced a crisis in 1986–87, when it was revealed that the US had sold weapons to Iran in exchange for release of US hostages being held in Lebanon and that subsequently some of the money was diverted to the Nicaraguan contras (Congress had barred aid to the contras). The scandal led to the resignation of leading White House aides. As Reagan left office in January 1989, the nation was experiencing its sixth consecutive year of economic prosperity. Reagan, however, was unable to control the high budget deficits that plagued him throughout his administration.

In 1994, in a letter to the American people, Reagan revealed that he was suffering from Alzheimer's disease.

* * * * *

President Reagan was elected for two terms. With his personal charisma he proved to be a popular President although his administration had its faults along with its successes. Many people feel that the Iran-Contra affair during his administration involving arms for hostages was a much more serious and dangerous policy for our country than President Clinton's later personal violations. After his terms, he developed Alzheimer's disease. He lives quietly in California with his always supportive wife, Nancy, and still at times receives visitors.

The "great communicator" is still greatly admired by his many fans.

George Herbert Walker Bush
1989–1993

George Herbert Walker Bush, forty-first President, Republican, was born on June 12, 1924, in Milton, Massachusetts, the son of Prescott and Dorothy Walker Bush. He served as a US Navy pilot in World War II. After graduating form Yale University in 1948, he settled in Texas, where, in 1953, he helped found an oil company. He was elected to the House of Representatives in 1966 and 1968. He lost a second US Senate race in 1970. Subsequently he served as US Ambassador to the United Nations (1971–73), headed the US Liaison office in Beijing (1974–75), and was Director of Central Intelligence (1976–77).

Following an unsuccessful bid for the 1980 Republican Presidential nomination, Bush was chosen by Ronald Reagan as his Vice Presidential running mate. He served as US Vice President from 1981 to 1989.

In 1988, Bush gained the Republican Presidential nomination and defeated Democrat Michael Dukakis in the November elections. Bush took office faced with the ongoing US budget and trade deficits as well as the rescue of insolvent US savings and loan institutions. He faced a severe budget deficit annually, struggled with military cutbacks in light of reduced cold war tensions, and vetoed abortion-rights legislation. In 1990 he agreed to a budget deficit-reduction plan that included tax hikes.

Bush supported Soviet reforms and Eastern Europe Democratization. He was criticized by some for keeping US policy tied closely to Mikhail Gorbachev as the Soviet leader lost power and for under reaction to China's violent repression of pro-democracy demonstrators in 1989. In December 1989, Bush sent troops to Panama; they overthrew the government and captured strongman General Manuel Noriega.

Bush reacted to Iraq's August 1990 invasion of Kuwait by sending US forces to the Persian Gulf area and assembling a UN-backed coalition, including NATO and Arab League members. After a month-long air war, in February 1991, Allied forces retook Kuwait in a four-day ground assault. The quick victory, with light casualties, gave Bush one of the highest Presidential approval ratings in history.

He was defeated by his Democratic opponent, Bill Clinton, in the 1992 election.

* * * * *

Except for his broken campaign promise not to raise taxes, "read my lips," his administration was a calm one. His wife, Barbara, was a charming First Lady and the book which their dog "Millie" wrote for her received everyone's compliments.

He was a popular President and his leadership during the war with the Iraq "Desert Storm" was an inspiration to all, particularly the work he did in getting the world's cooperation in this confrontation.

The Bush Family is still flourishing in politics and statesmanship, with sons Jeb Bush, Governor of Florida and Texas Governor George W. Bush, who is currently campaigning for the Republican nomination for President.

William Jefferson Clinton
1993–Present

President Clinton was the first Democratic President elected since Franklin Roosevelt to be elected for two consecutive terms. He did an excellent job in bringing our country to the best financial stability in many years with a balanced budget, and the lowest unemployment rate in years.

A Place Called Hope

Bill Clinton was born William Jefferson Blythe III on August 19, 1946, in the small town of Hope, Arkansas. He was named after his father, William Jefferson Blythe II, who had been killed in a car accident just three months before his son was born. Needing to find a way to support herself and her new child, Bill Clinton's mother, Virginia Cassidy Blythe, moved to New Orleans, Louisiana, to study nursing. Bill Clinton stayed with his mother's parents in Hope. There he was surrounded by many relatives who gave him love and support and who played a significant role in his upbringing.

Bill Clinton's grandparents, Eldridge and Edith Cassidy, taught him strong values and beliefs. They owned a small grocery store just outside of Hope, and despite the segregation laws of the time, they allowed people of all races to purchase goods on credit. They taught their young grandson that everyone is created equal and that people should not be treated differently because of the color of their skin. This was a lesson Bill Clinton never forgot.

His mother returned from New Orleans with her nursing degree in 1950, when her son was four-years-old. Later that same year, she married an automobile salesman named Roger Clinton. When Bill Clinton was seven-years-old, the family moved to Hot Springs, Arkansas. Known for its natural mineral hot springs, its scenic beauty, and its racetrack, Hot Springs was bigger than Hope and offered better employment opportunities. Roger received a higher paying job as a service manager for his brother's car dealership and Virginia was able to find a better job as a nurse anesthetist. In 1956

Bill Clinton's half-brother, Roger Clinton, Jr., was born. When his brother was old enough to enter school, young Bill had his last name legally changed from Blythe to Clinton.

In 1960 John F. Kennedy was elected President. Two years later, when Clinton was a senior in high school, he was selected to go to Washington, D.C. to be a part of Boys Nation, a special youth leadership conference. They were invited to the White House to meet President Kennedy. Clinton was one of the first in line to shake President Kennedy's hand in the Rose Garden. That event was one of the most memorable, important experiences of his youth. After that, he knew he wanted to make a difference in the lives of the people of America by becoming President.

Young Clinton thrived on the hard work that his academic and extracurricular activities required. As an active member of his church, he raised money and organized charity events. More important, he learned about working with people and being a good citizen. In his spare time, he enjoyed reading. Some of his favorite books were *The Silver Chalice, The Last of the Mohicans, The Robe,* and *Black Beauty.*

Playing the saxophone was his favorite pastime. He loved music, practiced every day, and played in jazz ensembles. Each summer, he attended a band camp in the Ozark Mountains. His hard work paid off when he became a top saxophone player at his school and won first chair in the state band's saxophone section.

Clinton recognized that although college would be expensive, it would give him the education he needed to accomplish his goals. His hard work in school, combined with his musical ability, earned him many academic and music scholarships. With the help of those scholarships and loans from the government, he was able to attend Georgetown University in Washington, D.C.

He chose Georgetown because it had an excellent foreign service program; he was also excited about going to school in the nation's capitol. While earning his Bachelor of Science degree in International Affairs, he worked as an intern in the office of

Arkansas Senator J. William Fulbright. There he learned how government worked and what it was like to be a politician. He admired Senator Fulbright for his accomplishments and beliefs.

When Clinton finished college in 1968, he won a Rhodes Scholarship, which allows select students to study at Oxford University in England. While at Oxford, he studied government and played rugby. Upon his return to the United States, he began law school at Yale University. At Yale, he continued to work hard. He maintained his interest in government by campaigning for a Senate candidate in Connecticut. He also met Hillary Rodham, whom he would later marry. When he graduated from law school in 1973, Clinton returned to Arkansas to teach law at the University of Arkansas at Fayetteville. There he could concentrate on his goal of running for political office. In 1974 he had his first opportunity when he ran for Congress against Republican incumbent John Paul Hammerschmidt. Although he lost the race, Clinton learned much about politics and met people who have remained his lifelong friends. Hillary had joined him in Arkansas and helped him campaign. She also began teaching at the University of Arkansas. They were married on October 11, 1975.

In 1970 Bill Clinton was elected Attorney General of Arkansas. Two years later, at the age of thirty-two, he became the youngest Governor in the United States. As Governor of Arkansas, he concentrated on improving the state's educational system and building better roads. On February 27, 1980, the Clinton's daughter, Chelsea Victoria, was born. The Clinton's describe this day as the happiest one of their lives. Later that year, in a close election, Governor Clinton lost the race for a second term to Republican Frank White. Feeling that he had not accomplished all that he wanted to do, he ran as the Democratic candidate in the next gubernatorial election. Campaigning throughout the state, he assured the voters that he would address their needs, and he was re-elected in November 1982.

Again, his most important goal as Governor was to enhance the quality of education in the state. He raised teachers' salaries and began a program of testing students after the third, sixth, and eighth grades. He also encouraged parents to participate in their children's education. His new educational standards ensured that every child in Arkansas, regardless of the size or wealth of his or her community or of family income level, would receive a quality education. From August 1986 to August 1987, Governor Clinton served as Chairman of the National Governors' Association. During that time, he led the Governors' efforts to reform the welfare system and the educational systems of the states.

By the fall of 1991, Governor Clinton believed that the country needed someone with a new vision and plan, and he decided to run for President. He also felt that he had the experience and the best ideas for changing our country for the better. He wanted to strengthen the health care system, to improve the school system, and most of all, to bolster the economy and create new jobs. He brought his message to the country by going door to door, holding one-on-one talks with people in town hall meetings, and appearing on various talk shows.

After a long primary process, Governor Clinton was nominated as the Democratic Presidential candidate. He asked Senator Al Gore of Tennessee to be his Vice Presidential running mate. Together, Bill Clinton and Al Gore campaigned on the concept of "putting people first"—preserving the American Dream, restoring future hopes of the middle class, and reclaiming the future for the nation's children. When election day arrived on November 3, 1992, voters turned out in record numbers to cast their ballots. Clinton was elected the forty-second President of the United States and Al Gore the forty-fifth Vice President.

Throughout his life, President Clinton has worked to make a difference in the lives of others. To him, Hope means more than a small town in Arkansas; it means working to ensure that each American has the opportunity to fulfill his or her dream. But his own dream became a nightmare.

* * * * *

Contrary to what you may be expecting, this is not another book on the Clinton debacle, although I spent over two months at my home in Washington at the height, or rather I should say, the "depth" of the Starr investigation.

This should be a time of peace, prosperity, and enthusiasm for the future of our beloved country, much of it attributed to the hard work of our very dedicated President.

I am just as shocked and ashamed as all American citizens at President Clinton's behavior and the terrible cost to his loyal supporters and to our world-wide reputation.

I sat in the galleries of the Senate and the House of Representatives during this tragic time in our history and wished I could take the floor to express my opinion. The atmosphere in our Capitol city seemed permeated with disillusion and disgust at the way the case has been handled. The $40 million+ worth of hearings, illegally taped telephone conversations, along with the meticulously preserved stained dress as evidence, seem to many to constitute entrapment. Even in the Simpson trial, O.J.'s lawyers had the right to be apprised of any evidence against him. The case against the President in the infamous Starr report, delivered in the *Washington Post,* was also issued on international web sites before the President could be notified. The video of his appearance before the grand jury was gleefully distributed around the world (this while a judge has yet to rule on Starr's illegal leaking of the earlier grand jury testimony). Washington feels the President has been crucified. He was never able to cross examine any one. Miss Lewinsky has been granted full immunity and although she earlier stated to Linda Tripp that she lies a lot, no one questions her statements.

Realizing that impeachment is a punishment for "high crimes and misdemeanors," we should recall the Iran Contra affair during President Reagan's Presidency; the clandestine dealings with the enemy and selling of weapons to them. Oliver North spent all night shredding valuable documents until the machine broke down, and even his secretary during the hearings made the statement that she thought they were "above the law." I remember well, too, both the treachery of Watergate and the pardon which Republican President Ford issued to President Nixon after his resignation.

President Clinton's popularity climbed to seventy-three percent approval of the public despite the two articles of impeachment enacted by the House of Representatives against him. Former Presidents Ford and Carter, as well as the Republican candidate who was defeated by him, Senator Bob Dole, all came out publicly for censure by the Senate and not impeachment of him. The Senate trial ensued and he was not convicted.

In spite of it all, President Clinton, at a recent United Nations meeting, received a standing ovation which he acknowledged and tried to stop, but which continued for several minutes. A reflection of where he stands with the leaders of the other countries of the world?

The poll taken three weeks before mid-term elections showed that by a margin of two-to-one, Americans disapproved of the way the Republicans conducted the investigation.

It will be of enormous importance to see where the remainder of his term takes him—and us.

CHAPTER FOURTEEN

Addresses of Presidential Libraries

Herbert Hoover Library
PO Box 488
West Branch, IL 52358-0488
Tel: 319-643-5301
Fax: 319-643-5825
(1929–1933)

Franklin D. Roosevelt Library
511 Albany Post Road
Hyde Park, NY 12538-1999
Tel: 914-229-8114
Fax: 914-229-0872
(1933–1945)

Harry S. Truman Library
500 West US Highway 24
Independence, MO 64050-1798
Tel: 816-833-1400
Fax: 816-833-4368
(1945–1953)

Dwight D. Eisenhower Library
200 SE 4th St.
Abilene, KS 67410-2900
Tel: 913-263-4751
Fax: 913-263-4218
(1953–1961)

John Fitzgerald Kennedy Library
Columbia Point
Boston, MA 02125-3398
Tel: 617-929-4500
Fax: 617-929-4538
(1961–1963)

Lyndon Baines Johnson Library
2313 Red River Street
Austin, TX 78705-5702
Tel: 512-916-5137
Fax:: 512-478-9104
(1963–1969)

The Richard Nixon Library and Birthplace
18001 Yorba Linda Blvd.
Yorba Linda, CA 92686
And
Nixon Presidential Materials Staff
National Archives at College Park
8601 Adelphi Rd.
College Park, MD 20740-6001
Tel: 301-713-6950
Fax: 301-713-6916
(1969–1974)

Gerald R. Ford Library and Museum
1000 Beal Avenue
Ann Arbor, MI 48109-2114
Tel: 313-741-2218
Fax: 313-741-2341
(1974–1977)

Jimmy Carter Library and Museum
One Copenhill Ave., NE
Atlanta, CA 30307-1406
Tel: 404-331-3942
Fax: 404-730-2215
(1977–1981)

Ronald Reagan Library
40 Presidential Dr.
Simi Valley, CA 93065-0666
Tel: 805-522-8444
Fax: 805-522-9621
(1981–1989)

George Bush Library
1000 George Bush Drive West
College Station, TX 77845
Tel: 409-260-9554
Fax: 409-260-9557
(1989–1993)

Author's Bio

Dorothye G. Scott was one of the highest ranking women on Capitol Hill and the one person who had her finger on the pulse of the Senate during the "glory days." In 1992, the Senate Historical Office in Washington, D.C. published her *Oral History Interview*, 350 pages of Dorothye's remembrances, anecdotes and insights into the period of time she worked in the Senate, 1945–1977. It is an extraordinary honor to have done such a book for any individual. Using many of these intimate, gripping, recollections, Ms. Scott has written a fascinating book, *When The Senate Halls Were Hallowed*.

From 1939, when she was graduated from high school in Silver Spring, Maryland, to subsequent graduation from the Washington School for Secretaries in 1940 as an honor graduate, she was swept into the government offices. 1941–45 saw her as secretary in the US War Department. After leaving the War Department, her Senate career began, was long lasting under six Presidential administrations. Her recollections of Democratic conventions, an intimate portrait of Lyndon Johnson, and many amusing stories, bring one to realize this tiny woman *was* the Senate, lived it, loved it and made it her entire life. Her knowledge of those days of respect and dignity in the government contrasts sharply with current politics and abuses today.

She presently lives a very active life in Palm Springs, California.

INDEX